Framing the Environmental Humanities

Studies in Environmental Humanities

Managing Editor

Mark Luccarelli (*University of Oslo*)

Co-editor

Steven Hartman (*Mid Sweden University*)

Editorial Board
Þorvarður Árnason (*University of Iceland*)
Eva Friman (*Uppsala University*)
Maunu Häyrynen (*University of Turku*)
David E. Nye (*University of Southern Denmark*)

Advisory Board

Sigurd Bergmann (*Norwegian University of Science and Technology*)
Lawrence Buell (*Harvard University*)
Thomas Hallock (*University of South Florida, St. Petersburg*)
Ursula Heise (*University of California at Los Angeles*)
Amanda Lagerkvist (*Stockholm University*)
Phillip Payne (*Monash University*)
Aaron Sachs (*Cornell University*)
Kate Soper (*London Metropolitan University*)
Sigríður Þorgeirsdóttir (*University of Iceland*)
Cary Wolfe (*Rice University*)
Donald Worster (*University of Kansas*)

VOLUME 5

The titles published in this series are listed at *brill.com/seh*

Framing the Environmental Humanities

Edited by

Hannes Bergthaller
Peter Mortensen

BRILL
RODOPI

LEIDEN | BOSTON

Cover illustration: "Wassergeist." Photograph by Peter Bergthaller.

The Library of Congress Cataloging-in-Publication Data is available online at http://catalog.loc.gov
LC record available at http://lccn.loc.gov/2017059464

Typeface for the Latin, Greek, and Cyrillic scripts: "Brill". See and download: brill.com/brill-typeface.

ISSN 2211-5846
ISBN 978-90-04-35884-3 (hardback)
ISBN 978-90-04-36048-8 (e-book)

Copyright 2018 by Koninklijke Brill NV, Leiden, The Netherlands.
Koninklijke Brill NV incorporates the imprints Brill, Brill Hes & De Graaf, Brill Nijhoff, Brill Rodopi, Brill Sense and Hotei Publishing.
All rights reserved. No part of this publication may be reproduced, translated, stored in a retrieval system, or transmitted in any form or by any means, electronic, mechanical, photocopying, recording or otherwise, without prior written permission from the publisher.
Authorization to photocopy items for internal or personal use is granted by Koninklijke Brill NV provided that the appropriate fees are paid directly to The Copyright Clearance Center, 222 Rosewood Drive, Suite 910, Danvers, MA 01923, USA. Fees are subject to change.

This book is printed on acid-free paper and produced in a sustainable manner.

Contents

1 Introduction: Framing Nature   1
   Hannes Bergthaller and Peter Mortensen

PART 1
Literary Frames

2 Framing in Literary Energy Narratives   15
   Axel Goodbody

3 Narrating in Fluid Frames: Overcoming Anthropocentrism in Zora Neale Hurston's Early Short Fiction on Rivers   34
   Matthias Klestil

4 320 Million Years, a Century, a Quarter of a Mile, a Couple of Paces: Framing the 'Good Step' in Tim Robinson's *Stones of Aran*   50
   Pippa Marland

PART 2
History, Politics, and National Frames

5 Ghosts, Power, and the Natures of Nature: Reconstructing the World of Jón Guðmundsson the Learned   67
   Viðar Hreinsson

6 Reframing Sacred Natural Sites as National Monuments in Estonia: Shifts in Nature-Culture Interactions   86
   Ott Heinapuu

7 Animals in Norwegian Political Party Programs: A Critical Reading   103
   Morten Tønnessen

8 Chemical Unknowns: Preliminary Outline for an Environmental History of Fear   124
   Michael Egan

9   Czeching American Nature Images in the Work of Robinson Jeffers and John Steinbeck   139
    Petr Kopecký

PART 3
Framing Nature on Screen

10 Black-and-White Telecasting? Water Pollution on Finnish and Estonian Television during the Cold War   157
    Ottoaleksi Tähkäpää and Simo Laakkonen

11 Who's Framing Whom? Surrealism and Science in the Documentaries of Jean Painlevé   175
    Kathryn St. Ours

12 Cognitivist Film Theory and the Bioculturalist Turn in Eco-film Studies   190
    David Ingram

PART 4
Teaching Frames

13 Framing the Alien, Teaching *District 9*   207
    Roman Bartosch

14 The Nature Study Idea: Framing Nature for Children in Early Twentieth Century Schools   221
    Dorothy Kass

15 Matter, Meaning, and the Classroom: A Case-Study   238
    Isabel Hoving

16 Postscript: Framing the Environmental Humanities   252
    Hannes Bergthaller and Peter Mortensen

    Index   255

CHAPTER 1

Introduction: Framing Nature

Hannes Bergthaller and Peter Mortensen

"There is no natural frame," Derrida notes in his essay on the "The Parergon" (1979: 39). In his argument, the frame is a figure that troubles the conceptual schemata which organize the discourse of aesthetics – a discourse which must, in order to move forward, presuppose a clear distinction between form and matter, between the example and that which it exemplifies, between the work itself and the medium in which it appears, between what is proper to it and what is not. The frame confounds these distinctions: it is not part of the work itself, but neither can it be merely an indifferent part of the environing "milieu," because if it were, it would not be able to fulfil the essential task of setting the work apart. Marking the boundary between the inside and the outside, it does not have a proper place: "In relation to the work, [...] it disappears into the wall and then, by degrees, into the general context. In relation to the general context, it disappears into the work [...]." (1979: 24) The frame is neither matter nor form – but one can trace its effects where the material intrudes on the form; it "warps," Derrida writes, "[l]ike wood": "It splits, breaks down, breaks up, at the same time that it cooperates in the production of the product, it exceeds it and deducts itself. It never simply exposes itself" (1979: 35).

Derrida was neither the first nor the only scholar to explore the potential of the frame as a figure of thought. There is a rich interdisciplinary research tradition (straddling anthropology, cognitive science, media studies, political science, semiotics, and sociology) for which framing constitutes one of the fundamental communicative processes by which social groups arrive at a shared sense of the world in which they live and act. Philosophy, pedagogy, art history, film and photography studies: all of these fields have conceptualized framing in distinctive, often divergent ways. The essays collected in this volume, which are based on talks delivered at the conference "Framing Nature," jointly organized by the European Association for the Study of Literature, Culture, and the Environment (EASLCE) and the Nordic Network of Interdisciplinary Environmental Studies (NIES) at the University of Tartu in 2014, rely on a wide range of different understandings of the term. In selecting them, our aim has been to give an impression of the remarkable disciplinary breadth of the work presented at this conference – a breadth that in itself speaks to the power of (re-)framing, as more and more scholars have begun to locate their intellectual endeavors no longer only within the various environmentally-inclined subfields of established disciplines (such ecocriticism, environmental history, or environmental ethics), but to also see them as part of the larger project of the environmental humanities.

And yet, in framing this volume, as an introduction must, it does seem apposite to begin by invoking Derrida – not only because he exemplifies a kind of thinking which, like that to which the environmental humanities aspire, is uncowed by disciplinary frames. Deconstructionism loomed large among the "bêtes noires" of early ecocriticism. Derrida's famous assertion that "there is no outside-text" was (mis-)read as a wholesale denial of the reality of the natural world, his popularity in literature departments interpreted as a symptom for the anthropocentric arrogance and narcissism of a largely urban-based academic elite. To some observers, however, it was clear from the outset that the effort to bring "nature" back into the picture (an effort which, it must be pointed out, historians and philosophers had already been engaging in for a decade or two before literary scholars joined the party) ran in certain ways parallel to Derrida's questioning of the philosophical tradition. Both were concerned with upsetting established metaphysical hierarchies and habits of perception. For the longest time, scholars in the humanities had viewed the non-human world as a mere background, an impassive surface on which the drama of human self-generation was inscribed. When someone like Alfred W. Crosby pointed out that the Europeans' successful conquest of the Americas resulted not so much from their superior mastery of the laws of nature, but rather from a kind of ecological dumb luck, he was effectively asking us to "see the painting from the side of the canvas or the wood" (Derrida 1979: 34). From there, it was but a small step to the many contemporary versions of ecological posthumanism, which argue that non-human actors have always been essential to the human story, that there is in fact no properly human history, but only the history of the assemblages of which humans form a part. Thus, the human comes to be seen as a creature within an ecological environment, within a frame that buckles and warps the figures appearing within its boundaries – a wider frame encompassing not just the "historical" time and space of human beings and their institutions, but evolutionary time and spatial scales both larger and smaller than those on which we are accustomed to think.

But still, mind you, a *frame* – and as such, not "natural." Reaching "[b]eyond the frame," Derrida insists, we do not find the world as it is in and of itself, not "the environment" or "nature" in the singular, but rather: "naturalization of the frame" (1979: 39). One can read this as cautioning against the desire which animates so much of recent theorizing in the environmental humanities: to slip from the frame altogether and achieve a sort of primordial intimacy that would overcome the distance which the very concept of "nature" seems to place between the human and its others. To speak of the non-human world in terms of "nature" is, in this view, already a way of "framing" it – not only in a philosophical, but also in the colloquial sense of setting it up for a fall. Among the most prominent proponents of such a view is Timothy Morton, who argues that the discourse of "Nature" (with a capital N) functions as a way of denying ecological interconnectedness: "Putting nature on a pedestal and admiring it from afar does for the environment what patriarchy does for the figure of Woman. It is a paradoxical act of sadistic admiration" (2007: 5). This is not far removed from Carolyn Merchant's earlier critique of the natural sciences which, as she attempts to show in a close reading of the rhetoric of Francis Bacon's programmatic writings, can be understood as a systematic effort "to put [nature] to the rack" (2006: 528).

If there is a prototype to such arguments, it is probably the late philosophy of Martin Heidegger who, in the essay "The Question Concerning Technology" ("Die Frage nach der Technik") (1953), employed the innocuous German word *Gestell* (meaning frame, rack, shelf or stand) to signify the mode in which Being discloses itself to western technological modernity. All modern thinking, Heidegger proposed, consisted essentially in acts of "enframing," of revealing nature as "stock," "supply" or "standing-reserve" (*Bestand*) (1977: 17). Unlike other, pre-modern modes of disclosure, such as the *poeisis* of the ancient Greeks, enframing is a form of "setting-upon" or "challenging-forth" (1977: 16) in which the world can no longer be viewed ecologically, as something that has a claim on us or with which we enjoy an organic relationship, but only as the "chief storehouse of the standing energy reserve" (1977: 21). *Gestell* is the instrumentalist, objectifying mode of thought that frames the world – its mineralogical reserves, its biodiversity, its human populations, even its chemical and atomic structures – as so many raw materials to be unlocked, manipulated, processed, transformed, stored, distributed and monetized. Although Heidegger drops tantalizing hints suggesting that an alternative "releasement toward things" (*Gelassenheit*) (1966: 55) might be possible, these tend to be overwhelmed by pessimism concerning the degree to which enframing has already more or less completely colonized our relation to Being. Contemporary theorists in the environmental humanities may generally eschew the eschatological mood of Heidegger's musings, yet many share the underlying assumption that the roots of today's environmental crisis are to be sought for in some sort of kinked ontology.

Such views stand in contrast with a rather different strand of thinking about framing – one which, rather than getting bogged down with the essence of things, is content to note that framing constitutes an ineluctable aspect of communication, and resolutely brackets the question of what lies beyond our frames, instead focusing attention on the sheer variety of their pragmatic uses and effects. The Canadian social psychologist Erving Goffman is often credited with originating this approach to framing. He understood frames as "schemata of interpretation" (1974: 21) which organize an otherwise meaningless succession of events into something coherent and meaningful. However, Goffman was building on the work of an earlier generation of scholars, such as Frederic C. Bartlett and Maurice Halbwachs, who had argued that the communication of individual experience necessarily involves stylizations and typifications. In his experimental studies on memory, Bartlett showed that individual retention of events relied on conventional schemata that were supplied by the social group (1932). Remembering was thus as much a social as it was a psychological process. Similarly, Halbwachs claimed that besides the individual memory, there was also a collective memory which could be studied in terms of "social frames" (*cadres sociaux*; 1925).

It must be emphasized that in such an account, framing is not a matter of distorting or falsifying the world. Rather, it is a necessary process of abstraction, given that the sheer specificity and complexity of private experience is, as such, incommunicable. The question whether the resulting abstractions are "true" to that which they represent is, from this vantage point, besides the point, since in raising and answering it we would have to employ schemata of the same general order as those whose truthfulness we are seeking to assess. Unframed, the world would be too much with us – we would not know what to pay attention to, how to distinguish the accidental from the significant, let alone how to convey our individual experiences to others. Whatever reality may be apart from our conceptual frames, it can become socially meaningful only after it has been tailored and cropped so as to fit the semantic templates provided by communication.

Importantly, this does not preclude the study of framing as a strategic quality of communication, and a critical assessment of its political effects. Whereas Goffman's work had focused largely on everyday life, one of his most prominent student, Todd Gitlin, went on to apply his insights to the analysis of political communication in the mass media. He proposed that frames should studied as devices which enable journalists to organize enormous amounts of information and bundle them effectively for lay audiences. They were "persistent patterns of cognition, interpretation, and presentation, of selection, emphasis, and exclusion" which capture the essence of an issue, define what the problem is, and imply how to think, how to feel, and what to do about it (1981: 7). In much the same vein, Robert M. Entman suggests that framing involves selection and salience: "To frame is to select some aspects of a perceived reality and make them more salient in a communicating text, in such a way as to promote a particular problem definition, causal interpretation, moral evaluation, and/or treatment recommendation for the item described" (1993: 52). Studying representations of nuclear energy, Gamson and Modigliani (1989) define "interpretive packages" and find that journalists routinely rely on five common framing devices when reporting the news: metaphors, exemplars, catchphrases, depictions and visual images. Contrary to the stipulations of rational choice theory, research shows that accentuating certain considerations in a message can influence the decisions that people make. Thus, in a 1981 study, psychologists Tversky and Kahneman demonstrated how presentations of equivalent information under different framing headlines inclined respondents to favor different courses of action. Again, communicative framing should not be equated with the use of lies, propaganda or spin, although journalists, politicians, spin doctors and many others do sometimes play fast and loose with the truth. Rather, framing is a necessity of communication that pares down complex information, charges it with emotional meaning, and gives greater weight to some considerations rather than others while conforming to what is commonly known about a subject.

Framing theory tells us that communication about environmental problems is never a simple matter of articulating facts that can be assumed to speak for themselves. Even such a relatively straightforward scientific matter of fact as the steadily increasing concentration of CO_2 in the Earth's atmosphere must be constructed as a matter of concern by invoking pre-existing cultural beliefs, narratives, metaphors and mythologies such as "lamenting Eden," "presaging apocalypse," "constructing Babel" or "celebrating Jubilee," to use some of Mike Hulme's examples in *Why We Disagree about Climate Change* (2009: 340–355). Scholars in the environmental humanities can use the concept of framing to better understand how specific meta-communicative strategies reflecting certain cultural traditions and preconceptions powerfully, productively and problematically shape perceptions of environmental crisis and of human-natural relations more generally. Framing can help us understand, for example, why Rachel Carson's *Silent Spring* (1963) became the most influential environmentalist text of the 20th century, as Carson successfully framed the hitherto non-existing problem of DDT pollution by tapping into already powerful anxieties about runaway technology and nuclear contamination. Environmental rhetoricians Kenny Walker and Lynda Walsh (2012) argue that Carson consciously employed scientific uncertainty as a framing device to destabilize scientific authority, amplify risk scenarios, and stimulate public debate. More recently, however, the scientific uncertainty frame was wielded with great effectiveness during George W. Bush's presidency, when anti-environmentalist pollster and policy strategist Frank Luntz wrote a now-notorious 2002 policy memo advising Republican legislators to start using the term "climate change" instead of "global warming," because the former sounded less frightening and left more scope for doubt (Burkeman 2003).

At the same time, awareness of the importance of framing should also allow those involved in the environmental humanities and the green movement more generally to become more effective and conscious active framers of debates and agendas. Successful "frame alignment" (Snow et al. 1986) is crucial to social mobilization, for only when the framing of an issue relates to the experience of a public and resonates in some way with existing cultural values, myths and narratives will it lead people outside the movement to change their political beliefs. The insight that "advocate frames" must complement "deep frames" (Crompton 2010: 46) in order to have a lasting effect ought to stimulate critical reflection and soul-searching on the part of environmental humanists concerned to transcend communicative barriers and engage with non-academic audiences in new ways. In particular, it should to make us wary of the tendency in environmentalist discourse to rehearse doom-and-gloom messages, or to assume that people would surely come around if only the scientific facts were explained with sufficient clarity and vehemence. But we also shouldn't underestimate the considerable difficulties of reframing environmental issues. Devoting oneself to the task of "build[ing] a visual and compelling vision of low carbon heaven," as the Futerra sustainable communications agency describes its goals (2009: 2), is all very well, but such exercises in prettifying the environmentalist brand will accomplish little unless they tackle the challenge of embedding their "sizzling" visions in deep frames which might endow them with lasting relevance and meaning. As cognitive linguist George Lakoff points out, frames should not be mistaken for simple ad-hoc messaging tricks, and they cannot be conjured out of nowhere. Rather, they must be built up over a long time, and require a good deal of concerted efforts to become powerful (2010: 79).

To be sure, the foregoing offers little more than a brief and cursory overview of the issues which the figure of the frame raises for the environmental humanities, and it hardly begins to cover the diversity of approaches and scholarly disciplines represented by the essays collected here. For purposes of convenience, we have grouped them into four thematic sections.

The first of these sections, "Literary Frames," brings together three essays addressing a subject matter which, as a rule, commands rather little attention from scholars who analyse framing in environmental communication, namely literary texts. In the contemporary world, novels and creative non-fiction play a marginal role in shaping public attitudes, yet the contributors in this section show that they nevertheless provide a particularly rich and complex medium for questioning and reflecting on the power of framing. In "Framing Literary Energy Narratives," Axel Goodbody compares media discourse on energy transition with the treatment of energy in three British novels: Charles Dickens's *Hard Times*, Jim Crace's *Harvest* and Ian McEwan's *Solar*. In representing energy transitions, journalists tend to invoke a consistent and relatively limited typology of frames, Goodbody finds. By contrast, the sheer plurality of frames in British novels, and the irony, ambiguity and self-awareness with which they are played off against one another, lead him to view creative literary texts as sites of experimental framing, de-framing and re-framing. The value of these works, Goodbody suggests, lies not in that they offer concrete solutions to problems, but rather in the manner in which they challenge the established frames structuring readers' self-perceptions and imaginatively reclaim forgotten but potentially fruitful ideas from the archives of cultural memory.

Matthias Klestil's essay "Narrating in Fluid Frames: Overcoming Anthropocentrism in Zora Neale Hurston's Early Short Fiction on Rivers" makes a similar case for the power of literary texts to challenge established framing strategies. His case rests on three early and mostly overlooked short stories by the African American writer Zora Neale Hurston, in which rivers inundate and disrupt characters' lives. Klestil finds that the unruly rivers in these narratives function as more than plot devices, as they facilitate a critical perspective on ideas of white supremacy and human dominance that were institutionalized in powerful early 20th-century discourses such as anthropology and sociology.

In "320 Million Years, a Century, a Quarter of a Mile, a Couple of Paces: Framing the 'Good Step' in Tim Robinson's Stones of Aran," Pippa Marland addresses a question of central importance to the environmental humanities: how can we avoid getting framed by our natural sensorium? Or, to put it differently, is it possible to overcome the biological parochialism of the human senses, which have evolved to perceive the world at spatiotemporal scales that are incommensurate with larger ecological processes? Tim Robinson's two books about the Aran islands (*Stones of Aran: Pilgrimage* and *Stones of Aran: Labyrinth*, published in 1985 and 1995, respectively), Marland contends, can be read as extended meditations on this problem. Robinson's ambitious and unwieldy work is place-bound but not rooted, connects local nature and topography to the planetary environment, and links the historical present to events of the deep geological past. While such a literature of spatiotemporal "derangement," with its dizzying shifts between the microscopic and the macroscopic, places high demands on both writer and reader, it also stimulates the environmental imagination in productive ways.

Our second cluster of essays is titled "History, Politics, and National Frames." While the four essays it encompasses cover widely different historical periods and bear the marks of divergent disciplinary traditions, they all testify to the continuing importance of a frame that has played an inestimable role in shaping the humanities, both conceptually and institutionally, namely that of the nation. In "Ghosts, Power, and the Natures of Nature: Reconstructing the World of Jón Guðmundsson the Learned," Viðar Hreinsson examines the life and writings of early modern Icelandic scholar Jón Guðmundsson, who is widely recoginzed as a key figure in the genesis of a distinctly Icelandic cultural identity. Hreinsson's lively account situates Guðmundsson not only amidst a good deal of dynastic and socio-political turmoil, but also at the center of conflict between rivalling framings of the natural world and its significance to human beings. Guðmundsson's life, Hreinsson argues, straddled the ever-widening schism between the "holistic" nature mysticism of the Middle Ages and the "objectifying" spirit of the incipient scientific revolution, which the Icelandic autodidact resisted even at the risk of being condemned as a heretic.

A similar conflict is the subject of Ott Heinapuu's essay "Reframing Sacred Natural Sites as National Monuments in Estonia: Shifts in Nature-Culture Interactions," which addresses the fate of Estonia's sacred natural sites in the age of the modern nation state. While great efforts went into protecting traditional sites of nature- and ancestor-worship, the meaning of these sites changed in the process of social and political modernization: They lost their connection to lived local practice and were incorporated into emergent narratives about the origins of the Estonian nation. Constructing a typology of romantic-era commodification strategies, Heinapuu assesses the gains and losses entailed by different ways of framing the significance of specific natural sites.

The third contribution to this cluster takes us into the present, and directly addresses issue of framing in environmental policy-making. In "Animals in Norwegian Political Party Programs: A Critical Reading," Morten Tønnessen draws on ecolinguistics, corpus linguistics and critical discourse analysis to investigate the status of animals and animal questions in Norwegian political debate, and in so doing he somewhat qualifies Norway's popular reputation as romantic, green and progressive. Looking at the actual words that left, right and centrist political parties use to convey their principles to voters, Tønnessen finds, reveals the almost complete dominance of the deep cultural frame that establishes animals as manageable and exploitable resources, relevant only insofar as they add to the value of human lives and enhance the nation's economic performance.

Michael Egan's "Chemical Unknowns: Preliminary Outline for an Environmental History of Fear" connects environmental history to the study of human affect by spotlighting toxic fear in the 1980s United States. This decade saw the widespread deregulation of industry, the de-legitimation of scientific authority, the marginalization of oppositional politics and the splintering of environmentalism under internal and external pressure. But the Reagan-era was also, Egan shows, a time when the fear of human-made chemical toxins reached a new pitch exceeding anything seen during the heyday of environmentalism in the 1960s and 1970s. Tracing this development, he argues, requires an approach that draws on a wider spectrum of methods than are usually applied by environmental historians and is, for that reason, an exemplary subject for the environmental humanities. Egan asks how these diffuse but overpowering toxic fears were manufactured, how their manifestations can be assessed, and what bearing their legacy has for the present.

In "Czeching American Nature Images in the Work of Robinson Jeffers and John Steinbeck," Petr Kopecký focuses on the reframing that occurs when the work of writers with specific national backgrounds – in this case the US writers Robinson Jeffers and John Steinbeck – are transferred to and recontextualized within a radically different setting. Kopecký attributes the remarkable popularity these particular writers enjoyed in communist Czechoslovakia, and the preference for certain kinds of text and imagery in their wide-ranging works, to anti-utilitarian frustration and budding environmental sentiment. Reframed by nature-starved Czech translators, editors, critics and readers, Jeffers' and Steinbeck's wild and mystical California of rocks, trees and ocean functioned as a counter-image to state-sponsored socialist realism, and became charged with romantic longing and utopian desire.

The question how (proto-)environmentalist sentiments could find expression in the repressive cultural climate that prevailed east of the Iron Curtain is also relevant for the first piece of the next section, "Framing Nature on Screen." In "Black-and-White Telecasting? Water Pollution on Finnish and Estonian Television During the Cold War," Ottoaleksi Tähkäpää and Simo Laakkonen discuss the role that the new mass medium of television played in educating publics and in framing environmental problems as issues of concern for audiences in two countries that were geographically, culturally, and linguistically close to each other, but were governed by very different political systems. Water pollution was a common and pressing problem in both capitalist Finland and communist Estonia between 1955 and 1974. After the mid-1960s, there was a rising tide of environmental concern in Finnish television programming. Although Estonian television producers were much more constrained in their ability to report stories which risked upsetting state-owned industries,

Tähkäpää and Laakkonen find that the contrast between the two neighbouring countries was much less monochromatic than the commonsense view of the Cold War might lead one to expect.

In "Who's Framing Whom? Surrealism and Science in the Documentaries of Jean Painlevé," Kathryn St. Ours employs Peircean semiotics to analyze the cinematic framing strategies of French biologist and experimental filmmaker Jean Painlevé, who in the 1920s and 1930s established himself as a pioneer of underwater photography. St. Ours shows how Painlevé's blurring of the boundaries between science and art reflects his critical involvement with the surrealist movement. While he was unafraid to anthropomorphize the octopi, sea urchins and sea horses which served as protagonists in his films, he also refused the temptation of turning them into mere symbols of the human unconscious. His aesthetic program of re-enchanting science by playfully and self-consciously combining scientific and imaginative methods of framing non-human beings, she argues, holds lasting interest for the environmental humanities.

The third and last essay in this section takes up a more theoretical set of questions. In "Cognitivist Film Theory and the Bioculturalist Turn in Eco-film Studies," David Ingram responds to the biocultural turn in recent film studies, which would reframe the study of film by highlighting how spectators' evolved cognitive and emotional apparatus mediates their encounter with and comprehension of film. Insofar as it presents human nature as relatively constant and unified, biocultural film theory departs from hitherto dominant historicist and culturalist film theories, which emphasize the social and ideological constructedness of human subjectivity. Seeking a middle course between these polarized arguments, Ingram positions the emergent field of eco-film criticism as pluralistic, flexible and comprehensive, open to many different dimensions of film's complex meaning-making.

The fact that many environmental humanists also teach for a living raises the crucial question how our pedagogical practices engage with, perpetuate or challenge different ways of framing nature. This is the topic of the fourth section of this volume, titled "Teaching Frames," which opens with another essay on a cinematic subject. Roland Bartosch's "Framing the Alien, Teaching *District 9*" discusses Neil Blomkamp's South African science fiction film from an ecopedagogical perspective. While the gory and action-packed *District 9* may not hold any obvious environmentalist message, Bartosch finds that the film works particularly well in teaching situations because it not only encourages student viewers to reflect on the power of genre conventions, but, through the figure of the disturbing alien "prawns," also raises questions of speciesism and environmental justice. It thus enables critical reflection on those "deep frames" whose effects on our judgements usually go unnoticed.

Rather than reflecting on the ecopedagogical challenges of the present, Dorothy Kass' essay "The Nature Study Idea: Framing Nature for Children in Early Twentieth Century Schools" revisits a time when "nature" held a far more prominent place in education than it does today. The subject of "nature study" was introduced to elementary school curricula throughout the English-speaking world in the years around 1900. Examining material from early 20th-century schools in New South Wales, Australia, Kass discovers a high degree of flexibility and openness within the subject of nature study. Much more than a tool of nationalist self-formation or the assertion of imperial dominance, nature study helped to imbue schoolchildren with conservationist values, and also played a crucial role in the formation of several of Australia's leading nature writers.

Finally, in "Matter, Meaning, and the Classroom: A Case Study," ecocritic Isabel Hoving brings us back to a central theme of both of the original "Framing Nature" conference and this introduction: the possibility that the environmental humanities can function as a disciplinary re-framing which enables new kinds of work and facilitates broader conversations about matters of pressing concern. Hoving presents her readers with field notes from an experimental course on the "material turn" in culture and theory, co-taught with a colleague from Art History and involving a diverse group of international masters level students with different disciplinary backgrounds. In delineating how the classroom debates and the students' projects which evolved from the latter both frustrated her expectations and surpassed them in surprising and productive ways, Hoving makes a compelling case for the environmental humanities as an open-ended pedagogical framework which allows for critical, cross-cultural engagement with today's environmental problems.

Bibliography

Bartlett, Frederic C. 1932. *Remembering*. Cambridge: Cambridge University Press.

Burkeman, Oliver. 2003. "Memo Exposes Bush's New Green Strategy" in *The Guardian* (4 March 2003). Online at: http://www.theguardian.com/environment/2003/mar/04/usnews.climate-change (consulted 27.11.2015).

Crompton, Tom. 2010. *Common Cause: The Case for Working with our Cultural Values*. Online at: http://assets.wwf.org.uk/downloads/common_cause_report.pdf (consulted 27.11.2015).

Derrida, Jacques. 1979. "The Parergon," in *October* 9: 3–41.

Entman, Robert M. 1993. "Framing: Toward Clarification of a Fractured Paradigm," in *Journal of Communication* 43 (4): 51–58.

Futerra. (2009). *Sizzle: The New Climate Message*. Online at: www.futerra.co.uk (consulted 27.11.2015).

Gamson, William A. and Andre Modigliani. 1989. "Media Discourse and Public Opinion on Nuclear Power: A Constructionist Approach," in *American Journal of Sociology* 95: 1–37.

Gitlin, Todd. 1981. *The Whole World is Watching: Mass Media in the Making and Unmaking of the New Left*. Berkeley: The University of California Press.

Goffman, Erving. 1974. *Frame Analysis: An Essay on the Organization of Experience*. Cambridge, MA: Harvard University Press.

Halbwachs, Maurice. 1952 [1925]. *Les cadres sociaux de la mémoire*. Paris: Presses Universitaires de France.

Heidegger, Martin. 1977. *The Question Concerning. Technology and Other Essays*. Translated by William Lovitt. New York: Harper and Row.

Heidegger, Martin. 1966. *Discourse on Thinking*. Translated by John M. Anderson and E. Hans Freund. New York: Harper and Row.

Hulme, Mike. 2009. *Why We Disagree about Climate Change: Understanding Controversy, Inaction and Opportunity*. Cambridge: Cambridge University Press.

Lakoff, George. 2010. "Why It Matters How We Frame the Environment," in *Environmental Communication* 4(1): 70–81.

Merchant, Carolyn. 2006. "The Scientific Revolution and *the Death of Nature*," in *Isis* 97: 513–533.

Morton, Timothy. 2007. *Ecology without Nature: Rethinking Environmental Aesthetics*. Cambridge, MA: Harvard University Press.

Snow, David A. et al. 1986. "Frame Alignment Processes, Micromobilization, and Movement Participation," in *American Sociological Review* 51(4): 464–481.

Tversky, Amos, and Daniel Kahneman. 1981. "The Framing of Decisions and the Psychology of Choice" in *Science* 211: 453–458.

Walker, Kenny and Lynda Walsh. 2012. "'No One Yet Knows What the Ultimate Consequences May Be': How Rachel Carson Transformed Scientific Uncertainty into a Site for Public Participation in *Silent Spring*," in *Journal of Business and Technical Communication* 26(1): 3–34.

PART 1

Literary Frames

CHAPTER 2

Framing in Literary Energy Narratives

Axel Goodbody

Abstract

This essay is part of a wider project exploring the ability of frame analysis to serve as a common methodology for the description and analysis of oral, media, historical and literary stories about energy, in the context of today's transition to renewables. Taking as starting point the typology of frames in Gamson/Modigliani (1989), it applies the theory and methodology of framing to three literary texts depicting and reflecting on our changing use of energy. The first is Jim Crace's recent historical novel, *Harvest* (2013), which tells the story of Britain's agricultural enclosures; the second Charles Dickens's classic depiction of the Industrial Revolution, *Hard Times* (1854). The third novel, which is examined in greater depth, is Ian McEwan's account of the challenge posed by the transition to renewable energy today in *Solar* (2010). Sensitivity is demanded in approaching narrative strategies which can involve multiple, conflicting framings and merely implicit narrative perspectives. However, a focus on framing can, it is argued, foreground neglected aspects of literary narration, and give insights into the part played by literature and imagination in energy debates.

1   Introduction: Framing in Energy Stories

In the Climate Change Act of 2008 the UK government set the country ambitious targets for decarbonising the economy, while simultaneously seeking to maintain energy security and affordability. While the British public in general accepts the need to switch from coal, oil and gas to renewable energy sources, there are significant forces of resistance to energy system change,[1] which must be understood if they are to be overcome. This essay is part of a wider project on stories about energy use and decarbonisation, 'Stories of Change: The Past, Present and Future of Energy.'[2] Over a period of three years starting in July

---

1   'Energy system change' is defined as "an interconnected set of transformations in the systems of supply, demand, infrastructure and human behaviour," in a recent study drawing on interviews with stakeholders, workshops and a public opinion survey (Parkhill 2013: 2).
2   UK Arts & Humanities Research Council, grant AH/L008173/1.

2014, an interdisciplinary team has collected, curated and analysed oral accounts by members of three different communities in England and Wales of their experiences with changes in the production and consumption of energy.

By giving voice to individuals and communities disadvantaged or otherwise affected by the consequences of our burning of fossil fuels and the transition to renewables, the project aims to raise awareness of the diverse impacts of change, stimulate debate, inform policy, and generally facilitate transition to the post-carbon economy. It has also pursued its aim to promote environmental literacy by commissioning artistic work involving the communities which it engaged with. Researchers in storytelling and personal narrative from the George Ewart Evans Centre for Storytelling at the University of South Wales worked together with environmental historians, sociologists and literary scholars on the project.[3] A key aim was to set the experiences, dilemmas and decisions captured in digital storytelling in a wider context, by juxtaposing them on the one hand with historical accounts of earlier socio-technical transitions such as the shift from the organic economy to coal power in the industrial revolution, and on the other with literary narratives describing, remembering, interpreting and imagining the implications of past, present and future changes in relations with energy.

Focusing on the framing of energy-related change provides a way of comparing oral, historical, media and literary narratives. The purpose of this paper is therefore to test the application of the principles of frame analysis to works of literature through exploratory case studies. Because energy is abstract and intangible, issues connected with it gain much of their significance for the general public through discursive construction. Exemplification and the association of situations and choices with those encountered in other social issues play a key role in energy stories. The media play a central part in shaping debates on energy, typically linking matters of energy production and use with worldviews and political ideologies. However, literature also feeds into the social construction of energy relations, with its staging of scenarios and imagining of the consequences of actions through fictional depiction.

The premise on which the literary dimension of the 'Stories of Change' project is founded is that literary texts make a distinctive contribution to contemporary discourses on energy through their focus on the social, psychological and cultural implications of energy system change rather than its economic and political dimensions (although these last are by no means ignored in novels of social realism and speculative future fiction). Representing and dramatizing individual and collective experiences, novels in particular explore the

---

3 See https://www.storiesofchange.ac.uk.

complex consequences of energy system change, and issues of agency and responsibility. They frame energy choices by embedding them in moral and religious frameworks and aligning them with traditional patterns of thought and cultural narratives. A second common (though not universal) feature of literary texts is their mediation of alterity,[4] here for instance in the form of overlooked or suppressed experiences of energy system change. Working with personalisation, dramatization and emotional focalisation, plays and novels expose the public to the experiences of others, and distribute readers' empathy in ways leading them to identify with new perspectives on energy dilemmas and choices. Conveying alterity can alternatively consist of breaking down existing habits of thought, finding words for thoughts hitherto unformulated. Concreteness and vividness of depiction give novels the ability to push the boundaries of what is imaginable by the public at a given moment.[5]

In the final part of this essay, Ian McEwan's *Solar* is read in the light of these considerations as a re-imagining of the search for a technical solution to the problem of meeting our ever-increasing demands for energy in the age of global warming. McEwan frames energy system change as a matter of the tension between altruism and self-interest. He challenges his readers by rejecting the master narrative of progress and resisting the temptation to indulge in either idealised notions of scientific practice or shallow optimism about human nature. However, before proceeding to discussion of literary texts, it is necessary to explain the concept of framing. William Gamson and André Modigliani's study of shifting public attitudes towards nuclear energy in the United States (Gamson/Modigliani 1989) is one of the more thoughtful and developed analyses of the framing of an environmental issue. In the following, I ask what their work has to offer for classifying literary energy narratives and understanding the structures and mechanisms by means of which changing patterns of energy use are perceived and evaluated, before looking briefly at two English

---

4   The term 'alterity' is borrowed from Derek Attridge, who has argued that the 'specificity' of literature lies in its characterisation by innovation, uniqueness, and alterity, describing these qualities as "a trinity lying at the heart of Western art as a practice and as an institution" (2004: 2). Attridge sees as further inherent dimensions of literature its occurrence as a 'performance' or 'event' which can be endlessly repeated but is never exactly the same, and its engagement with ethical concerns (2004: 2).

5   Attridge's conception of literature as distinguished by vividness, immediacy, cogency, complexity, a congruence of form and content, and an appeal to the emotions as well as the intellect is unobjectionable. However, his insistence that it demands mental and emotional expansion and change in the reader (2004: 77), and that it resists instrumentalisation, its effects being too unpredictable to serve as a political or even moral programme, (2004: 7) is a selective one which excludes many works normally classified as 'fiction.'

novels depicting past energy system changes, and finally examining McEwan's account of the current energy predicament in greater detail.

2 Frame Analysis in Media Studies, and Its Application to Literature

In their study of media discourse and public opinion on nuclear power in America over four decades after the Second World War, the sociologists Gamson and Modigliani argue that discourses compose 'interpretive packages' which offer meanings for significant social events, and that they do so through a mix of rational arguments and moral appeals, metaphors and images. They distinguish between three broad types of discourse on issues such as energy: technical/scientific discourses, the 'political' discourse of officials and administrators, and what they call 'challenger' discourses in the media, in which interpretive packages seek to mobilise audiences and shape public opinion. Media discourses dominate contemporary cultures, reflecting their formation, but at the same time reconfiguring it. Journalists tend to derive ideas and terms from other forums, paraphrasing or quoting, and to draw on the popular culture which they share with their audience. But they also contribute their own frames, and exercise influence by coining clever catchphrases encapsulating their views (3).

At the heart of media packages, whose function is to make suggested meanings available to the public, are frames. These are central organising ideas, which make sense of events by suggesting what is at stake, for instance:

- progress (whether in terms of scientific knowledge or human emancipation)
- financial advantage
- security
- individual liberty
- justice

Media frames are normally unspoken and unacknowledged, but they organise the world for journalists, and through them for their readers and viewers. Frames imply a hierarchy of concerns, but within what they posit as the key concern they typically offer a range of positions rather than any single one, allowing for a degree of controversy among those who share a common frame (ibid.). Frame packages make extensive use of condensing symbols, which suggest the core frame and positions in shorthand. Gamson and Modigliani argue that a package can be summarized in a signature matrix that states the frame, the range of positions within it, and its use of eight different types of signature element which point towards its core in a condensed manner. Five of these signature elements are framing devices, which suggest how to think about the issue: metaphors, exemplars (i.e. historical examples from which lessons are drawn), catchphrases, descriptions, and visual images. The other three are reasoning devices, which justify what should be done about the issue: roots (analysis of causes), consequences, and appeals to principle (moral claims).

Gamson and Modigliani distinguished between seven key framings of nuclear energy in the American media: 'progress'; 'energy independence'; 'runaway science'; 'the devil's bargain'; 'not cost effective'; 'public accountability'; and 'soft paths.' In the first quarter of a century after the Second World War, the 'progress' package went practically unchallenged. By the mid-1970s, the energy crisis meant that it was replaced increasingly by a second pronuclear argument, that it provided 'energy independence.' Simultaneously, however, it was challenged by the rise of an anti-nuclear discourse. One group of environmentalists offered a 'soft paths' package, calling for harmony with the natural environment and decentralised production, and raising health and safety issues. A second, less radical group stressed the threat to individual liberty and democracy as a result of the lack of 'public accountability' inherent in the organisation of nuclear production by profit-making corporations. A third group presented a more pragmatic cost-benefit package describable as 'not cost effective.'

From the second half of the 1970s on, Gamson and Modigliani note the emergence of a new package, which they call 'runaway science.' This is fatalistic or resigned rather than actively opposed to nuclear power. The argument is that we did not understand what we were getting into, and sooner or later there will probably be a terrible price to pay. The runaway science frame has an antinuclear flavour, but is characterised by gallows humour rather than anger or the will to take preventative action. In the 1980s the once dominant progress frame continued to give way to runaway science and public accountability framing. A final new frame also emerged, characterizing nuclear power as a Faustian 'devil's bargain.' In this thoroughly ambivalent package the pronuclear argument of benefits in terms of energy supply is followed sequentially by the runaway contention that sooner or later there will be a terrible price to pay. Gamson and Modigliani concluded that it would be wrong to attempt to characterise American media discourse in the 1980s as either pro- or anti-nuclear: the dominant package in the media was rather the fatalistic combination of the two in the devil's bargain frame.

It cannot of course be assumed that the same frames will be found in other times or places, or in debates over other forms of energy. And they may only relate indirectly to the framing of energy issues in literature. Gamson and

Modigliani are only marginally concerned with literature, film and art: they do not regard these as playing a significant part in shaping or even mediating what they call the 'culture' of social issues such as nuclear power. They do, however, discuss the impact of one film, *The China Syndrome* (1979), commenting that this provided a vivid concrete image of how a disastrous nuclear accident might happen, and that the lead actress Jane Fonda became a figurehead of the anti-nuclear movement, giving it a public face and promoting it through her celebrity status. More significantly, they also write that to remain viable, packages must prove themselves capable of incorporating new events into their interpretive frames, and maintaining their attraction over time. To do this they need a storyline or scenario which is flexible at the same time as being consistent and plausible. Meeting this challenge calls for the ingenuity and skill of what they call 'cultural entrepreneurs' (1989: 4–5). Writers, artists and feature film makers belong to the category of cultural entrepreneurs alongside journalists and the formulators of political policy.[6]

Whereas novelists, poets, dramatists and cultural critics differ from journalists and media workers in attaching greater importance to aesthetics, they are not merely formal and aesthetic innovators: they are also concerned with knowledge and truth in the wider sense, and in particular with the ethics of human behaviour. The philosopher and literary critic Martha Nussbaum has stressed the contribution of literature (more specifically the novels of Henry James, Marcel Proust, Charles Dickens and Samuel Beckett) to moral debates, arguing that moral life is too delicate to be fully and adequately stated in the language of conventional philosophical prose. It demands, she argues, a language and forms which are more complex, allusive, and attentive to particulars. Only fiction possesses the emotive force, the subtlety, and imagination appropriate to moral life: it is an indispensable vehicle for moral enquiry (Nussbaum 1990: 3).

Needless to say, Nussbaum's conception of 'literature' as "carefully written and fully imagined" texts, formulated in a dense, concrete and subtle language, and structured as narrative, in which there is an "organic connection between form and content" (1990: 4–5), excludes works of popular culture on a par with *The China Syndrome*.[7] More important for my argument that literature should

---

6   The social movement theorist Mayer Zald has similarly used the term 'moral entrepreneur' to describe journalists, ministers, community and associational leaders, politicians and writers who provide new perspectives and problem-perceptions by reattributing blame, redefining tactics, and generally reframing social issues through use of new metaphors, symbols and iconic events (1996: 269).

7   Nussbaum acknowledges that while the novels she has in mind cultivate perception and responsiveness by illustrating them in the characters, and engender them in the reader by

be regarded, like the media, as a significant site of contestation over the social construction of reality, and that it should therefore be subjected to frame analysis (albeit in modified form), are the *cultural resonances* which Gamson and Modigliani discuss as prime determinants of the success of a given interpretive package, alongside *sponsor activities* and *media practices*. Certain packages, they argue, have a natural advantage because their ideas and language resonate with larger themes familiar in the culture. Citing the social movement theorists Snow and Benford, they note that some frames "resonate with cultural narrations, that is, with the stories, myths, and folk tales that are part and parcel of one's cultural heritage" (1989: 5, with reference to Snow and Benford 1988). Two (diametrically opposed) frames in debates on nuclear energy are singled out as having benefited particularly from cultural resonances in America: *progress* (from narratives celebrating technical progress, efficiency, adaptability, innovation and expansion, images of the inventor as a cultural hero, and tales of mastery over nature), and *soft paths/ runaway science* (which reflect scepticism/ hostility to technology, benefitting from appeals to harmony with nature by the Transcendentalists Emerson and Thoreau, and from instantiations of the narrative of technology out of control such as *Frankenstein, Modern Times, Brave New World,* and *2001: A Space Odyssey*). Novelists, poets, dramatists and literary essayists make both conscious and unconscious use of cultural resonances in their work, finding new formulations which draw on a reservoir of cultural models. Their work feeds in turn into the popular culture from which journalists derive inspiration.

Although there is, as this suggests, no rigid boundary between literary and media discourses, there are, when it comes to framing issues, differences of degree between them. Journalism is more likely to be directly exposed to the (material) interests of sponsors than literature, and to be under pressure to conform to the publisher's political philosophy. Literary writers often construct a counter-discourse to dominant social positions, but are normally granted the licence to defer closure and withhold judgement in the face of complexity. Whereas journalists tend to simplify their message and shape their material to match the formulae of familiar news stories, for instance making an official interpretation package their starting point in discussing an issue, and seeking to give the impression of objectivity by striking a balance between this and a rival package (thereby reducing controversies to two competing positions). Literary writing is likely to be more experimental and ambivalent than media writing,

---

setting up a similar complex activity, it is not the case that all novels facilitate experiential learning in this way. Neither novels with an omniscient authorial posture nor ones full of dramatic action are helpful. Certain dramas, biographies and histories can on the other hand give the necessary attention to particularity and emotion (1990: 44–46).

offering the reader positions (implicitly as well as explicitly), but simultaneously relativising or undermining them with ironic detachment. While journalism commonly serves as an inter-discourse, engaging with and mediating between scientific, administrative, economic and other discourses, metadiscourse (i.e. reflection on the process of discursive construction) is likely to play a more prominent role in literature (particularly in prose fiction and essays).

In novels and plays, the issues are exemplified by constellations of figures who are sometimes overtly constructed so as to represent a range of attitudes and patterns of behaviour. These characters direct the reader's emotional engagement by linking positions with personal characteristics which are more or less attractive. The consequences of positions and behaviours are then dramatized and played out through plots in ways which also contribute to the construction of the literary interpretive package. In addition to the metaphors, historical exemplars, catchphrases and descriptions encountered in the media, representational conventions and narrative forms (which are often associated with a particular cultural tradition and a related set of values) predispose readers' understanding of literary texts: mode of writing and genre are not the least of the devices which guide our interpretation of the given issue. Intertextual references and other cultural allusions possess a similar function, as already noted.

While literary framing may be assumed to share basic structures and mechanisms with interpretive packages in the media, Gamson and Modigliani's methodology for examining public attitudes towards nuclear energy as reflected in the media cannot therefore be followed too closely, without running the risk of losing sight of the leanings of literature towards ironic detachment, ambivalence, and the direction of readers' attention to the process of framing itself (rather than mobilising them within the parameters of a given ideology). The list of media frames will have to be adapted and the catalogue of framing devices expanded to include allusions to cultural narratives, personification, plot and genre. With these considerations in mind, I now turn to the novelistic depiction of three different energy system transitions.

3   Literary Depictions of Past Energy System Changes

The first important energy system change in human history was, as Vaclav Smil writes (2010: 6), the shift from human to domestic animal muscle power which accompanied the transition from hunter-gatherer to agricultural society. Food provides the primary energy which is converted into mechanical energy by humans and animals, and food production remained the most important part of the energy system until quite recently, despite the gradual introduction of mechanical (inanimate) prime movers. In the English context, the first wave of enclosures, which started with the rise of the wool trade in the late fifteenth century, and continued sporadically up to the nineteenth, marked a caesura in food production. Enclosure was a necessary precondition for the move from a community-based, largely self-sufficient economy organised around arable farming to the large-scale sheep grazing needed to service domestic textile manufacturing and the lucrative export of wool to the continent. It led to control of the means of agricultural production by a class of landowners, in whose interest villages were disbanded and the countryside was depopulated. The devastating impact of enclosure on rural communities, which was recorded in contemporary accounts ranging from passages in Thomas More's *Utopia* (1516) to the eighteenth-century poems of John Clare and Oliver Goldsmith, is the subject of Jim Crace's recent historical novel, *Harvest* (2013). Giving voice to the English countryfolk who were so painfully disadvantaged by this process of modernisation over the centuries, Crace tells the forgotten story of the loss of the land and a far-reaching shift in patterns of economic activity, energy production and consumption without which the Industrial Revolution could not later have taken place.

In an interview, Crace has revealed that he was prompted to write *Harvest* by reading a newspaper article on rural dispossession by soya barons in South America: "I wanted to write about loss of the land and people's relationship with the land" (Wroe 2013). While he sought to raise readers' awareness of the losses and injustices incurred in ordinary people's lives in processes associated with energy system change by means of a historical parallel, he renders the action timeless by avoiding reference to specific historical events, and by writing in a language which combines archaic words and expressions with terms and concepts possessing a modern ring. His portrait of a remote hamlet in Middle England is also geographically universal, a near-mythical deep place in deep time. Readers are encouraged not only to recall, imagine and vicariously experience an incident in the past, but also, by inference, to reflect on parallels in the present.

In Crace's framing, the act of enclosure is a tale of the absence of moral courage, justice and solidarity leading to belated and ill-conceived resistance to change, with disastrous results for the villagers. Whereas his narrator initially adopts an open stance towards the changes which begin to come over the village when the manor house passes into new ownership, these are depicted in increasingly negative terms as the action progresses. Village life prior to the change is described in terms of unremitting toil and hardship, and shown to be in a state of decline. It is nevertheless idealised in passages in the bucolic mode as a relatively egalitarian community enjoying simple earthy pleasures. Enclosure is presented as one step in a quasi-universal deterioration of the human condition in the course of modernisation. Towards the end of the book, Crace's elegy to an unalienated way of life in proximity with nature acquires a religious dimension. The unravelling of the old world of the village takes place, like the Creation, over seven days. Although the villagers are already paying "the penalty of Adam" (2013: 37) at the outset, toiling in the sweat of their brow, their fate is depicted as a repetition of expulsion from the Garden of Eden. And the destruction of the entire village by fire in an act of revenge by outsiders wronged by the villagers echoes divine punishment in the Apocalypse. Crace thus frames the transition from a sustainable economy based on mixed subsistence farming to a (locally) unsustainable one dependent on international trade through master narratives, metaphors and other literary techniques which accentuate the injustice of this rural dispossession and growing social inequality.

Crace's framing mechanisms differ from those employed by Charles Dickens in *Hard Times*, a mid-nineteenth-century account of life in the industrial revolution. However, the overall framing is similarly backward-looking and declensionist, despite the hopes associated with the partial restoration of justice at the end of the novel. A classic of social realism, *Hard Times* is as good a place as any to look for a depiction of the impact of the transition from wood, wind and water power to coal as the 'new' energy source, and of the advent of the carbon economy. Set in a fictional manufacturing city in the North of England, but based on the author's first-hand observation of conditions in Preston on a visit in January 1854, the book is a passionate indictment of the circumstances in which the workers lived, describing urban constriction, pollution, and the enslavement of men and women in the cotton mills. 'Coketown' is the name Dickens gives to this world of coal-driven machinery and the resultant bondage of workers to economic calculation and rigid work routines. The action in the novel is underpinned by the new pattern of energy conversion and consumption in Coketown's cotton mills. However, energy production in the coal mines is also present on the margins. Dickens describes the once idyllic landscape surrounding the city as 'blotted' with slag heaps, coal shafts and associated machinery, and he narrates, in a key scene towards the end of the book, how his representative mill worker, Stephen Blackpool, falls to his death down a disused mineshaft.

Hard Times, which is dedicated to the political reformer Thomas Carlyle, drew the soul-destroying regimentation of the workers' lives, unhealthy living conditions in the city, poor safety regulations in the coalmines, and the social injustice of the class system to the attention of contemporaries. However,

Dickens interpreted these circumstances as a consequence of the Utilitarian philosophy of Jeremy Bentham, which is encapsulated in the opening pages of the novel in the stultifying educational philosophy of the wealthy merchant Thomas Gradgrind, who urges the teacher in his school, Mr M'*Choakumchild*, to impart to the children "nothing but Facts, sir, nothing but Facts" (1969: 47). In reality, the problem lay less with the aims of Utilitarianism (which supported and achieved important social reforms) than with its implementation by proponents who combined it with laissez-faire capitalism. Dickens has been much criticised for lack of political insight into industrial relations and failure to recognise the importance of collective action of the workers. *Hard Times* nevertheless provided shorthands for many conversations about the social problems associated with the industrial revolution.[8]

Dickens's characters, which are distinguished by bold, vivid, repeated traits, his use of catchphrases, and his effective linking of themes all serve to structure the text and frame the social changes accompanying energy system change. However, it is especially his use of gloomy images and ominous metaphors of imprisonment and spent energy which serve as markers of a perceived moral decline threatening the cohesion and sustainability of British society in the Industrial Revolution. Glowing coals dying and turning to ash is a recurring motif in *Hard Times*. The girl Louisa Gradgrind is repeatedly (1969: 91, 94, 129) depicted as sitting at twilight in the prison-like children's room in Stone Lodge, watching red sparks from the fire drop on the hearth, whiten and die. The scene evokes the extinction of the children's imagination by their exclusively fact-based education, and the looming emptiness of the dutiful Louisa's life. Coal and education go hand in hand: "Combustion, calcination, calorification" are among the subjects taught to Thomas Gradgrind's children (1969: 94). In a wider sense, the reduction of coal to ash also symbolises the joyless lives working people are forced to lead in industrial Britain (e.g. 1969: 135). The business of the nation is described not as an active process generating energy by burning coal, but as groping in ashes. Parliament is referred to as the "national dust-yard," and Thomas Gradgrind's work as a member of parliament is described as "sifting and sifting at his parliamentary cinder-heap in London (without being observed to turn up many precious articles among the rubbish)" (1969: 222).

---

8 Karl Marx, an admirer of Dickens's novels, echoed them in his depiction of factory work in Chapters 14 and 15 ('Division of Labour and Manufacturing' and 'Machinery and Modern Industry') of Vol. 1, Part 4 of *Das Kapital*, which was published thirteen years after *Hard Times*. A century later, the American historian and authority on urban life, Lewis Mumford, similarly referenced Coketown in works including *The Culture of Cities* (1940) and *The City in History* (1966).

Seen in this light, the opening sentence of the famous passage describing Coketown acquires added significance: "It was a town of red brick, or of brick that would have been red if the smoke and ashes had allowed it [...]" (1969: 65).

Thinking back to the framings of nuclear energy identified by Gamson and Modigliani, we see that while neither the position of 'progress'-type endorsement nor 'soft paths' opposition to energy system change is closely replicated in the overall framing of the two novels examined so far, there are certain parallels with 'runaway science' and 'the devil's bargain.' Through his narrator, Crace initially adopts a neutral position on modernisation, balancing the benefits it brings against the losses incurred. However, drawing increasingly on biblical narratives, he ultimately paints an overwhelmingly negative picture of the unstoppable nature of change and the inability of humanity to manage it in such a way as to benefit the collective rather than wealthy and powerful individuals. Dickens was for his part deeply troubled by what he perceived as the threat posed by the transition to a fossil fuel-based economy to public health and wellbeing. His images of the combustion of coal expressed contemporary anxieties about the dissipation and loss of national energies through social division and conflict. On a more personal level, he framed energy system change as a manifestation of the threat he perceived of the extinction of human warmth, imagination and affective concern for others in a world dominated by efficiency and economic calculation, self-interest and the machine.

A final point worth noting before moving on to Ian McEwan's novel is that *Hard Times* reveals the potentially limiting effects of literary framing. Dickens modelled the figure of the power loom-worker Stephen Blackpool on St. Stephen the Martyr, thereby presenting him as a paragon of passive virtue and saintly forbearance, and appealing to readers' pity, rather than seeking as a political activist to persuade them of the importance of workers' rights. The constraints of the literary market, which favoured a melodramatic genre imposing trite, unrealistic solutions on conflicts explored in the novel are apparent here.

4 *Solar*: Framing the Transition to Renewable Energy

How then does a contemporary novelist frame today's faltering transition to renewable energy? Must he or she fall back on such tried and tested (but simultaneously limiting) strategies, echoing the pastoral in a lament of what is being lost to climate change, seeking to convey a sense of the urgency of action through apocalyptic imagery, or relying on the power of emotional identification and moral exhortation? Can he or she avoid the limitations imposed by traditional narrative forms and generic conventions while still drawing on the persuasive power of narratives, images and cultural resonances?

While *Harvest* makes a parable of a historical socio-technical transition, and *Hard Times* critiqued a contemporary one, *Solar* presents responses to the challenge of an energy system change which has yet to come about. At stake here is the "imminent industrial revolution" (2011: 244) of "affordable clean energy" (2011: 150), that is, the replacement of coal, oil and gas by a process of artificial photosynthesis invented by the Nobel Prize-winning physicist, Michael Beard. Implicitly, the novel is also about the ability of humanity to adopt a way of life reversing ever-increasing energy consumption. In other ways too, McEwan's novel differs from Crace's and Dickens's. Whereas these depict the ambivalent consequences of progress and modernisation, castigate abuse of the opportunities which they offer for self-enrichment at the expense of others, and call for justice and compassion in their implementation, McEwan examines the reasons why humanity appears incapable of taking a step which is urgently needed for the benefit, indeed survival of future generations. Where they use affect and pathos to move and persuade readers, he works with humour and irony, and is at pains to avoid the charge of writing with an environmentalist message.

McEwan does not call in question the necessity for decarbonisation. However, rather than exhorting readers to take action, he illustrates forms of naïve optimism and evasion of the implications of climate change. In the course of the novel, he exposes, in turn, the tendency of politicians to simulate concern in their environmental policies rather than take real action, that of the business world to defend existing investments rather than support change, and that of individuals to put their careers and pleasures before obligations to the welfare of less fortunate others. The implication of the story is that the necessary energy change is not likely to emerge from processes of reasoning and argument. Nor will it be achieved by idealistic environmentalists relying on moral exhortation and artistic agitation to mobilise the public. If the world is to be saved (and McEwan leaves open whether it will be), he implies it will be against the odds, because we are deeply divided, and altruistic aspirations are outweighed by laziness and selfishness.

The issue of global warming and the need to replace fossil fuels by other energy sources is not addressed directly, but rather obliquely, using multiple distancing mechanisms. The proponents of change are minor figures, who are quickly dismissed or made fun of. First there is the 'pony-tail' Tom Aldous, a goofy Physics postdoc in his mid-twenties, whose brilliant ideas for modelling photosynthesis are later stolen by Beard. "Coal and then oil have made us, but now we know, burning the stuff will ruin us," Aldous argues. "We need a different fuel or we fail, we sink. It's about another industrial revolution. And there's no way round it, the future is electricity and hydrogen, the only two energy carriers we know that are clean at the point of use" (2011: 26). At this point, Beard dismisses Aldous's arguments: put off by the young man's "bucolic" Norfolk accent and holier-than-thou diet of salad and yoghurt, he is suspicious of his talk of "the planet." The irritating enthusiasm with which Aldous insists the world is in peril is encountered again in the artists and writers in whose company Beard is invited to "see global warming for himself" (2011: 59) in the Arctic, by witnessing a dramatically melting glacier. They are convinced they can enhance public awareness of global warming and trigger "profound inner change" (2011: 66) in individuals through their work. Sceptical about both the urgency of change and its viability, Beard is touched by the artists' good intentions, but doubly alienated by their assumptions about the impact of their efforts, and the moral puritanism of their appeal to austerity.

While vaguely deploring climate change and expecting governments to meet and take action, Beard thus reacts allergically to environmentalist apocalypticism (2011: 15). Through a chain of circumstances he becomes an unlikely proponent of solar energy. Eloquent arguments for transition are put into his mouth, but at moments and in contexts which undermine them. At the midpoint of the novel, he echoes Aldous's words in a set-piece speech to investors explaining the necessity for decarbonisation (2011: 148–156). It is a *tour de force*, operating with a sequence of different frames to appeal to his listeners. However, the whole speech is overshadowed by indications that the nauseous Beard, who has gorged himself on smoked salmon sandwiches, is about to throw up. Similarly, at the end of the novel, the reader's attention is distracted from Beard's stirring words to site workers on the eve of the inauguration of his revolutionary solar energy plant, by hints that everything is about to go spectacularly wrong (2011: 249f.).

More space in the book is in any case devoted to the breakup of Beard's marriage and his relationships with other women, and to his uncontrolled appetite, than to his efforts to generate solar energy. The narrative focuses on the psychology of infidelity and Beard's reluctance to commit to the responsibilities of fatherhood. Beard is an allegorical figure, standing for a humankind constantly deflected from the goal of addressing the world's most important problems by laziness and self-indulgence, repeatedly giving in to the calls of food and sex. (On 2011: 170f. he is described as "comfortably" sharing all of humanity's faults.)

McEwan's message is underlined in an overtly allegorical passage about the quasi-entropic circumstances of growing disorder in the boot room of the ship in the Arctic where the climate artists and scientists are accommodated: "How were they to save the earth – assuming it needed saving, which he doubted," Beard asks himself, "when it was so much larger than the boot room?" (2011: 78) If Beard's relationships with women symbolise the mis-management of our lives in general, and his appetite for sex and food are metaphors for the consumer society, the book contains a series of further metaphors for our creeping destruction of the environment. These include Beard's bloated body, the cancer on his hand, and congested cities like London, which is described as a vast organism consuming the environment. "How could we ever begin to restrain ourselves?," Beard reflects, looking down on the city from a circling aeroplane. Humanity appears "like a spreading lichen, a ravaging bloom of algae, a mould enveloping a soft fruit – we were such a wild success. Up there with the spores!" (2011: 111)

McEwan adopts a writing strategy which, like that of Dickens, personifies positions in the energy debate in graphically delineated characters, but he combines Dickens's blend of social realism and allegory with a greater measure of satire. Like Crace, he builds suspense, but he substitutes rhetorical brilliance for the sensuous richness of *Harvest*'s landscape descriptions. McEwan forces readers to acknowledge conflicting desires and human weakness as barriers in human nature to transition from the carbon economy to renewables. If the book reveals any activist intention, it lies in his sarcasm challenging us to reaffirm our will to change.

5 In Conclusion: The Applicability of Media Frames to Literary Accounts of Energy System Change

How, finally, does the framing of energy system change in *Solar* then compare with Gamson and Modigliani's media frames and related hierarchies of concerns? They list, as noted above, 'progress,' 'financial advantage,' 'security,' 'individual liberty' and 'justice' as quasi-universal frames in the presentation of environmental problems and their solutions, each with its own implications for who should take action, what should be done, and how. Viewed in this light, McEwan's book presents a strikingly complex picture. It operates within the 'progress' frame inasmuch as it engages with treasured notions of the accumulation and rational application of scientific knowledge – but only to challenge them. While acknowledging that scientific and technological innovation have a central role to play in satisfying future energy needs, McEwan is far from either idealising scientific practice or writing a paean to solar energy.

The 'financial advantage' frame is present on two levels: on the one hand, the financial argument for renewables is found alongside others in Beard's speech to potential investors. On the other, his own efforts to develop solar energy are driven throughout by a quest for personal gain. McEwan also describes the machinations of leaders of research teams seeking to maximise funding streams for their work on renewable energy and the cynical behaviour of politicians seeking public approval. While 'energy security' also features as an argument in Beard's London speech to investors, it does not otherwise play a large role in the novel. Nor does McEwan present resistance to the transition to renewable energy as dominated by fear of 'loss of individual liberty,' unless one interprets as such Beard's defence of his freedom to indulge his needs and desires. The issue of 'justice' is, however, present throughout the novel, in the sense that the monstrous Beard provocatively denies responsibility for future generations, but in the end has to learn to accept the demands of the child he has tried so hard not to conceive.

There remain the three further, more specific framings observed by Gamson and Modigliani in their analysis of nuclear energy debates: 'runaway science,' 'soft paths,' and the 'devil's bargain.' ('Progress' is present in both sets of terms, and 'energy independence,' 'cost effectivity' and 'public accountability' can be regarded as respective subsets of 'security,' 'financial advantage' and 'individual liberty.') Tom Aldous and the artists and writers whom Beard meets on his trip to the Arctic represent variants of the 'soft paths,' holistic environmentalist frame. They introduce alternatives to Beard's 'financial advantage' perspective, but are marginalised. 'Runaway science' (fear of the dangers of technology), and the 'devil's bargain' (fatalistic combination of acceptance of the benefits of technology with a sense there will be a terrible price to pay in the future) are frames of special significance for nuclear debates, but not for solar energy, and do not feature in this novel. However, *Solar* shares the "gallows humour" observed by Gamson and Modigliani in the 'runaway science' frame. It is not a book written in anger or seeking to stir readers into climate activism. McEwan's position on the conflictedness of human nature ("the old parliament of [Beard's] selfhood was in uproarious division," we are told on 2011: 262) also corresponds to the ambivalence of the 'devil's bargain' frame.

Solar then juxtaposes and stages conflicts between different frames, and McEwan critically interrogates them rather than simply applying a readymade frame in the fashion of classical journalism. On a deeper level, his treatment of energy system transition might be said to approximate to the 'justice' frame, inasmuch as he implicitly challenges readers to reflect on the morality of denying the implications of climate change for individuals' lives.

Space does not permit closer analysis of how McEwan's literary practice relates to the way media frames are constituted (through condensing symbols, metaphors, exemplars, catchphrases, and images). Suffice it to say that Beard stands out as an allegorical figure, and the scene in the 'boot room' as an image for the difficulties which face environmental governance initiatives. McEwan refreshes familiar symbols, by investing them with surprising and amusing new meanings. The polar bear, for instance, cuddly icon of global warming campaigns, becomes a dangerous presence when encountered by Beard in the Arctic, and a crucial prop in the slapstick scene where Beard takes Aldous to task for sleeping with his wife.

In terms of literary form as an element framing the issue of energy change and guiding our interpretation, McEwan does not draw on any of the three literary genres and cultural traditions normally associated with depictions of environmental change: the epic (associated with the 'progress' frame and confidence in human ability to solve problems); the tragic or apocalyptic (which frequently accompanies the 'runaway science' counter-tradition warning of the dangers of technology), and the pastoral (often found as a vehicle for the 'soft paths' or 'harmony with nature' frame). Instead, he resorts to comedy, social satire, and the picaresque genre. Beard's actions can be read as exemplifying the behaviour of a humanity which may be weak and foolish, but proves capable of survival through adaptation to circumstances. The protagonist in the picaresque novel is not presented as a virtuous character in charge of his own fate, but as an ignoble one, driven by events, making his way through life in a world of change and uncertainty by means of cunning and deception. At the end of *Solar*, as in the picaresque novel, no problems are solved, no enemies are defeated, no new truths are discovered. But Beard can be seen as the ultimate realist, living off his wit and powers of invention.

Crace presents the dispossession and displacement which drove peasants into the towns and created the English proletariat in the light of the biblical narratives of Edenic expulsion and apocalyptic punishment: the villagers' cowardice in the face of change and their indifference to outsiders appear as parts of human nature which cannot be changed and as manifestations of original sin. *Harvest* exemplifies the continuing shaping presence of the pastoral mode and Biblical narratives in current thinking, and shows how traditional concerns such as the loss of place can be mapped onto changes in the economy of energy.

The newly released energies of the coal-powered economy in the mid-nineteenth century and its potential for both good and evil prompted awe, but also anxiety and abhorrence. Dickens interpreted the exploitation and suffering accompanying energy system change in the Industrial Revolution as a consequence of the tyranny of reason and the triumph of calculated self-interest over empathetic identification with and support for others, implying that things could be changed for the better by the exercise of moral will.

In comparison, the ending of McEwan's book is ambivalent. It allows interpretation of the narrative trajectory as an inexorable movement towards catastrophe, resulting from inborn human flaws. But the novel can equally be read as a picture of humanity at the mercy of its weaknesses, nevertheless finding inspiration in the hour of need and muddling through – as a picaresque tale of erring but also Faustian striving and dogged perseverance. The latter interpretation finds support in McEwan's comments in an interview. Climate change poses a particular problem for our nature, he noted, because we are being asked to do things for people we'll never meet, people who are unborn: "This requires a scale of long-term thinking that lies outside our biology. I'm hoping to take the reader on that journey of what it means actually for us, how uniquely difficult it is for us, and how our cleverness might win through." (McEwan, 'Interview with Friends of the Earth')

This essay set out to explore how a typology of narratives of energy system change might draw on categories arrived at in environmental media analysis, and adapt them for the classification of literary narratives (and their comparison with oral and historical ones). My examination of *Harvest*, *Hard Times* and *Solar* has shown that while all three novels frame change in such a way as to counter hegemonic narratives of progress, and ultimately seek to activate marginalised forms of experience in imagined counter-worlds, *Solar* complicates this by simultaneously critiquing the naïve assumptions about human nature which underlie well-intentioned appeals to the public to support decarbonisation, and by challenging simplistic notions of the social agency of artists. Literary framing in at least some texts may be too complex and fragmented to serve as a workable basis of classification. Approaching literary texts with the tools of frame analysis nevertheless brings to the fore their conceptual orientation and structuring through metaphors, condensing symbols, genre choice and adaptation, resonances with familiar cultural narratives, and other textual mechanisms. This permits comparisons with the interpretation of energy relations in oral, historical and media narratives, and has the potential to throw new light on the special part which literature plays in energy debates – whether it be a matter of pluralising them by giving voice to marginalised groups and drawing attention to tensions and conflicts in individuals ignored by policy makers, or one of mobilising readers through emotional engagement and inducement to reflect our ethical responsibilities. Alternatively, the principal contribution of literary energy narratives to public debate may lie, in the spirit of the "complex particularity" which Nussbaum regards as the key to literature's uniqueness, in eliciting from readers, through the example of "tentative and uncontrolling relation to the matter at hand, one that holds open the possibility of surprise, bewilderment and change" (1990: 33), an open-ended activity of searching and nuanced understanding grounded in both cognition and emotion.

Bibliography

Primary Sources

Crace, Jim. 2013. *Harvest*. London: Picador.

Dickens, Charles. 1969 [1854]. *Hard Times. For These Times* (ed. David Craig). London: Penguin.

McEwan, Ian. 2011. *Solar*. London: Vintage.

McEwan, Ian. 'Interview with Friends of the Earth on climate change and *Solar*.' On line at: http://www.ianmcewan.com/bib/books/solar.html (consulted 19.03.2015).

Scholarly Publications

Attridge, Derek. 2004. *The Singularity of Literature*. London: Routledge.

Gamson, William A. and André Modligiani. 1989. 'Media Discourse and Public Opinion on Nuclear Power: A Constructionist Approach' in *American Journal of Sociology* 95(1): 1–37.

Nussbaum, Martha C. 1990. *Love's Knowledge. Essays on Philosophy and Literature*. New York and Oxford: Oxford University Press.

Parkhill, Karen et al. 2013. *Transforming the UK Energy System: Public Values, Attitudes and Acceptability – Synthesis Report*. London: UKERC. On line at: http://psych.cf.ac.uk/understandingrisk/docs/SYNTHESIS%20FINAL%20SP.pdf (consulted 19.03.2015).

Smil, Vaclav. 2010. *Energy Transitions: History, Requirements, Prospects*. Santa Barbara: Praeger.

Snow, David A. and Robert D. Benford. 1988. 'Ideology, Frame Resonance, and Participant Mobilization' in Klandermans, Bert, Hanspeter Kriesi and Sidney Tarrow (eds) *From Structure to Action: Social Movement Participation Across Cultures*. Greenwich, CT: JAI Press: 197–217.

Wroe, Nicholas. 2013. 'Jim Crace: "At the Watford Gap it hit me that the English landscape was absolutely drenched in narrative." Interview with Jim Crace' in *The Guardian* (16 August 2013). On line at: http://www.theguardian.com/culture/2013/aug/16/jim-crace-interview (consulted 19.03.2015).

Zald, Mayer N. 1996. 'Culture, Ideology and Strategic Framing' in McAdam, Doug, John D. McCarthy and Mayer N. Zald (eds) *Comparative Perspectives on Social Movements: Political opportunities, mobilizing structures, and cultural framings*. Cambridge: Cambridge University Press: 261–274.

CHAPTER 3

Narrating in Fluid Frames: Overcoming Anthropocentrism in Zora Neale Hurston's Early Short Fiction on Rivers

Matthias Klestil

Abstract

Despite prolific scholarly engagement with Zora Neale Hurston in African American studies and, more recently, in ecocriticism, many of the author's early short stories have remained largely underrepresented. Adding to an emerging ecocritical Hurston scholarship, this essay focuses on the central role of rivers in three of these texts, "John Redding Goes to Sea" (1921), "Magnolia Flower" (1925), and the only recently recovered "Under the Bridge" (1925). I employ the idea of fluid frames, conceptualized as frames that challenge human perceptive and epistemological boundaries, to describe the de-anthropocentrizing function of rivers in Hurston's tales and to show how her texts critique some of the dominant racist as well as anthropocentric assumptions of early twentieth-century (physical) anthropology and sociology. "John Redding" and "Under the Bridge" hint at nonhuman forms of agency through their employment of rivers and implicitly challenge the (pre-Boasian) anthropological idea of a hierarchical ladder leading up to civilization through their celebration of a holistic Black folk culture. "Magnolia Flower" uses anthropomorphized streams as narrators to deconstruct the predominance of human perceptive modes and suggests the constructedness of the racial hierarchies proposed by several early twentieth-century anthropologists. Thus, Hurston's environmentalism becomes visible as a multidimensional strategy that simultaneously subverts both racisms and anthropocentrisms of her day.

1   Introduction

Since Zora Neale Hurston's rediscovery and reappraisal in the 1970s, scholarship has overwhelmingly focused on her novels – especially the highly acclaimed *Their Eyes Were Watching God* (1937) – and has traditionally approached her texts along the themes of race, gender and anthropology. Moreover, such critical perspectives have been complemented by the recognition of another vital dimension of Hurston's *oeuvre*, her portrayal and appreciation of the natural world in general, and of her native Florida in particular. Critics such as Goodwin (1990), Morris/Dunn (1991), Brown (1991), Jones (1992), Stein (1997: 53–83) or Levy (2001), and, more recently, Davis (2006) and Hicks (2010), are increasingly drawing attention to this aspect of Hurston's work; their approaches attest to (and in the latter two cases explicitly argue for) the author's importance to ecocriticism, which now includes a growing sub-field engaged in recovering specifically African American perspectives.[1]

Despite these developments, however, both African American studies and environmentally oriented literary criticism have displayed a tendency to overlook much of Hurston's short fiction of the 1920s, the beginning years of her writing career. The former continues, under the influence of scholarship from the 1970s that assessed these texts as "apprentice work" (Bone 1975: 144), to dismiss much of her early short prose, with the exception of "Drenched in Light" (1924), "Spunk" (1925), and "Sweat" (1926).[2] The latter, lamenting that Hurston "by all accounts, remains largely unheralded as an 'environmentalist,'" likewise exhibits much more fervor with respect to interpreting her novels, whilst so far focusing much less on the shorter works (Hicks 2010: 113).[3]

Turning thus to a generally underrepresented and, in part, only recently retrieved set of texts, and adding an additional dimension to emerging ecocritical Hurston scholarship, this essay focuses on three short stories, "John Redding Goes to Sea" (1921), "Magnolia Flower" (1925), and "Under the Bridge" (1925; rediscovered in 1996). In all three texts, rivers play a central role as what I call "fluid frames."

---

1 Apart from a steadily growing number of articles and an essay collection (Mayer (2003)), major book-length studies demarcating this young branch of ecocriticism can be found in Myers (2005), Smith (2007), Outka (2008), Finseth (2009), Ruffin (2010), and Wardi (2011). An early forerunner concerned with some of the themes the field currently addresses can be seen in Dixon's *Ride Out the Wilderness* (1987).

2 Under the influence of works such as Hemenway's seminal Hurston-biography (1977), scholars have traditionally read the early tales as (yet unaccomplished) writing experiments. Higher literary value has only been attributed to the three above-mentioned texts; for an overview of scholarly approaches to these cf. Davis/Mitchell (2013: 101–107). The texts treated in this essay are generally mentioned only in passing; two exceptionally extensive readings of "John Redding Goes to Sea" are given by Bone (1975: 141–150) and Perry (1976: 110–124).

3 Ecocritical approaches to *Their Eyes Were Watching God* include e.g. Rieger (2009: 92–134), Norwood (1993: 173–188), and Stein (1997: 53–83). Moreover, environmentally oriented criticism has turned to Hurston's use of folk culture (Clark (2003)) and her relation to Florida (Willis (2012: 103–123)); Hicks (2010) more generally argues for Hurston's inclusion in the ecocritical canon. While several critics have turned to the role of nature in Hurston's short fiction, the only ecocritical approach to some of the stories considered in this essay to date is Davis (2006).

Generally, frames can be understood as "schemata of interpretation" (Goffman 1974: 21). They are fundamental sets of (often tacit) knowledge and ideas organizing social experience, i.e. unconscious "primary" frameworks "seen by those who apply [...] [them] as not depending on or harkening back to some prior or 'original' interpretation" (1974: 21). By "fluid" frames I mean to describe specifically such frames that challenge human perceptive and epistemological boundaries. Fluid frames occur in moments in which the social nature of primary frames as such is being problematized, for instance by narratively suspending human – or by hinting at alternative, non-human – modes of perception. In this sense, fluid frames fulfil a de-anthropocentrizing function.

In Hurston's stories, the functioning of rivers as fluid frames can be traced on both a narrative and a discursive level. On the one hand, the construction of rivers as fluid frames is the primary instrument of Hurston's de-anthropocentrizing narrative strategy: "John Redding Goes to Sea" and "Under the Bridge" weave rivers into their plots and diegeses as non-human agents in their own rights; "Magnolia Flower" employs streams themselves as narrators, seeking to blur perceptive modes. On the other hand, I argue that Hurston's stories thereby challenge a racially and environmentally hegemonic discursive framework of their time, as it was articulated and popularized through the disciplines of (physical) anthropology and sociology. In this sense, Hurston's fluid frames fulfil not only a de-anthropocentrizing function but simultaneously bear a de-racializing potential in the context of dominant assumptions of a set of transforming discourses.

In the following, I will first outline three of these assumptions as they became challenged through the "father" of modern American anthropology and Hurston's later anthropological mentor, Franz Boas. Boas is treated as part of a broader discursive context rather than as an immediate influence on Hurston (who only came into direct contact with Boas in 1925), even though my reading suggests that both could be seen as moving in a similar direction even prior to their meeting.[4] Subsequently, I will turn to Hurston's river-stories and read their fluid frames as instances of resistance against a racialized anthropocentrism,

---

4   There is no clear evidence, however, that Hurston was already drawing directly from Boas for the texts I discuss – too scarce are the available sources with respect to the period in question (only one Hurston-letter pre-1925 is known to have survived), and too unreliable is Hurston's own assessments of her early life in her autobiography *Dust Tracks On a Road* (1942) (cf. Kaplan 2002: 35–49). Nonetheless, it is highly probable that Hurston came in contact with Boas' influential ideas during her College-years in Washington, D.C., and as she became part of the "New Negro Movement" in New York – i.e. even before she began conducting fieldwork for Boas in 1926 (on Hurston's relation to Boas more generally see e.g. Boyd (2002: 142–155) and Plant (2007: 55–84)). In this sense, I understand Boas, for the purposes of this essay, as

therein suggesting a revaluation of this set of texts on the basis of more contextualizing environmentally oriented readings.

2   Contexts: Pre-Boasian Discursive Formations

Hurston's early stories emerged at a time that was marked by a persistently held set of simultaneously racist and anthropocentric ideas formed primarily during the nineteenth century, but still characteristically articulated by a variety of dominant discursive formations of the first decades of the twentieth century. One may identify (at least) three such ideas in the disciplines of (physical) anthropology and sociology.

(1) Firstly, there was the central idea of an *essentialist universalistic evolutionism*: Drawing from a tradition of social Darwinist thought and still influenced by pseudo-scientific concepts of the "American School of Polygenesis" (Morton, Nott, Agassiz), one persistent notion in turn-of-the-century anthropology was the *a-priori* assumption of a timeless constant of human (societal) development. As David Brinton, then President of the *American Association for the Advancement of Science*, pointed out in 1895,

> [t]his discovery is that of the physical unity of man, the parallelism of his development everywhere and in all time; [...] the absolute uniformity of his thoughts and actions, his aims and methods, when in the same degree of development, no matter where he is or in what epoch living.
> qtd. PÖHL 2009: 8

The assumption here is a simple (and simplifying) notion of "same causes – same effects," which – even though the idea of the "physical unity of man" prepared the ground for (Boas') modern anthropology – was turned by many of the leading theorists of the time such as Lewis H. Morgan, John Wesley Powell, or William John McGee, into an essentialist theory of racial difference. From their perspective, the assumption of "the physical unity of man" primarily facilitated the recognition of certain undeniably existing and all-embracing stages of development, several of which could – and according to this view in fact *did* – occur synchronically across the North American continent of that given moment. Perhaps most visibly, this view, which did not focus on the geographic or environmental contexts of a given culture but was primarily concerned

---

part of a transforming context, Hurston's short stories being – to some extent – parallel reactions against the same frameworks against which Boas set his new stance of anthropology.

with tracing human culture-evolutionary "Progress," found expression in such bizarrely appearing projects as the exhibition of "living objects" at the Chicago World's Fair of 1893, which portrayed and visualized graphically "the stages of development of man on the American continent" (Frederick Putnam, qtd. Hoxie 1989: 88), or William John McGee's "Congress of Races," an exhibition of living ethnological and anthropological curiosities during the "Louisiana Purchase Exhibition" of 1904 (cf. Pöhl 2007; Rydell 1984). It was such phenomena and their underlying conceptual premise of a universalistic evolutionism against which Boas came to vehemently argue throughout his career, with his diverging focus on the specificity of distinct cultures – read in their distinct social as well as nonhuman environments – and in his idea of cultural relativism.

(2) Intimately connected with the idea of a constant and traceable human societal development including the assumption of different but possibly synchronically occurring stages, was a second idea endorsed by many early-twentieth-century anthropologists and sociologists: the assumption of a *hierarchical relation* among such stages of development. Whether still rooted in (polygenist) arguments that assumed and constructed racial difference on the basis of primal physical distinctions, in terms of racial "character" as Broeckmann (2000) has suggested, or on the basis of Brinton's and others' ideas of culture-evolution and "Progress," an overwhelming majority of anthropologists and sociologists proposed a hierarchical order in terms of the "value" of the groups of humans synchronically being attributed to different societal stages. Euro-American "civilization," from this perspective, was held to be the climax of human societal development, i.e. the highest rank of a teleologically understood ladder.

This thought was expressed by no means exclusively regarding African Americans, but especially also with respect to Native American populations. Roswell Johnson, for instance, an American eugenics professor who joined Carnegie Institution's "Station for Experimental Evolution" in 1905, conceded in his *Applied Eugenics* (1918) that "[w]e do not mean, of course, to suggest that all natives who have died in the New World since the landing of Columbus have died because the evolution of their race had not proceeded so far in certain directions as that of their conquerors," only to continue: "But the proportion of them who were eliminated for that reason is certainly very large" (qtd. Pöhl 2009: 16). Even though expressed here in terms of a "tendency" by Johnson, the underlying impetus appears clear: Synchronically existing but presumably distinctly far developed and therefore not equally "progressed" and "valuable" groups at different "evolutionary stages" will inevitably (and not just metaphorically) "struggle for life" in the social arena, with civilization as the "fittest" element surviving. Boas critically drew attention precisely to this second concept, when he pointed out in the *American Anthropologist* in 1920, how "it may be recognized that the hypothesis [of a linear and universal social evolutionism] implies the thought that our modern Western European civilization represents the highest cultural development towards which all other more primitive cultural types tend" (Boas 1988: 282). His own stance of cultural anthropology, by contrast, was set against such hierarchies, which is reflected not only in his claim for a holistic view – and a particular value – of *each* culture, perceived in its specific societal, historical and geographic context as a phenomenon of its own, but also in his engagement in the African American struggle for equality throughout his career.[5]

(3) What generally followed from the described reasoning for many leaders within the scientific disciplines that formed the immediate backdrop for the emergence of Boas' cultural anthropology was, thirdly, a *deductive and prescriptive methodology*: deductive, because the methodological frameworks largely applied were not based on working from the observation of phenomena actually found through fieldwork in a specific culture, but primarily aimed to validate the pre-assumed hierarchical ladder leading up to "civilization"; and prescriptive, on the other hand, as supposed findings, especially regarding African Americans, were sought to be actively turned into political and social practice. Concrete policies were proposed both on the basis of a residual biological essentialism that assumed an innate (physical) inferiority, and in connection with a recognized physical "unity" of an evolutionarily understood human race. An example of the former can be found in Robert Bean's widely disseminated article "Negro Brain" (1906), which proposed openly racist education policies on the basis of the assumption that "due to a deficiency of gray matter and connecting fibres in the negro brain [...] we are forced to conclude that it is useless to try to elevate the negro by education or otherwise except in the direction of his natural endowments" (qtd. Baker 2009: 123). On the other hand, it was also prominent scientists such as Brinton – whose work is permeated with racist hierarchies and the idea of an unsurmountable inferiority of Blacks despite his argument for the "physical unity of man" (cf. Baker 1998: 32–37) – who opened the gates for (racist) political action via the rather unspecific, but all the more prescriptive general claim that anthropology "offers a positive basis for legislation, politics and education as applied to a given ethnic group" (Brinton 1896: 69).

---

5   While Boas actively supported "racial uplift" and conversed with Black leaders such as W.E.B. Du Bois or Booker T. Washington on the "Negro problem," his involvement with the African American intelligentsia of his day was certainly ambivalent and to some extent problematic. See Hyatt (1990: 83–102), Williams (1996), and Baker's recent work (2009, 2010).

3 Stories: Hurston's Rivers as Fluid Frames

In a variety of ways, then, the ideas of a universalistic evolutionism (1), in conjunction with persistent social Darwinist hierarchies (2) and a corresponding deductive and prescriptive methodology (3) permeated scientific and public discourse and marked the climate against which Boas modernized anthropology and Hurston produced her first short fiction. Such ideas were vital elements of what Lee Baker describes as the "ideological cement that fused capitalist development, imperialism, scientific progress, racism and the law into a rock solid edifice within US society" in the first decades of the twentieth century – a "cement" that Hurston was undoubtedly becoming aware of as she began studying and working in Washington D.C. in 1919 and then moved to New York in January 1925 to become part of the circles of the "Harlem Renaissance" and to be trained as an anthropologist at Barnard College (2009: 112).

It was at D.C.'s Howard University, namely in a student organization and literary magazine called *Stylus*, which had been established in 1915 by Montgomery Gregory and Alain Locke for the purpose of "stimulating and producing authors and artists within the race," that Hurston's first known published piece of short fiction, "John Redding Goes to Sea," appeared in May 1921 (qtd. Boyd 2002: 84).[6] The event gave Hurston access to a literary salon hosted by poet Georgia Douglas Johnson on Washington's S street, which enlisted distinguished members such as poets Sterling Brown and Angelina Grimke, writers Jean Toomer and Rudolph Fisher, and racial leaders such as James Weldon Johnson and W.E.B. Du Bois. "John Redding Goes to Sea," often underestimated by critics in the legacy of Hemenway's dismissal as Hurston's "groping, stumbling attempt to capture the folk ethos," is the story of an outsider-protagonist living in a Southern Black community, who is fatally equipped with a persistent longing for the sea and for exploring the world (1977: 19). Having been perceived from the start by the villagers of a typical Hurstonian Eatonville[7] as a "queer child," due to his overarching wanderlust and dreaminess, John's character is fundamentally linked – as his name suggests – with a fictionalized "St. John's River" (Hurston 1921: 925).

---

6 Five years later, in January 1926, "John Redding Goes to Sea" was republished in *Opportunity*, the much more widely read National Urban League Magazine edited by Charles Spurgeon Johnson.

7 Eatonville, Florida, one of the first all-black settlements in the U.S. and Hurston's hometown, recurs throughout her *oeuvre* and can hardly be overrated as a source of inspiration. Eatonville may easily be recognized as the setting of "John Redding" (cf. Plant (2007: 33) and Boyd (2002: 85)); in "Under the Bridge," the influence seems more subtle (cf. Boyd 2002: 138).

Read as a symbol, the "St. John's" primarily stands in for John's longing, as it is able to do exactly that which John desires most of all: it moves away, down "to Jacksonville, the sea, the wide world" (Hurston 1921: 925). Signifying on Frederick Douglass's 1845 *Narrative of the Life of Frederick Douglass*, Hurston's story portrays John Redding as wandering restlessly "down to the water's edge, and, casting in dry twigs, watch them sail away," referring to these twigs as his "ships" (925). However, just as for the young Douglass, still a slave in the famous apostrophe-scene of the *Narrative*, the sails at the distance remain unattainable (cf. Douglass 1997: 46), so John's "ships," too, encounter various obstacles. As metaphors for the protagonist's own stagnation, "these twigs [...] did not always sail away. Sometimes they would be swept in among the weeds growing in the shallow water, and be held there" (Hurston 1921: 925–926).

In addition to functioning as a signifying symbol, however, Hurston's river in "John Redding" also expresses a de-anthropocentrized sense of agency. With John being "home-tied" (930), at first by his mother Matty, who will not give the required blessing to her son's wandering off into the "wide world," and then by mother and John's newly-wedded wife Stella in unison, who vehemently oppose his desire, the river ultimately becomes the only means by which the protagonist is able to escape – even if it is through death. The story builds up to its climax as John is being asked to help fortify a bridge over the "St. John's" in order to fend off an approaching storm. Before embarking on this last (or maybe rather the first *real*) adventure of his life, John gives an insightful description of his state of mind and his dilemma in a conversation with his father. He explains:

> I feel that I am just earth, *soil*, lying helpless to move myself, but *thinking*. I seem to hear herds of big beasts like horses and cows thundering over me, and rains beating down; and winds sweeping furiously over – all acting upon me, but me, well, just soil, *feeling* but not able to take part in it all. Then a soft wind like love passes over and warms me, and a summer rain comes down like understanding and softens me, and I push a blade of grass or a flower, or maybe a pine tree – that's the ground thinking. Plants are ground thoughts, because the soil can't move itself. Whenever I see little whirls of dust sailing down the road I always step aside – I don't want to stop 'em 'cause they're on their shining way – moving! Oh, yes, I'm a dreamer.... I have such wonderfully complete dreams, papa. They never come true. But even as my dreams fade I have others.
> HURSTON 1921: 933–934, emphasis in original

John, the dreamer, the "queer child" closely associates himself with nature, entrusting to his father – the only character in the story who empathizes with

John's wanderlust – his sense of a fragmentariness of modes of perceiving the world that extend beyond the human sphere. He implies and muses on a variety of possible perspectives of experience, which, he feels, fundamentally escape socially framed human perception, but which may be accessible through a deeper sensual understanding. Although John, at this point, uses the idea of being "*soil*," "just earth" (Hurston 1921: 933), as an expression of his own non-agency, he does see – and eventually will find – the agency necessary for the fulfilment of his desire within another part of that natural world: the "St. John's." It is only as the river eventually swells up towards the end of the story and sweeps away not just the bridge but a crucified John Redding with it that the protagonist's life wish is fulfilled. That is, only by actually turning *into* pure "*soil*," into "just dust" of a floating body, does his liberation occur. The storm and swell of the river, read in this sense, represents more than a "deus ex machina of an approaching hurricane" to resolve the conflict and bring the story to some kind of ending, as West has suggested (2005: 24).[8] As a fluid frame, it also stands in, beyond being a mere symbol for a human being's longing, for a sense of agency possibly lying beyond human life.

The second story, "Under the Bridge," first published in 1925 in "The X-Ray: The Official Publication of Zeta Phi Beta Sorority" of Howard University, but only recovered in 1996,[9] similarly embraces a more holistic perspective through its employment of an unnamed river. Ending not on top, but "under" a bridge, as the title implies, the plot revolves around a tragic love-triangle including a 58-year-old father, Luke, his newly-wed 19-year-old wife, Vangie, and his 22-year-old son, Artie. After a month's living together through a sweltering Florida summer, more-than-platonic feelings begin to develop between the son and the young stepmother. Luke, pained by jealousy, decides to rely on conjure to prevent his marriage from failing. With a "small parcel sewed up in red flannel" and purchased for 10 dollars, he believes the seller of the item, a local "conjure man," that

> [...] nobody can't ever cross you. Wait till sundown, sprinkle it wid a drop or two of water and nobody kin git twixt you 'thout water gittin' him.

---

8 Other critics have perceived the ending of the tale as either tragic (e.g. Fisher Peters 1998: 24–25) or ironic (e.g. Howard 1980: 58–59); Boyd sees in it "a final act of perverse justice" (2002: 85).

9 Discovered in a cardboard box of Hurston memorabilia, the text has not been included in Gates and Lemke's *The Complete Stories* (1995). However, it underscores their assessment of Hurston's storytelling as evolving around the themes of "love, betrayal, and death," which are undoubtedly central to "Under the Bridge" (1995: xxiii). Regarding the process of the text's discovery cf. Houston Day (1997); the text is also briefly mentioned in Boyd (2002: 138–139), Croft (2002: 164), Cronin (1998: 23), and West (2005: 230).

But don't sprinkle it tell youse sho' you wants somethin' done, cause it's bound to come after de sprinklin.' And don't never take it off once you put it, else it will work the other way.

HURSTON 1925b: 16

Eventually, the latter happens, when Luke, as a last resort, sprinkles and activates the "parcel" intending to tragically harm his beloved son, but loses the conjuring device during a boat trip on the river. The charm unfolds and works, as foretold, the opposite way: In the climactic scene under the bridge we find the young couple embracing and kissing, while Luke, a victim of his own backfiring scheme, ends up lying dead in the rear of the boat and "was not" (Hurston 1925b: 19).

As in the case of "John Redding Goes to Sea," "Under the Bridge" ends with a dead protagonist floating away on a river and taken over by the stream: "The boat drifted on, for Destiny, the grim steersman, had seized the rudder and they were bound – whither?" (Hurston 1925b: 19) Thus, both stories leave human agency exposed as ultimately potentially open to failure – adrift, without a "rudder" – or, at least, as certainly not a sole guiding principle that could be seen as separate from alternative dimensions of agency such as the "water gittin' him" (16). In this sense, Hurston's de-anthropocentrizing fluid frames – in opposition to the premises of a dominant universalistic evolutionism infused with a hierarchization of cultures and focused on human societal "Progress" – imply not only a radical focus on the inner values of the portrayed Black folk culture of her own origin, which is being celebrated in its peculiarities (use of the vernacular; conjure). Moreover, they also echo a Boasian particularism as they combine this more holistic notion of a specific culture with an environmentalism that resists modes of thought based on a merely human perspective (as well as a purely biocentric one), emphasizing instead contingencies between the agency of both the human and the non-human.

A third short story, "Magnolia Flower," published in the 1925 July-issue of a magazine called *Spokesman*, is even more radical in its employment of de-anthropocentrizing rivers, as it directly subverts human perceptive frameworks through its narrative technique. The text, literally reduced to a footnote in Hemenway's Hurston-biography (1977) and unfavourably received by subsequent critics,[10] is significantly not a tale *about* a river, but is told, for the most part, *by* an anthropomorphized river as first-person narrator.

---

[10] Hemenway references "Magnolia Flower" as "[a]nother less-than-successful ZNH story from this period" (1977: 83). Others, being somewhat more appreciative, have perceived the tale as sentimental love story – a "happier version of *Romeo and Juliet* set in Florida" (Croft 2002: 93) or a "story of love conquering all" (Boyd 2002: 103).

The story starts out in heterodiegetic narration with a nightly squabbling among the large "St. John's," also referred to as "The Mighty One," and a small brook, who unnerves the former by laughing and singing away loudly at nighttime (Hurston 1925a: 33). In the ensuing conversation, the "Mighty One" tells its younger companion that it has borne lovers "up and down, listened to those things that are uttered more with the breath than with the lips" (34). The brook, intrigued, convinces the "St. John's" to relate a tale, which makes up the major part of Hurston's text, entitled "The River's Story" (34).

Apart from "Magnolia Flower's" anthropomorphism, two aspects are particularly striking with respect to the rivers' role as de-anthropocentrizing and de-racializing fluid frames. Firstly, the way in which the idea of a racist hierarchization of cultures leading "up" to civilization is being deconstructed through the intra-diegetic narrative; and, secondly, the means by which Hurston's text, more radically than the previously discussed stories, challenges the perceptive boundaries of experiencing the world, the means by which perceptive frames are mutually and continually blurred.

With respect to the first aspect, it is crucial how the intra-diegetic story told by the "St. John's" reverses the relations between "white," "black" and "native American" – i.e. between the supposedly fixed, because "naturally" or "culture-evolutionarily" explicable human (racial) groups. The river's voice recounts the fate of a former fugitive slave named Bentley, "large and black and strong," who subsequently turns himself into a tyrant in a Florida jungle setting (Hurston 1925a: 34). Here, Bentley "had many to serve him, for now he had built a big house such as white men owned when he was in bondage" (35). He takes a native for a wife, oversees a large workforce by which he is "hated" and "feared," and seeks to marry his beautiful daughter Magnolia Flower away (35). Eventually, Bentley dies of his own rage when she falls in love and elopes with a teacher named John, whose complexion is a shade lighter than his own. Throughout, the river's tale thus emphasizes how Bentley excessively and quasi-symmetrically repeats the ways of American "civilization" during African American enslavement: Bentley becomes precisely the kind of oppressor he had originally fled from. Hence, "The River's Story" takes a critical position with respect to the delineated discursive background. It stresses, against the ideas of essentializing and racist evolutionary theories of Hurston's time that it is neither "necessary" to be white (i.e. to be marked as "civilized" according to the dominant hierarchical logic) in order to be a "commanding" (or oppressive) race, nor that it is impossible to relatively quickly reverse – Bentley's "career" from fugitive to oppressor takes a mere four years – currently dominant race relations, which are thus unveiled as non-essential and constructed.

The second way in which "Magnolia Flower" resists culturally dominant premises of its time is the text's deconstruction of the centrality of human consciousness as prime perceiver of the world, which is implied in Brinton's "discovery [...] of the physical unity of man" (qtd. Pöhl 2009: 8) and in culture-evolution's anthropocentrism that omits contextualizing specific cultures environmentally. Throughout its tale, the "St. John's" displays a distinct sense of time and history: It repeatedly refers, for example, to the ways in which "men love to clip Time into bits" (Hurston 1925a: 34), creating "man-made time notches" (35), and mocks the idea of human historicity, as historical events are continuously described in a detached mode as something that occurs but that is not vital or necessary to the river's own creation of a meaningful world. Moreover, the St. John's perspective de-emphasizes the importance of naming, as protagonists' names are mentioned only belatedly, in passing, and as if coincidentally. The latter, in this context, appears to be not so much a (perhaps expectable) qualitative deficit of a young writer's apprentice work, but seems part of Hurston's deliberate narrative strategy – a strategy implying that, from the perceptive point of view of the stream, even that which humans call identity may be void and shallow.

How truly "fluid" Hurston's river-frames become in this last piece may be seen most clearly in the closing scene of the text, in which the voice switches back to heterodiegetic narration. Here, the protagonists of the St. John's tale return, having been absent from the vicinity for a period of 40 years, and indulge, as an aging couple, in their life memories on the river's banks where they used to secretly meet. The last sentence of the story, uttered by Magnolia Flower herself to her lover, is an answer – and at the same time technically and significantly a question – to his inquiry why the river appears to be making oddly unsettling sounds, why it is "murmuring" or "talking" in a way John has never heard rivers sound before (Hurston 1925a: 40). Her response is: "Maybe it's welcoming us back. I always felt that it loved you and me, somehow?" (40) Ending the text on a "somehow" and a question mark re-emphasizes not only the existence of two (or more) distinct ways of perceiving and being in the world, but also hints at the difficulties of communication between the two perceiving and narrating entities of the text: the river and the human. The story, by investing rivers with a framing function, thus ultimately leaves us with the notion of a fluidity of perception; it celebrates an openness between both frames, the human and the nonhuman, as mutually shaping each other's fate.

4   Conclusion

In Hurston's stories, rivers function neither as simple elements of a local color-celebration of the author's native Florida, nor as mere symbols and literary motifs. Instead, read in the suggested discursive contexts, Hurston's rivers may also be seen as part of a broader, subversive critique of some of the fundamental notions pervading racially and environmentally hegemonic discourses of her time – a critique that suggests her affinity with a Boasian stance of anthropology even prior to their meeting and collaboration. Hurston's stories employ streams of water as de-anthropocentrizing and de-racializing fluid frames: "John Redding Goes to Sea" and "Under the Bridge" question and deconstruct notions of a universalistic evolutionism by suggesting a more holistic understanding of African American folk culture, and by environmentalizing agency through their rivers. Hurston's underlying suggestion is that human societal phenomena cannot be explained by a notion of "Progress" or a universal law of culture-evolution, but must take into account specific cultures within their specific human as well as non-human environments. "Magnolia Flower" employs a more radical narrative technique in order to unsettle notions of a prioritization of human perceptive frameworks, as it openly challenges the idea and possibility of a hierarchization of human (racial) groups on the basis of a single trajectory heading towards "civilization."

Reading and re-assessing Hurston's short fiction anew within broader discursive contexts and from an ecocritical perspective therefore not only adds to recovering environmental dimensions of an African American literary tradition. Rather, it also demonstrates more generally the potential that lies in conjoining ecocriticism and African American studies, as it may lead to the recovery of so far unthought of dimensions of meaning in otherwise less prominent texts, help uncover the interconnections between the histories of racism and anthropocentrism, and draw attention to narrative strategies that artfully link writing against racism with resisting anthropocentrism.

Bibliography

Baker, Lee D. 1998. *From Savage to Negro: Anthropology and the Construction of Race, 1896–1954*. Berkeley: University of California Press.
Baker, Lee D. 2009. 'The Location of Franz Boas within the African-American Struggle' in Friedrich Pöhl and Bernhard Tilg (eds) *Franz Boas: Kultur, Sprache, Rasse: Wege einer antirassistischen Anthropologie*. Wien: LIT: 111–129.
Baker, Lee D. 2010. *Anthropology and the Racial Politics of Culture*. Durham, NC: Duke University Press.
Boas, Franz. 1988. *Race, Language and Culture*. Chicago: University of Chicago Press.
Bone, Robert. 1975. *Down Home: A History of Afro-American Short Fiction from Its Beginning to the End of the Harlem Renaissance*. New York: Putnam.
Boyd, Valerie. 2002. *Wrapped in Rainbows: The Life of Zora Neale Hurston*. New York: Scribner.

Brinton, Daniel G. 1896. 'The Aims of Anthropology' in *Popular Science Monthly* 48(1): 59–72.

Broeckmann, Cathy. 2000. *A Question of Character: Scientific Racism and the Genres of American Fiction, 1892–1912*. Tuscaloosa: University of Alabama Press.

Brown, Alan. 1991. '"De Beast" Within: The Role of Nature in *Jonah's Gourd Vine*' in Steve Glassman and Kathryn Lee Seidel (eds) *Zora in Florida*. Orlando: University of Florida Press: 76–85.

Clark, Suzanne. 2003. 'Narrative Fitness: Science, Nature, and Zora Neale Hurston's Folk Culture' in Mayer (2003): 45–71.

Croft, Robert W. 2002. *A Zora Neale Hurston Companion*. Westport, CT: Greenwood Press.

Cronin, Gloria L. 1998. 'Introduction: Going to the Far Horizon' in Cronin, Gloria L. (ed.) *Critical Essays on Zora Neale Hurston*. New York: G.K. Hall & Co.

Davis, Cynthia. 2006. 'The Landscape of the Text: Locating Zora Neale Hurston in the Ecocritical Canon' in Steve Glassman et al. (eds) *Florida Studies: Proceedings of the 2005 Annual Meeting of the Florida College English Association*. Newcastle upon Tyne: Cambridge Scholars Press: 149–156.

Davis, Cynthia, and Verner D. Mitchell. 2013. *Zora Neale Hurston: An Annotated Bibliography of Works and Criticism*. Lanham: Scarecrow Press.

Dixon, Melvin. 1987. *Ride Out the Wilderness: Geography and Identity in Afro-American Literature*. Urbana, IL: University of Illinois Press.

Douglass, Frederick. 1997. *Narrative of the Life of Frederick Douglass, An American Slave, Written by Himself* (eds William L. Andrews and William S. McFeely). New York: Norton.

Finseth, Ian Frederick. 2009. *Shades of Green: Visions of Nature in the Literature of American Slavery, 1770–1860*. Athens, GA: University of Georgia Press.

Fisher Peters, Pearlie Mae. 1998. *The Assertive Woman in Zora Neale Hurston's Fiction, Folklore, and Drama*. New York and London: Garland.

Gates, Henry Louis, Jr., and Sieglinde Lemke (eds). 1995. *Zora Neale Hurston: The Complete Stories*. New York: HarperCollins.

Goffman, Erving. 1994. *Frame Analysis: An Essay on the Organization of Experience*. Cambridge, MA: Harvard University Press.

Goodwin, Floyd. 1990. 'Nature Imagery in *Their Eyes Were Watching God*' in *Publications of the Mississippi Philological Association* 1990: 90–96.

Hemenway, Robert E. 1977. *Zora Neale Hurston: A Literary Biography*. Urbana, IL: University of Illinois Press.

Hicks, Scott. 2010. 'Zora Neale Hurston: Environmentalist in Southern Literature' in Plant, Deborah G. (ed.) *"The Inside Light": New Critical Essays on Zora Neale Hurston*. Santa Barbara: Praeger: 113–125.

Houston Day, Wyatt. 1997. 'Under the Bridge' in *American Visions* 11(6): 14.

Howard, Lillie P. 1980. *Zora Neale Hurston*. Boston: Twayne.

Hoxie, Frederick E. 1989. *A Final Promise. The Campaign to Assimilate the Indians 1880–1920*. Cambridge, MA: Cambridge University Press.

Hurston, Zora Neale. [1921] 'John Redding Goes to Sea' in Cheryl A. Wall (ed.) *Zora Neale Hurston. Novels and Stories*. New York: The Library of America: 1995: 925–939.

Hurston, Zora Neale. [1925a] 'Magnolia Flower' in Gates and Lemke (1995): 33–40.

Hurston, Zora Neale. [1925b] 'Under the Bridge' in *American Visions* 11(6): 1997: 15–19.

Hyatt, Marshall. 1990. *Franz Boas Social Activist: The Dynamics of Ethnicity*. New York: Greenwood Press.

Jones, Evora W. 1992. 'The Pastoral and the Picaresque in Zora Neale Hurston's "The Gilded Six-Bits"' in *CLA* 35(3): 316–324.

Kaplan, Carla. 2002. *Zora Neale Hurston: A Life in Letters*. New York: Doubleday.

Levy, Valerie. 2001. '"That Florida Flavor": Nature and Culture in Zora Neale Hurston's Work for the Federal Writers' Project' in Thomas S. Edwards and Elizabeth A. DeWolfe (eds) *Such News of the Land: U.S. Women Nature Writers*. Hanover, NH: University Press of New England: 85–94.

Mayer, Sylvia (ed.). 2003. *Restoring the Connection to the Natural World: Essays on the African American Environmental Imagination*. Münster: LIT.

Morris, Ann, and Margaret M. Dunn. 1991. 'Flora and Fauna in Hurston's Florida Novels' in Steve Glassman and Kathryn Lee Seidel (eds) *Zora in Florida*. Orlando: University of Florida Press: 1–12.

Myers, Jeffrey. 2005. *Converging Stories: Race, Ecology, and Environmental Justice in American Literature*. Athens, GA: University of Georgia Press.

Norwood, Vera. 1993. *Made from this Earth: American Women and Nature*. Chapel Hill: University of North Carolina Press.

Outka, Paul. 2008. *Race and Nature from Transcendentalism to the Harlem Renaissance*. New York: Palgrave Macmillan.

Perry, Margaret. 1976. *Silence to the Drums: A Survey of the Literature of the Harlem Renaissance*. Westport, CT: Greenwood.

Plant, Deborah G. 2007. *Zora Neale Hurston: A Biography of the Spirit*. Westport, CT: Praeger.

Pöhl, Friedrich. 2007. 'Tote und Lebende. Im fremden Raum der Anthropologie' in Thomas Gimesi and Werner Hanselitsch (eds) *Das Fremde im Raum*. Wien: LIT: 127–157.

Pöhl, Friedrich. 2009. 'Einleitung' in Friedrich Pöhl and Bernhard Tild (eds) *Franz Boas – Kultur, Sprache, Rasse: Wege einer antirassistischen Anthropologie*. Wien: LIT: 1–25.

Rieger, Christopher. *Clear-Cutting Eden: Ecology and the Pastoral in Southern Literature*. Tuscaloosa: University of Alabama Press.

Ruffin, Kimberly N. 2010. *Black on Earth: African American Ecoliterary Traditions*. Athens, GA: University of Georgia Press.

Rydell, Robert W. 1984. *All the World's a Fair: Visions of Empire at American International Expositions, 1876–1916*. Chicago: University of Chicago Press.

Smith, Kimberly K. 2007. *African American Environmental Thought: Foundations*. Lawrence: University Press of Kansas.

Stein, Rachel. 1997. *Shifting the Ground: American Women Writers' Revision of Nature, Gender, and Race*. Charlottesville: University of Virginia Press.

Wardi, Anissa J. 2011. *Water and African American Memory: An Ecocritical Perspective*. Gainesville: University Press of Florida.

West, Genevieve M. 2005. *Zora Neale Hurston & American Literary Culture*. Gainesville: University Press of Florida.

Williams, Vernon J. Jr. 1996. *Rethinking Race: Franz Boas and His Contemporaries*. Lexington: University Press of Kentucky.

Willis, Lloyd. 2012. *Environmental Evasion: The Literary, Critical, and Cultural Politics of 'Nature's Nation' 1823–1966*. Albany: SUNY Press.

CHAPTER 4

320 Million Years, a Century, a Quarter of a Mile, a Couple of Paces: Framing the 'Good Step' in Tim Robinson's *Stones of Aran*

Pippa Marland

Abstract

Tim Robinson's *Stones of Aran* diptych takes the reader on a journey that first circumnavigates the coast and then delves into the interior of the island of Árainn, the largest of the Irish Aran islands. In its sustained focus and wealth of detail it represents an extraordinary piece of landscape-writing. At the heart of the work is the motif of the "good step," an image Robinson uses to explore human "dwelling," and of particular significance is his insistence on the spatiotemporal frames he uses to discuss that step. He proposes that we hold in our minds, as the ultimate contexts for all the other spans of space and time that occur in the narrative, the beginning of time and the horizon of the visible universe. In its reading of *Stones of Aran,* this chapter explores the implications for ecocriticism of Robinson's expansive framework, assessing this in terms of recent concepts such as Timothy Clark's "derangements of scale," Ursula Heise's "eco-cosmopolitanism" and Timothy Morton's "thinking big." It suggests that Robinson's cosmic framing might potentially assist us in making sense of the kind of scales involved in the consideration of contemporary environmental issues, but that at the same time it also works to diminish our sense of the importance of the human species, ultimately and perhaps paradoxically focusing renewed – but valuably deterritorialised – attention on the "segment of home-planet" we each inhabit.

1 Introduction

"Cosmologists now say that Time began ten or fifteen thousand million years ago, and that the horizon of the visible universe is therefore the same number

---

* This essay develops ideas first explored in my PhD thesis "The island imagination: an ecocritical study of 'islandness' in selected post-1960 literature of the British and Irish archipelago," and shares some concepts and phrasing with this work. The research was funded by the University of Worcester, UK.

of light-years from us" (Robinson, 2008: 5). So begins Tim Robinson's extraordinary two-volume feat of landscape-writing, *Stones of Aran: Pilgrimage* and *Stones of Aran: Labyrinth* (first published in 1985 and 1995, and re-issued in 2008 and 2009 respectively), which takes as its subject Árainn, the largest of the Irish Aran islands. Described by Robinson himself as being like "two mirrors face to face" (2009: 7), and as a "diptych" by Robert Macfarlane (2005: n.p.) – perhaps in recognition of the kind of passionate (though resolutely secular) devotion Robinson brings to the island – the work is made up of two complementary parts. The first sees the author tracing on foot the entire coastline of Árainn, while the second sees him working his way through its non-coastal interior, recording throughout both volumes, and in as much detail as he can possibly accrue, the landscapes through which he passes. Thus, at any one point of his exploration Robinson's rich description might include an assessment of the particular geologies of the place, a discussion of the nature of its flora and fauna, a summary of its myths and folklore, a dissection of its cultural and political histories, and a sense of its interrelationships with other locations, near and far. This comprehensive account is augmented by Robinson's observations of the place's impact upon his own psyche, and the whole picture is presented within a spatiotemporal framework that, as the opening lines of the work suggest, reaches back to the beginning of time and out to the furthest extent of the known universe. The ensuing narrative runs to almost a thousand pages, and attempts what John Wylie calls "the total description of landscape" (2012: 366).

While Robinson immediately acknowledges that the figures he cites at the beginning of the work are based on our current understanding of the history of the cosmos, and will in all likelihood be superseded at some point by another perhaps equally speculative set of numbers, he proposes that this immense span of space-time should provide us with the framework for our reading of the text. He writes,

> But for the moment let it stand as the context, the ultimate context, of other spans of time and space mentioned throughout this book (320 million years, a century, a quarter of a mile, a couple of paces, are measures that recur, I note, on thumbing through my manuscript). (2008: 5)

This contextualisation involves a challenging act of imaginative orientation, moving as it does from the furthest extent of space and time to a couple of footsteps, but it is one that Robinson thinks is a necessary prelude to our reading of a work that puzzles constantly over the very large question of what it means to be human on this earth. The dominant motif of the books is the "good step" (Robinson, 2008: 20), a concept Robinson uses to explore the relationship between humanity and the world. The inspiration for the step is his sighting of dolphins off the coast of Árainn – creatures that seem to him to be "wave made flesh, with minds solely to ensure the moment-by-moment reintegration of body and world" (19). Conscious that such integration is, for the human animal, hard to achieve, Robinson sees the experience as presenting him with a puzzle that he formulates as follows: "Let the problem be symbolized by that of taking a single step as adequate to the ground it clears as is the dolphin's arc to its wave" (20). On the basis of this formulation he poses two questions that haunt the entire work: "Is it possible to think towards a *human* conception of this 'good step'?" (19); and is it possible to achieve "a state of consciousness even fleetingly worthy of its ground?" (20).

In his interest in forging an "adequate" human response to the earth and in his sense of the importance of the ways in which we conceptually frame our being-in-the-world, particularly in spatiotemporal terms, Robinson's themes can be seen as ecological in the broadest sense, and also as anticipating some of the specific concerns of contemporary ecocritical enquiry. Timothy Clark, for example, writes of the "derangements of scale" (2012: 148) that occur when we try to make sense of the massive discrepancy between space and time as experienced by individual humans and the spatial and temporal dimensions implied by climate change, and Ursula Heise identifies a tension between the kind of environmentalist perspectives that foreground the importance of local attachments and the more globalised views she believes are necessary for the development of an "ecocosmopolitan" imagination adequate to the kinds of socio-environmental problems facing us in the 21st century (2008: 10). Axel Goodbody argues that literature may have a role to play in providing us with a means of negotiating such conceptual challenges. Citing Timo Müller, he writes, "literature frames our notions of the natural environment in a continuous process of adapting and reformulating existing frames and proposing new ones" (2012: 23). These frames may take the form of cultural tropes: Mike Hulme suggests that we might make use of our human instincts for "nostalgia, fear, pride and justice" (2009: 239) – instincts that he characterises as "lamenting Eden, presaging Apocalypse, constructing Babel, and celebrating Jubilee" (329)[1] – in our attempt to develop a response to the particular conceptual challenge of climate change. Timothy Morton, by contrast, eschews such cultural tropes, encouraging us to move beyond the discourse of apocalypticism and to

---

1 As Goodbody notes, two of these tropes – Eden and Apocalypse – have been identified (among others) by Greg Garrard (2012a) as having a broader application to the question of human being-in-the-world, acting as "extended metaphors representing and reflecting on human interaction with the environment" (Goodbody 2012: 21).

think big, "as big as possible, and maybe even bigger than that, bigger than we can conceive" (2010: 20).

In the paragraphs that follow I explore the potential of Robinson's flexible and expansive spatiotemporal framework for mitigating some of the difficulties involved in processing and reconciling the scales of time and space involved in the consideration of contemporary environmental issues. I assess the way in which Robinson engages with and re-negotiates certain cultural frames, but at the same time, like Morton, moves beyond these through his insistence on situating human dwelling in the context of the entire cosmos. Lastly, I investigate the implications of the way in which, somewhat paradoxically, Robinson's cosmic contextualisation ultimately seems to orient him back towards the local and the immediate, but from a valuably deterritorialised perspective. This trajectory enables him to see Árainn as what he calls "a segment of my home-planet" (2009: 608) – a formulation that perhaps dispels in a single phrase some of the tension between 'place' and 'planet' identified by Heise. I argue that in the Aran diptych Robinson thus provides a model by which we might move conceptually between the local and the global, while at the same time encouraging us to witness more closely, and perhaps to tread more lightly upon, the ground beneath our feet.

2 Taking the Good Step

It is difficult to single out any particular section of the Aran diptych to demonstrate Robinson's method, since his approach is consistent throughout, but as a brief example I will trace the trajectory of a short section of *Pilgrimage* entitled 'Leviathan' (2008: 162–166). This passage finds Robinson covering a single mile of coastline. He begins by establishing its geographical orientation:

> The north-western coast of Árainn, from the wind-shadow of the Brannock Islands to the point where it turns east and faces Connemara, is open to the Atlantic and rises in cliffs to stand against the gales and look out onto the ocean beyond Slyne Head. (162)

He then moves on to analysing the geological formation of the rocks, both individually (in the case of a single forty foot long block on the shoreline) and collectively (in their arrangement in the cliff-face). He then recounts an occasion on which he witnessed from this cliff a basking shark "rolling lazily in the sun-filled water" (163), an anecdote that leads him into a discussion of the rendition of the names of this species of shark in Irish and English and their possible semantic roots. He then turns his attention to the history of shark fishing on the islands, and to its methods, referencing, as he goes, Tom O'Flaherty's account of a shark hunt in *Aranmen All,* and digressing to explain how oil harvested from the sharks' livers was used in Aran as fuel for little lights or "*muiríní*" (164). He also alludes to Robert Flaherty's famous Árainn-based film, *Man of Aran* (1934), and its iconic (but anachronistic) shark hunt sequence, noting Flaherty's own interest in the possibility of reanimating the shark fishing industry on the islands in the 1930s. This idea is one, Robinson tells us, that also occurred to a modern-day islander he met on the clifftop on the same day that he sighted the shark. Together they witnessed a Norwegian trawler in the North Sound of the island harvesting a shoal of sharks. This islander then attempted to go into the shark hunting business himself, supplying a small company on Achill Island, who marketed the liver oil and the fins – the oil as an engineering lubricant (of the kind used, Robinson notes, on the Apollo space missions) and the fins as an ingredient for Chinese shark's fin soup.

3 Ecological Framings: Place, Planet, Cosmos

The passage above has a spatial trajectory that sees Robinson's attention move from a single rock on the Árainn shoreline to the history of space exploration. Furthermore, in his mention of Norwegian trawlers and Chinese shark's fin soup, he hints at the island's implication in a global economic system. As these elements might suggest, Robinson's devotion to recording the features of the landscape applies not only to his immediate environment, but moves far beyond it, placing the island in what might be seen as a valuably global context. He provides a model that might be seen as anticipating Doreen Massey's call within cultural geography for "a global sense of the local, a global sense of place" (1994: 156),[2] and as displaying the kind of breadth of imaginative scope that Ursula Heise seeks in her concept of "eco-cosmopolitanism" – an approach that enables us to consider environmental and socio-environmental issues "in terms that are premised no longer as primarily on ties to local places but on ties to territories and systems that are understood to encompass the planet as a whole" (2008: 10). While Robinson evinces a passionate attentiveness to the local in a manner that may seem to conflict with Heise's rejection of ties to local places, it is a mistake to overstate the implications of his apparent localism, particularly in terms of its relationship with nation-based understandings

---

2 This formulation was developed in response to Massey's reading of another island text: Dorothy Carrington's *Granite Island.*

of place. Jos Smith describes the contextualisation of Árainn in terms of its geological history as offering a "pre-national understanding of the archipelagic space" (2013: 11), and Robinson himself is certainly not interested in nationalistic claims. These claims are, in his view, rendered irrelevant in the face of the time scales of geological history. He writes, "So the geographies over which we are so suicidally passionate are, on this scale of events, fleeting expressions of the earth's face" (2008: 7). It is a perspective that functions, effectively, to deterritorialise the island, to unhinge it from limiting ties to nationhood, and instead to place it in a more far-reaching planetary context.

Moreover, for Robinson, and notwithstanding his attempt to know a place profoundly, rootedness is emphatically *not* a component of the good step. He firmly states:

> In all this the step is to be distinguished, maximally, from those metaphorical appendages of humanity [...]: roots – a concept which, though obviously deep, is to me unacceptably vegetable. (2008: 364)

When I asked Robinson to expand on this assertion in an interview, he explained:

> Roots spread out from a centre they themselves fix in place, lay claim to a territory, suck up historical and political poisons, limit the access of nomads, passers-by and explorers. I exaggerate, of course, and there is much to be said for settled communities in their familiar old places, but as a human being I claim the freedom of the globe's surface and accept responsibility for it. (2014: n.p.)

These clarifications of his position align Robinson more firmly with Heise's eco-cosmopolitanism, since she herself identifies scepticism "vis-à-vis local rootedness" (2008: 5) as a vital element in the search for the counter-models to the kind of nation-based concepts of identity that, in her view, impede the development of eco-cosmopolitanism. She sees this scepticism as instrumental in fostering new conceptualisations that validate "individual and collective forms of identity that define themselves in relation to a multiplicity of places and place experiences" (5). Robinson, as we have seen, while intensely devoted to his island home, defends his cosmopolitan right to define himself in relation to the entire surface of the globe.

Robinson's approach may also help to mitigate the "derangements of scale" Timothy Clark identifies (2012: 148), which occur when we try to make sense of the massive discrepancy between space and time as experienced by individual humans and the spatial and temporal dimensions implied by contemporary environmental issues such as climate change. To illustrate the problem Clark provides us with an imaginative scenario. We are lost in a small town. A helpful stranger offers us a map: "'The whole town is there,' he says. It turns out to be a map of the whole earth" (148). This, of course, is of no help whatsoever: it's "The wrong scale." (148). We cannot obtain the localised information we need to navigate our way through our immediate environment from a map on a global scale. Neither could we orient ourselves globally from a large scale map of an individual town. Clark goes on to argue that cartographic scale is in itself an inadequate concept, unable to accommodate the non-linear nature of environmental problems and the frequent disjunctions and discontinuities between small and large scale environmental models. He takes as his epigraph for his discussion of scale a quotation from Simon A. Levin's 1989 lecture 'The Problem of Pattern and Scale in Ecology,' in which Levin argued: "When we observe the environment, we necessarily do so on only a limited range of scales; therefore, our perception of events provides us with only a low-dimensional slice of a high-dimensional cake" (1992: 1945).

In the Aran books Robinson might be seen as presenting a "slice" of the landscape that is simultaneously low-dimensional and high-dimensional, local and global, temporally immediate and far distant. Like Clark, and despite his own skills in this area, he sees the limitations of cartography, arguing that maps lack an important dimension for him: the ability to represent both the "tiny details" of the natural world and the "huge overarching forms that bring it all together" (Robinson 2013: 7). Instead he pursues his project through "the world-hungry art of words" (Robinson 2008: 19). One of the advantages of this literary approach is the flexibility it seems to offer for moving between his objects of attention. Heise suggests that Google Earth – the satellite view with "infinite zooming tools" (2008: 21) – offers an aesthetic model "for considering ecological crisis and environmental as well as cultural connectedness across different spatial scales" (209). In its elasticity, and well before the advent of Google Earth, Robinson's literary exploration of the good step similarly allows us to zoom in and out, at any point able to move quickly from minutiae to global forms, "through all the subspaces of experiences up to the cosmic" (Robinson 1996: vi). Macfarlane argues, quite rightly, that the "continual vibration between the particular and the universal" (2008: xi) is one of the work's most distinctive elements.

This flexible, expansive vision is undoubtedly fostered by the qualities of Árainn itself. Describing his immediate attraction to the island, Robinson explains that what captivated him first were "the immensities in which this little place is wrapped" (2008: 17): the elemental forces of the weather, the Atlantic

FRAMING THE 'GOOD STEP' 57

breakers, and the "wildly starry" (17) nights. However, it is not only the breakers and the stars that connect Robinson with a larger sense of space, time and history. A significant contribution to the vast temporal framework of the diptych comes from the island's rock – the "stones of Aran" that give the work its title, and put Robinson in touch with geological deep time. In *The Book of Barely Imagined Beings,* Caspar Henderson writes: "Even if we accept the idea of deep time as a reality, it is still hard to *understand* because its dimensions are still so far outside our cognitive range" (2012: 33, emphasis in original). In order to *feel* deep time he recommends "a walking meditation among ancient rocks so that their solidity and presence can be felt through vibrations in your feet, legs, hips and spine" (34). Robinson's journey on foot across the stones of Aran conjures up for him the time span of three hundred and twenty million years – the time, according to Robinson, that has elapsed "since the limestone of which Aran is formed was being laid down as layer upon layer of sediment in a tropical sea" (2008: 5). Even then, this does not represent the beginning of the Aran islands, since "that sea was already ancient and full of intricate lives, the heirs of a previous three thousand million years of evolution" (6). Through his contact with these geological histories, Robinson shows himself able conceptually to deal with a range of scales, including, potentially, those involved in the consideration of contemporary environmental issues: the spans of time and space that, according to Clark, can elude the grasp of the human imagination.

However, there is also a sense in which this contemplation of the ancient rocks moves Robinson beyond the scale even of the environmental issues with which Clark and Heise are concerned. It is perhaps important to note here that although his work has been described as presenting "an ecological imagination of localities and environments" (Brannigan 2014: 232), Robinson does not identify himself as an environmentalist *per se*. In fact he actively discourages the application of this label to himself (2009: 8), and writes with apparent reservation about the "secular eschatologies" (1992: xxxix) of our age, presumably referring to the apocalyptic tone associated with some strands of contemporary environmentalist discourse. Moreover, the good step is not, for him, primarily concerned with fostering ecological sensibility. Resisting narratives of a lost human connection with the earth, and of religious interpretations of such a pre-Fall state of grace, he declares:

> For the dolphin's ravenous cybernetics and lean hydrodynamics induce in me no nostalgia for imaginary states of past instinctive or future theological grace. Nor is the ecological imperative, that we learn to tread more lightly on the earth, what I have in mind – though that commandment, which is always subject to challenge if presented as a mere facilitation of

survival, might indeed acquire some authority from the attitude to the earth I would like to hint at with my step. (2008: 19–20)

I would argue that it is perhaps the eschatologies of our time rather than concern for the environment itself that Robinson resists, and that he is trying to think on an altogether larger ecological scale, evoking even greater spatiotemporal frameworks than those implied by concerns for human survival in a time of "environmental reckoning" (Daniels and Lorimer 2012: 5). In its notion of treading lightly on the earth as a tangential, lateral effect, Robinson's good step suggests a form of ecology without instrumentalist imperatives, or perhaps, as Timothy Morton recommends, an *"ecology without environmentalism"* (2010: 6, emphasis in original).

In the process of trying to establish this bigger picture Robinson can be seen to be disrupting and reframing two of the tropes that Hulme recommends as stories through which we might negotiate a response to climate change: Eden and Apocalypse. In his initial contextualisation of Árainn, Robinson enters into a discussion of the science of 'plate tectonics,' and the ways in which the fractional movements in the plates that form the earth's crust have resulted in the formation of the continents and their mountain chains. He gradually works his way back to a point in history at which the earth consisted simply of one land mass and one sea:

Two hundred million years ago the Atlantic did not exist and all the landmasses of today were clasped together in one continuity, in pre-Adamite innocence of the fact that one day scientists inhabiting its scattered fragments would give it the lovely name of Pangaea, all-earth, and that its unbounded encircling ocean was Panthalassa, all-sea. (2008: 7)

But even having reached such a moment of planetary unity, Robinson pushes still further back in time:

But even great Pangaea is not the beginning; it is no more than a halfway house, inadequate but indispensable, for the mind travelling back in search of Eden. The rocks of Aran, for instance, pre-date it, as do many others. (2008: 7)

Robinson's mention of going further back in search of Eden is an apparent contradiction of his previous assertion that Pangaea was "pre-Adamite." It implies that Eden represents for him something other than the biblical garden-home of Adam and Eve. Macfarlane describes the opening chapter of *Pilgrimage* as a "creation myth" (2008: xi), but it is one that insistently looks back to a time that vastly pre-dates the arrival of the human. Eden appears to connote nothing less than the beginning of time itself.

In a similar trajectory, Robinson can also be seen to be looking beyond the existence of the human – or at least the human as we know it – on planet earth. Pondering the gradual erosion of the island's limestone, he comments that

> Unless vaster earth-processes intervene Aran will ultimately dwindle to a little reef and disappear. It seems unlikely that any creatures we would recognize as our descendants will be here to chart that rock in whatever shape of sea succeeds to Galway Bay. (2008: 28)

In effect he is presenting us with a time scale so vast that it dwarfs human concerns, including those tied up with the discourse of environmental apocalypse, and renders them, in the greater scheme of things, irrelevant. This perspective resonates with Morton's assertion that "The ecological thought must transcend the language of apocalypse" (2010: 19). Greg Garrard argues that one of the strengths of Morton's *The Ecological Thought* is the way in which it "admits the notion of urgent environmental crisis – haunted as it always is by apocalypticism – while looking way beyond it" (2012b: 203). For Morton, as for Robinson, it is perhaps only through freeing oneself from the powerful influence of apocalyptic dread that one can approach a fully ecological perspective: a two-way vista that looks both before and after the existence of *homo sapiens*.

A comparable shrinking of the stature of human concerns can be seen in the spatial framework of the text, which travels far beyond the limits of the globe's surface, reaching, as we have already seen, to the furthest extent of the visible universe. This is a deliberate move on Robinson's part. Indeed in the Preface to *Setting Foot on the Shores of Connemara* he asks specifically that we consider his work not as landscape writing but in more cosmic terms. He states: "'Landscape' has during the past decade become a key term in several disciplines; but I would prefer this body of work to be read in the light of 'Space'" (2006: vi). He expresses a fascination with "the amplitude of actual Space, in which one can without contradiction build deep-eaved Heideggerian dwellings" (vi), and argues that

> ultimately there is no space but Space, 'nor am I out of it'[...], for it is, among everything else, the interlocking of all our mental and physical trajectories, good or ill, through all the subspaces of experience up to the cosmic. (vi)

While this statement might be viewed as ultimately eliding the kinds of pressing socio-environmental issues with which Heise calls us to engage, in terms of broader ecological perspectives it could also be seen as establishing a conceptual framework that might benefit our thinking. For Robinson, it appears, only such a cosmic vision could allow one to build without contradiction those "deep-eaved Heideggerian dwellings" he evokes. The good step, then, implies taking into consideration, to the best of our human perceptive capacity (augmented at any given moment by the latest scientific speculations), all of the aspects of our experience, from the touch of our feet on the ground to our apprehension of the universe that surrounds us.

4 Thinking Big, Then Thinking Small Again

In this respect Robinson's view once again seems to correspond with Morton's "ecological thought." An important element of Morton's concept of "thinking big" is his insistence that we must place ourselves imaginatively in the context of Space: "Space isn't something that happens beyond the ionosphere. We are in Space right now" (2010: 24). He states, "Seeing the Earth from space is the beginning of ecological thinking" (14). But what exactly *is* the value for ecological thinking of this immense cosmic frame? I would argue that for both Morton and Robinson, while the vastness of the cosmos is a genuine object of fascination and source of valuably expanded perspectives, its evocation here can also be seen as something of a gambit. Morton's reading of a passage from John Milton's *Paradise Lost* is telling in this respect. In the excerpt we see the angel Raphael attempting to persuade Adam of the perils of idle speculation, which could distract his attention from "just and temperate action" (Morton 2010: 21). Raphael uses as an example of this kind of dangerous speculation the idea that our solar system may not be unique: there may be "other suns perhaps / With their attendant moons" (Milton, cited in Morton 2010: 21). Morton interprets Raphael's overt argument as a ploy. By telling Adam not to think of other suns, Raphael inevitably conjures them into his mind, with the effect, Morton argues, of making Adam see human life from a perspective that radically shrinks its stature. Morton extrapolates an ecological message from this. He writes, "If [humans] refrain from thinking that they are too important, [they] will resist Satan's setting [them up] at the centre of a universe that, like the apple, is there for the taking" (22). The result, Morton claims, is that in this expanded context we also see Satan and his temptations as diminished and ridiculous, viewing him "as if through the wrong end of a telescope" (23).

Robinson is perhaps producing a similar effect when he asks us to carry the furthest reaches of time and space in our mind as the context of our footsteps on the earth. Though, in the light of Space, we might potentially experience what he calls "the interlocking of all our mental and physical trajectories through all the subspaces of experience up to the cosmic" (2006: vi) and so build without contradiction our deep-eaved Heideggerian dwellings, the opening of *Stones of Aran* works in reverse: we go from fifteen thousand million light-years down through 320 million years, a century, a quarter of a mile, to a couple of paces – a pattern that is repeated with variations at other points in the text. Far from denoting a universe we can frame as ready for the human taking, it is one that often frames us, and shrinks us against unfathomable infinities. It is indeed like looking at human dwelling through the 'wrong' end of a telescope. As Robinson argues in the midst of establishing his cosmic scale, a natural reaction to this immensity "is to immerse oneself in the intense implication of the whole in the particular, if only to make the most out of every square foot of allotted ground" (2008: 5).

Thus, although Robinson is clearly genuinely interested in exploring out relationship with landscape in the context of space, this framing can perhaps ultimately also be seen, as I have suggested elsewhere (Marland 2015), as a ploy. Perhaps Robinson is not looking to build those deep-eaved Heideggerian dwellings in Space after all, but has evoked this vast frame, at least in part, in order to bring us to a sharpened existential awareness, both of our dwelling on the earth and of the particular part of the earth that sustains that dwelling. In a passage from *Labyrinth* he describes an episode in which he and his wife experience a moment of planetary connection, rich with the potential for transcending its earthly bounds. He writes:

> We would lie starwise on the pavement by it and close our eyes and let the sun or the breeze or even the first drops of a rain-shower explore our faces. After a few minutes our shoulder-blades would have fused with the limestone and we would be whirled along by the earth's turning, the dynamo that generates all our little norths and souths and easts and wests. (2009: 325)

But rather than pursue his transcendental flight out to the furthest reaches of the cosmos, Robinson returns with renewed intensity to the ground beneath his feet: "But I soon tire of transcendental flight and start poking about again, questioning the ground I stand on" (325).

5 Conclusion

This chapter has discussed the ways in which Tim Robinson establishes a vast spatiotemporal framework for his exploration of the good step and dwelling. It has argued that this framing offers us a literary means by which we might develop something approaching Heise's sense of planet, and also *feel* our way into the concept of deep time and the scales implicated in environmental change, perhaps mitigating some of those cartographic limitations and conceptual derangements of scale that Clark identifies. The temporal and spatial dimensions evoked by the island also enable Robinson to disrupt and reframe some of the existing cultural tropes we use to negotiate our being in the world, such that Eden is seen as vastly pre-dating the human, and we are provided with a temporal horizon that moves far beyond any notion of anthropogenically precipitated environmental apocalypse. It is a move that resonates with several aspects of Morton's *The Ecological Thought*. At the same time, I have suggested that, by thinking big in this way, Robinson also returns us, paradoxically, to the notion of thinking very small indeed – to paying attention to every square foot of our allotted ground. However, the effect of this is not only to return us to the earth. Once you have zoomed out in order to see the big picture, you might find, upon zooming in again, that your perspective on the human, and on the earth, and on the place of the mortal human upon that earth, has subtly changed. In something of an ecological sleight of hand, your gaze has been returned with renewed intensity to your allotted ground, but it is ground that has been deterritorialised, unhinged from concepts of nation, and reterritorialised as a "segment of [...] home planet" (Robinson 2009: 608).

Perhaps, then, the overriding message of the Aran diptych is that we can only begin to approach the good step – that state of consciousness adequate to the ground we walk – through an understanding that the vastness of the cosmos frames our, by comparison, infinitesimal existence: individually, as a civilisation, and as a species. In the light of this apprehension, we find that our eyes are inevitably turned back to the earth, but with a renewed attentiveness and appreciation, in ways that may prove beneficial to our ecological imagination. As we have seen, Robinson is not overtly environmentalist. He states that "the ecological imperative, that we learn to tread more lightly on the earth" (2008 [1985]: 19–20) is not at the forefront of his mind. He does, however, concede that "that commandment [...] might indeed acquire some authority from the attitude to the earth I would like to hint at with my step" (19–20). I would argue that his work does indeed imbue that commandment with authority, both providing us with the means to reflect on ecology on a planetary scale, and at the same time potentially fostering an attitude to the earth that might well involve treading more lightly on the segment of home-planet we each inhabit.

Excerpts from the unpublished interview by the author with Tim Robinson quoted with permission.

Bibliography

Brannigan, John. 2014. *Archipelagic Modernism: Literature in the Irish and British Isles, 1890–1970*. Edinburgh: Edinburgh University Press.

Clark, Timothy. 2012. 'Derangements of Scale' in Tom Cohen (ed.), *Telemorphosis: Theory in the Era of Climate Change. Volume 1*. Open Humanities Press: 148–166.

Daniels, Stephen and Hayden Lorimer. 2012. 'Until the End of Days: Narrating Landscape and Environment' in *Cultural Geographies* 19 (1): 3–9.

Garrard, Greg. 2012a. *Ecocriticism*. London: Routledge.

Garrard, Greg. 2012b. 'Ecocriticism.' In *The Year's Work in Critical and Cultural Theory* 20 (1): 200–243.

Goodbody, Axel. 2012. 'Frame Analysis and the Literature of Climate Change.' In Timo Müller and Michael Sauter (eds.), *Literature, Ecology, Ethics: Recent Trends in Ecocriticism*. Heidelberg: Universitätsverlag Winter: 15–33.

Heidegger, Martin. 2010 [1953]. *Being and Time*. Translated by Joan Stambaugh. Albany: SUNY Press.

Heise, Ursula. 2008. *Sense of Place and Sense of Planet*. New York: Oxford University Press.

Henderson, Caspar. 2012. *The Book of Barely Imagined Beings*. London: Granta.

Hulme, Mike. 2009. *Why We Disagree About Climate Change: Understanding Controversy, Inaction, Opportunity*. Cambridge: Cambridge University Press.

Levin, Simon A. (1992). 'The Problem of Pattern and Scale in Ecology: The Robert H. MacArthur Award Lecture 1989' in *Ecology* 73 (6): 1943–1967.

Macfarlane, Robert. 2005. 'Rock of Ages' Online at: http://www.guardian.co.uk/books/2005/may/14/featuresreviews.guardianreview3. May 14 2005 (consulted November 1 2015).

Macfarlane, Robert. 2008. 'Introduction' to Tim Robinson *Stones of Aran: Pilgrimage* London: Faber and Faber.

Marland, Pippa. 2015. 'The "Good Step" and Dwelling in Tim Robinson's *Stones of Aran*: the Advent of "*Psycho-Archipelagraphy*"' *Ecozon@* 6 (1): 7–24.

Morton, Timothy. 2010. *The Ecological Thought*. Cambridge, MA: Harvard University Press.

Robinson, Tim. 2008 [1985]. *Stones of Aran: Pilgrimage*. London: Faber and Faber.

Robinson, Tim. 2009 [1995]. *Stones of Aran: Labyrinth*. New York: New York Review of Books.

Robinson, Tim. 2006 [1996]. *Setting Foot on the Shores of Connemara & Other Writings*. Dublin: Lilliput Press.

Robinson, Tim. (2013). 'A Step Towards the Earth: Interview with Tim Robinson' by Jos Smith *Politics of Place: a Journal for Postgraduates* 1: 4–11.

Robinson, Tim. 2014. Interview by Pippa Marland via email May 5 2014.

Smith, Jos. 2012. *An Archipelagic Environment: Re-Writing the British and Irish Landscape 1972–2012*. PhD thesis. University of Exeter.

Smith, Jos. 2013. 'An Archipelagic Literature: Reframing "The New Nature Writing"' in *Green Letters: Studies in Ecocriticism* 17 (1): 5–15.

Wylie, John. 2012. 'Dwelling and Displacement: Tim Robinson and the Question of Landscape' in *Cultural Geographies* 19 (3): 365–383.

PART 2

History, Politics, and National Frames

∴

CHAPTER 5

Ghosts, Power, and the Natures of Nature: Reconstructing the World of Jón Guðmundsson the Learned

Viðar Hreinsson

Abstract

The meaning and usage of the word *nature* in the Middle Ages and the Renaissance was qualitative rather than quantitative and objectifying. The qualitative meaning of the word is reflected in the ideas and works of the 17th century Icelander Jón Guðmundsson the learned (1574–1658). He was a self-educated farmer and fisherman as well as a poet, scholar and artist who led a rough life due to his critical writings and occult activities. A pioneer in Icelandic literary history, he was the first to write a critical account of contemporary events and the first to write a description of Icelandic nature in Icelandic. In some of his poetry and especially in his later writings, he articulates a conception of nature which is fascinated by organic diversity and stands in sharp contrast to the then-ascendant tendency to frame nature as object.

1   Nature, Medieval and Modern

In the Middle Ages, nature was seen as eluding human comprehension, just like the God who was its first cause. This is how Isidore of Seville defined nature in the 7th century: "Nature (*natura*) is so called because it causes something to be born ... for it has the power of engendering and creating. Some people say that this is God, by whom all things have been created and exist." (2006: 231) Later in the Middle Ages, "natural law" was assumed to simply command people to strive for God and for perfection. All creatures seek the fulfillment of their natures but man only is aware of it, which can be painful (McInerny and O'Callaghan 2014). The original Latin meaning of the term nature is dynamic and organic, related to birth and creation. The Ancient Greek word "physis" has a similar meaning: "origin," "birth," "nature," "quality." In English dictionaries, the various meanings seem to be either qualitative and organic, or objectifying: that is, nature either refers to a condition where no sharp distinction is made between humans and a nature they belong to, or nature is regarded as an object external to humans, "the external world in its entirety." (Merriam-Webster)

The meaning of the Icelandic loan word "náttúra" (nature) is also twofold. In medieval Icelandic, it seems to have been exclusively qualitative, implying the innate qualities of phenomena in general, often in relations to surroundings. Humans were not thought to be separated from nature, but dependent on natural forces outside human control, although humans were sometimes able to acquire special, usually magical relations to these forces (Ordbog over det norrøne prosasprog). The modern, objectified meaning appeared only much later in Iceland, in the early 19th century (Ritmálssafn).

In an early 17th-century Danish academic definition of the word "natura" (in Latin), the meaning is almost exclusively qualitative: (a) "natura naturans" being the spirit of God as father and creator (master builder) of all things, (b) the intrinsic essence or meaning of all things, (c) the complete whole of all created things, (d) natural causes, since God and Nature never act without a reason, which excludes the possibility of a vacuum, (e) every spiritual being's temperament, as when the doctors talk about the temperament as a blend of the four elements, and (f) the becoming of living beings, the literal meaning of birth (Schepelern 1971: 101).

This was Ole Worm's definition in a series of lectures based on classical ideas that he delivered in 1613–1614, at the beginning of his career at the University of Copenhagen. Ole Worm was a Renaissance polymath, a professor at the University of Copenhagen, a physical doctor, antiquarian, expert in runes, and a great collector who established a cabinet of curiosities (*Wunderkammer*). He was a transitional figure in Danish intellectual life (Scheplern 1971, Hafstein 2003, Shackelford 1999), not least given that the 17th century was the period when the quantification of reality might be said to have had its breakthrough, at the expense of the organic frame of mind (Crosby 1997; Merchant 1989). The collection of curiosities and the empirical interest in objects was the first sign of modern ways of framing nature; it was no coincidence that this happened simultaneously with the concentration of state power in Denmark and Iceland following the so-called Reformation (Hafstein 2003: 6–8), and in Europe more widely.

The flip-side of modern, Western prosperity is the environmental crisis. It is rooted in the rationalism which followed the Scientific Revolution and the Enlightenment and resulted in a totalitarian domination of nature, based on an instrumentalist, reductionist and fragmenting world view. In past decades, criticism of this development has increased greatly, often along with the rejection of some basic assumptions such as Cartesian dualism, or dualist thinking in general. Although it is impossible to reject the modern mindset entirely, it is imperative to reach back into the past and investigate pre-modern ways

FIGURE 5.1   *The cabinet of curiosities.*
FRONTISPIECE OF OLE WORM'S *MUSEUM WORMIANUM* (1655). PUBLIC DOMAIN.

of thinking in order to consider what was lost in the long development from the Middle Ages to modernity. It was not merely a happy transition from a blend of scholasticism and superstitions to reason and progress. An attempt at a reconstruction of the world of the Icelandic autodidact Jón Guðmundsson, nicknamed the "learned," provides insights into earlier ways of thinking which may relativize the modern conception of nature. The ideas and experiences he grappled with reveal a recognition of the diversity and intrinsic significance of nature, and a sense of nature as a whole of which humans form a part, rather than as something to be dominated and exploited.

2   Iceland's Vernacular Literary Landscape

17th-century Iceland was a backward peasant society, predominantly rural with no towns or real urban centers and no centers of higher learning except for the two Latin schools at the bishoprics of Skálholt and Hólar. The peasantry was oppressed by a ruthless class of landowners and the country was under Danish rule, which had been considerably strengthened by the conversion to Lutheran Protestantism in 1550, with a Danish monopoly on trade being established in 1602. This was also the period, however, when Iceland's medieval sagas and poetry (in the vernacular) were introduced to Scandinavian and other European academics; Iceland subsequently became renowned for its medieval literary glory. This medieval literary heritage also forms the background for the 17th century material discussed here.

The sagas give an account of the settlement of Iceland in the late 9th to 10th centuries, and the establishment of a new society that was progressive and conservative at the same time in the way that it adjusted to new geographical circumstances. Icelanders preserved traditions and stories from the old countries, but they also created new narratives about the formation of their society which reflected the latter's distinctive interests, contexts, meanings, and approaches to reality. The island's settlement and the conversion to Christianity which followed around the year 1000 formed the preconditions for the writing of the sagas. Settlement provided narrative material, but Christianity brought the technology of writing and the first religious texts (in Latin, but later translated into vernacular Icelandic). The Church thus introduced the entire Christian system of beliefs, ideas, and knowledge. This influenced the shape which vernacular historiography took on, when the writing of these texts began early on in the 12th century, with short accounts of the history and settlement of Iceland. Sagas of Norwegian kings followed, the Old Norse mythology and poetry were put into writing, and a variety of saga genres gradually developed, the most important being the so-called Sagas of Icelanders, often also called Family Sagas. The canon of that genre comprises 40 sagas dealing with conflicts and feuds during the saga-age, i.e. from around the time of settlement until shortly after the conversion to Christianity (roughly 870–1050 CE).

The Icelandic sagas, which as a corpus range in scope from the anecdotal to the epic, deal directly with the experiences of a new and often strange and hostile environment – nature, landscape, strange beings – expressed within the broader framework of the medieval mind. The most productive period for saga-writing were the 13th and the 14th centuries, when some of the most highly esteemed sagas were written.

The early 14th century also saw the compiling of sagas and other material in large manuscripts, meaning that these texts were effectively edited and placed into new contexts: examples here include the *Möðruvallabók*, which contains sagas of Icelanders, and the very interesting *Hauksbók*. The *Hauksbók* contains a version of *The Book of Settlement* (a register, sometimes including narrative anecdotes, of all known settlers, organised on the principle of geography, and moving clockwise around the country), a few other sagas and poetry, intertwined with a variety of medieval theological, arithmetical, philosophical and other texts, including material originating from Pliny, Isidore of Seville's *Etymologies*, The Venerable Bede, and a few later authors. This remarkable compilation combines down-to-earth Icelandic historiography with more abstract, philosophical and sacral knowledge, ultimately constructing and presenting a specifically Icelandic medieval world view which prevailed for centuries (Jakobsson 2007).

Original saga-writing diminished in the following centuries, but the composing and copying of sagas, poetry, genealogies, law-codices, encyclopedia and theology can be seen as semi-organized literary activities, conducted in cloisters, bishoprics, manor farms, and even among common farmers, peasants and farmhands who occasionally operated as professional scribes (Springborg 1977). The material thus continued to be reproduced and circulated in an organic rhizome, a literary wayfaring or *"meshwo*rk of entangled lines of life, growth and movement," to use well-known, dynamic concepts from Deleuze and Guattari (1987: 3–25) and Tim Ingold (2011: 148, 63). Manuscript culture in Iceland was, to some extent, like uncontrolled growth along unpredictable paths and lines, although traditional philological methods and the quest for the original work or "Urtext" have neglected the dynamic aspects until the recent emergence of material philology (Driscoll 2010). The process of handwriting was not only the act of writing itself, but the entire production process of books involved manual labor and close contact to natural materials (vellum, and paper, ink, quills). Literary culture in Iceland was always partly driven by the spontaneous activities of autodidacts who acquired manuscripts and material here and there, read, copied and composed, capturing worlds in letters and books. The concept of social authorship (Ezell 1999: 18–19) rather than individual creation in a modern sense is a more useful one in this context of circulation and (re)production of manuscripts.

3   Jón the Learned – Life and Writings

Jón Guðmundsson, nicknamed 'lærði' ('the learned,' 1574–1658), was born in the Strandir district of North-West Iceland. He grew up among literate peasants and fishermen but was a distant relative of the most powerful and wealthiest family in his part of the country, the Svalbarð-clan, whose members were king's representatives, county sheriffs and extremely rich landowners. Importantly, this was a literate clan, some of whose members were educated abroad, especially in Hamburg. According to a family legend, the wealth of the family had

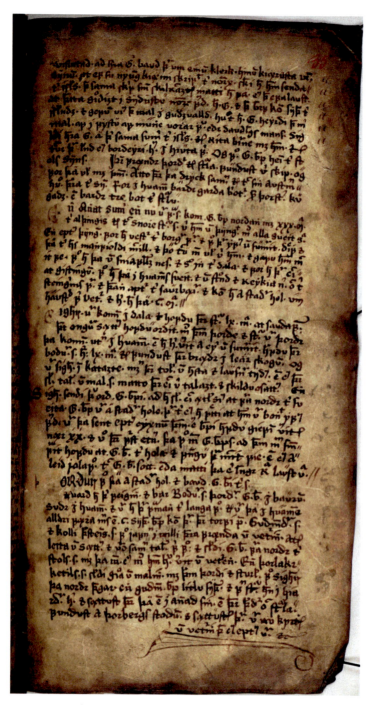

FIGURE 5.2 *A page from the parchment manuscript of the* Saga of Bishop Guðmundur the Good, *copied and compiled by Jón lærði in 1592, at the age of 18.*
© THE ÁRNI MAGNÚSSON INSTITUTE, REYKJAVÍK AM 394 4TO FROM 1592. PHOTOGRAPH BY JÓHANNA ÓLAFSDÓTTIR.

been acquired thanks to the magical skills of an ancestor, a 15th century priest. Two brothers in this family, Staðarhóls-Páll Jónsson and Magnús Jónsson prúði ('the elegant'), both of whom Jón had contact with in his youth, were well-known poets; other members of this clan initiated and supported some interesting literary activities in the 17th century, producing handwritten volumes of poetry, annals, law-books and sagas (Springborg 1977).

Jón lærði was moulded by the organic manuscript culture described above and insatiably curious about the surrounding, natural world. He was self-educated and by the age of twenty, he had already produced a number of manuscripts, among them four copies of the law-book *Jónsbók*, though unfortunately none of these copies is preserved. Extant manuscripts presumably in Jón's hand from before he turned twenty are an illustrated parchment manuscript containing "rímur," or traditional narrative poetry, mainly erotic; a parchment copy of the *Saga of Bishop Guðmundur the Good* which to some extent is his own version of the saga; a paper manuscript containing medieval chronology with Jón's marginal notes indicating that by copying the book he was enhancing his own education in time reckoning; and finally "Hieronymi psaltare," a collection of prayers from David's psalms, in a small format, and probably

FIGURE 5.3 *Two pages from a manuscript of sermons and epistles, copied and illustrated by Jón lærði in 1596–1597.*
PHOTOGRAPH BY AUÐUR VIÐARSDÓTTIR.

meant for use when travelling. In 1596–1597, at the age of 22, he produced a small, extremely well-written copy of a printed book of sermons end epistles, with a number of beautifully illuminated capitals. There are no illustrations in the printed original, so the illuminations must be his own creation. It is not unlikely that Jón undertook some writing and copying for certain members of the Svalbarð-clan, for instance some of the law books.

The already-mentioned *Hauksbók* is among the medieval manuscripts that Jón must certainly have read, possibly through his connections with the Svalbarð-clan; the cosmology, philosophy and natural history from *Hauksbók* are echoed in many of Jón's later writings, in which he also mentions a number of books and manuscripts, domestic and foreign, that he had seen and read such as printed German books on stones and herbs.

Jón married in 1600 and became a farmer and fisherman in the following years, but probably also made his living with handicrafts, carving wood as well as walrus and whale teeth or tusks, and writing. In 1606–1611 he was at Skarð, one of the richest manor estates in Iceland at that time, where he had access to books and interesting documents. He was known for his rare abilities to deal with evil powers, and in 1611 and 1612 he was believed to have driven back down into the earth ghosts with two long poems, purportedly the most powerful invocations in verse ever composed in Iceland.

In the fall of 1615, the sheriff, King's representative and richest landowner in the Westfjords, Ari Magnússon of the Svalbarð-clan, led the brutal slaying of 31 shipwrecked Basque whalers, an event regarded as amongst the worst atrocities committed in Icelandic history. Jón had been on friendly terms with Ari but now he wrote a critical and vividly detailed and realistic account of the killings, thus undermining Ari's local power. Jón subsequently had to flee his home district and lost all his books and belongings, but found shelter on the Snæfellsnes peninsula, where he remained for most of the next 12 years, working as a fisherman. In 1627, a local provost accused him of being a servant of Satan and Jón had to flee further south, to the Reykjanes Peninsula in the south-west. In 1631, Jón was exiled for having written a booklet describing occult practices, including 30 remedies against evil attacks. He found shelter on Bjarnarey, a small island off the northeast coast of Iceland where he stayed for a few years. He managed to travel to Copenhagen in 1636 to attempt to have his banishment annulled. In Copenhagen, he was interrogated by the board of the University of Copenhagen, led by the aforementioned Ole Worm. The board recommended that the sentence be reconsidered. Nevertheless, the charge was upheld in the spring of 1637. Jón was, however, allowed to live out the rest of his life in eastern Iceland, where he wrote many of his surviving works. In that period, he collected and annotated (in his own way) ancient lore for his greatest benefactor, Bishop Brynjólfur Sveinsson, the most learned man in the country.

Apart from the works discussed here, Jón wrote genealogical and historical accounts, interpretations of the Old Norse mythology, leechbooks, magic, and a great variety of poetry, including a long autobiographical poem which is a kind of a biographical passion relating how he was persecuted in long periods by otherworldly and worldly powers.

4 Jón's World

Jón had a lifelong passion for books. Referring to the Reformation as a catastrophe, he said: "While the catastrophe of darkness was raining over Skálholt, when all of the Church's silver and jewellery was plundered and books were destroyed, one of these books ended up in my parish, and at a young age I learned to read from it" (Tíðfordríf: 9r). Jón, and a few other autodidacts, especially farmer Björn Jónsson of Skarðsá who was born the same year as Jón, were held in high esteem by leading Renaissance intellectuals in Iceland, as they were able to assist in interpreting much of the old material, such as runes, mythology and poetry. Jón was especially renowned for his knowledge of runes, and learned Icelanders mentioned him in letters to Ole Worm around 1630, ironically enough, when he was about to be exiled for magic.

It is impossible to gain a complete understanding or overview of Jón's writings and ideas, since his situation was difficult for long periods of time, his works are variegated, and their ideas often seem to be quite fragmented. His earlier writings and his poetry confirm, however, that he was perfectly capable of constructing and composing longer works.

Jón's first work with philosophical or cosmological content is *Fjandafæla*, composed in 1611 in order to drive away a ghost. In this poem, he conveys the religious world picture he had adopted through his autodidactic learning, based on the medieval or Renaissance vertical system of values, with God at the top, the angels below God, Satan and Hell at the bottom and the humans torn in between. In the first part of the poem, Jón describes the heavenly spheres inhabited by angels, Lucifer's revolt and fall, and the nether regions where Satan's soulless devils live. The demons, he writes, are as many as motes in a sunbeam or the drops in nine days' rain. In the next chapter, Jón describes the earth, and Adam who was created out of the four elements, but endowed with spirit. When Adam was still alone, his seed impregnated the earth, so the elves were conceived and consequently lived underground. The poem then proceeds to Eve and the fall caused by Satan, and Christ's great victory over Satan in his resurrection. In the third and last part of the poem, the actual exorcism, Jón follows in the footsteps of Christ by verbally thrashing Satan or knocking him down to the lower depths, tormenting him with powerful rhetoric and curses. The exorcist reached new heights one year later when another ghost appeared in the same area and Jón cursed him down with another even more powerful exorcist poem.

By adhering to the idea of the elves being Adam's descendants, Jón maintained an organic link between humans and the elves, who represent nature and the earth. He was thus assuming a carnal connection between humans and nature, combining the flesh and the spirit, in a heretic manner that the Church could not accept.

After having fled his home district in 1615 as noted, Jón stayed in the Snæfellsnes peninsula for over a decade, earning a reputation as a healer and teaching fishermen in the fishing camps. Then, suddenly it seems, the poem *Fjandafæla* was brought up. Apparently, Jón had become a threat to the established powers and in 1627, the district provost, Guðmundur Einarsson, one of the most learned men in Iceland at that time, wrote a fierce pamphlet denouncing Jón and this poem, as well as his assumed magic activities. He claimed that two pastors from the district had brought him a manuscript containing *Fjandafæla* and books of magical symbols and formulas. The official subject of the pamphlet was the serpent's crooked and straight walk through life, that is, Satan's evil tricks and atrocities through history. Satan's most prominent representative in Iceland and consequently the greatest of God's enemies was Jón lærði, Guðmundur claimed. Guðmundur also refuted eight theories he found to be false in Jón's poem, such as the number of devils, the number of heavenly spheres, and the origin of elves. He criticized the worldly authorities for being too tolerant of magic and openly demanded that Jón be captured and burned at the stake. Sheriff Ari Magnússon welcomed the attack on magic but defended himself and the other sheriffs. The pastors were not particularly good or conscientious at fighting the magicians either, Ari argued: the scoundrel Jón lærði had been practicing magic in Guðmundur's own parish. Ari thought that torture would be an effective method to get the magicians to confess.

The era of witch-hunting only began decades later in Iceland, connected to the strengthening of central power following the Reformation. However, Guðmundur's attack was a step in that direction, and Ari's reply confirmed the secular aspect of this strengthened central power. Both of them were eager to identify enemies of the authorities such as Jón, who seems to have been regarded a threat to worldly as well as secular powers.

5 Late Writings on Nature

After the long period of perils and persecution, Jón lærði eventually found shelter in some tenant cottages in East Iceland from 1638 until his death 20 years later He was near his son Guðmundur, who was a pastor there, and also under some kind of protection from Bishop Brynjólfur Sveinsson, who set Jón to work on scholarly projects on his behalf. Consequently, Jón was only able to communicate his world view and ideas as responses to inquiries from his benefactor, the Bishop. Jón's writings thus appear fragmentary because of this situation, but he was not an unorganized collector of knowledge, even though he had not received any academic training. The three or four rather fragmented works he composed for the Bishop indicate that he possessed extensive knowledge which circumstances did not allow him to write down in full: he often mentions that he did not have the opportunity to write in any detail about certain subjects. All through his life, Jón experienced censorship directly, not least in being forbidden to read certain books. On one occasion, excusing himself for his worthless scribbling, he writes: "[Books] and all entertainment that knowledge brings was so strongly taken away from me" (*Tíðfordríf*: 1r). He says that in some clerical books, many secrets were kept away from poor and common people, so he hardly dared to look at these books, whether to quote from them or copy them. He complains that nobody taught him but many forbade him to handle papist books, or consider their content. Because of this censorship, it is hard to discuss great matters, or the things that people wanted him to remain silent about (*Tíðfordríf*: 1v–2v)

The works that Jón wrote for the bishop gradually became more concise and coherent wholes. The first piece, written in 1641, was a compilation aimed at interpreting the mythological Edda texts, comprising a copy of the text of *Snorra Edda* (the Old Norse mythology traditionally assigned to Snorri Sturluson) as well as his original and peculiarly critical annotations which include moral criticism of the heathen gods, folk-beliefs, and some very interesting moral concepts, such as "alfrí" (total freedom, or freedom without responsibility) and "orðhelgi" (preferring words to deeds).

In *Tíðfordríf,* Jón conveys his views of nature more thoroughly and refers to books he had read, handwritten and printed. Although rather unstructured at first sight, the text reveals his views of the world and a pluralist sense of infinity, e.g. when he states that only God but no earthly or mortal human can know the full number of species and the nature of the spirits and hidden things that God originally created in his omnipotent wisdom. Since the time of the creation of the world, no men have been able to comprehend the world, its beasts and natural phenomena, either internally or externally: "Just as no master painter is so skilled at his craft as to be able in one sketch to portray everything that is internal and invisible inside a human being, the secrets of the earth's crafting and its invisible filling and nature will never be explained by observing its external appearance," he writes (*Tíðfordríf*: 11r)

Jón discusses herbs, stones and animals, especially birds, in a qualitative, even moral manner, blending what he had read in books with his own observations, describing the virtues of the various phenomena, virtues that were transferred between them, seeking balance. The quest for balance by taking in remedies carrying different virtues of herbs, animal parts and fluids, is the method or theory behind older, traditional herb- or leechbooks (medical books), of which Jón wrote at least two. His writings are in a constant tension between his reading and his experiences, thus connecting medieval learning with the emerging emphasis on experiment and empirical knowledge, on the one hand, and the farmer's and fisherman's practical sense of reality, on the other. In referring to old books and texts he had seen and read (some of them long ago), retelling various tales and stories and even drawing folkloristic creatures, discussing the attributes and virtues of the different types of angels and other spiritual beings (sometimes in a peculiarly lyrical style), the relations between flesh and spirit, and the strange occurrence of spirits in the flesh, Jón always weaves together book-learning and first-hand experience.

After discussing the spirits and their abodes, Jón turns to the nature of the earth, full of holes, fissures and channels, and tells stories about people who were able to travel inside the earth. He mentions hidden attributes or qualities of the earth – mines, crystals, mineral springs –and continues with a lengthy discussion of stones, where he again blends his learning from books (some of which can be traced all the way back to St. Isidore's *Etymologies*) with his own experiences with the precious stones that he owned and lost over the course of his difficult life. Once, his wife found a stone floating on a pool by a rocky beach. She picked it up and observed it, a nature-stone, with a pink drop on the top, surrounded with red but green on the bottom. She took it to another pool and there it was as if a group of men appeared in the water. She knew that Jón had read about such a stone and wanted to put it into her mitten to take it home, but it fell to the ground with a rattle and disappeared (*Tíðfordríf*: 8r).

Stones were closely connected to birds. Attributes of birds blend with attributes of the stones, and some birds were poisonous. A stone was in the stomach of the wagtail – an evil bird. It was risky to kill the wagtail because it was poisonous and vengeful. One harsh spring, a wagtail that had frozen to death was brought to Jón. He dissected it and found a strange, black stone with a wavy surface in its stomach. That stone went into his treasure chest which was lost when his persecutions began (*Tíðfordríf*: 6r–6v).

The most precious stone was the stone of life, the bezoar. Jón had read in books from Frankfurt that it was produced by the sorrowful lachrymal gland of the stag but in reality, the bezoar forms in the intestines of animals and was introduced to Europeans by Arabs in the twelfth century. Jón writes that it could also be found in the raven's head, and he describes cunning tricks to get the stone from the raven. If the chick was captured and the mother made to believe the chick was dead, she would drop the stone into the chick's beak. Once, Jón said, a good farmer had saved the life of a raven's chick. The chick disappeared but three years later, it returned and brought the farmer a stone of life. He put it under the skin of his left armpit and kept it there. He stopped growing old and had lived three normal lifespans when his wife removed the stone. Then he immediately grew old and died. (*Tíðfordríf:* 9r)

Jón had read in old books that the bezoar carried all the virtues, attributes and healing power contained in other stones and herbs. The bezoar was a microcosmos that contained the holy spirit and the creation and order of the world, and nobody could ever fully grasp all of its secrets. It was located in Paradise, which place in turn contained everything that was to be found on earth.

Despite the often fragmentary character of Jón's accounts, his ideas and poetic visions of nature are fascinating. He observed qualitative forces, virtues, and effects of nature, without strictly categorizing them. These natural phenomena – stones, herbs, birds and other animals – carried active attributes that created whole universes of meaning that had to be observed in contextual relations: a vast semiosphere (Lotman 1990: 123–130). His writings are imbued with a sense of the infinity of nature and its endless meanings. Jón's poem about the island Bjarnarey, his place of exile from 1634–1636, describes a living, interacting world where animals and plants were indeed a source of food but also constituted a world for themselves. The noisy birds, the never-withering grass, the flowers, the whales, seals and the fishes are all presented as being in unity, and the poem conveys the sense that humans are a part of this unity. (Lbs. 2131 4to: 130–134).

6   Nature, Framed or Unframed

Ein stutt undirrétting um Íslands aðskiljanlegar náttúrur ("A brief description of Iceland's various natures") is the last piece Jón wrote for Bishop Brynjólfur Sveinsson, probably in 1646. Its composition is more focused and organized than his previous writings, perhaps due to more pointed questions, or otherwise to Jón's improved training in writing this kind of material. Bishop Brynjólfur's interest in Icelandic nature was probably influenced by Ole Worm's

FIGURES 5.4A AND 5.4B *Two pages, showing a blue whale and a walrus, from Jón lærði's manuscript on the various natures of Iceland.*
PHOTOGRAPH BY THE NATIONAL AND UNIVERSITY LIBRARY OF ICELAND.

interest in nature and his collection of natural artifacts. But there is a great difference in Jón's holistic views and Ole Worm's fragmenting and objectifying approach when collecting for his Wunderkammer, which literally attempted to "frame" nature (Hafstein 2003: 9).

After an opening chapter on the hidden inhabitants of Iceland, there is a chapter on the geography of the north, in which a number of mystical inhabited lands and islands around Iceland are mentioned. This section concludes with a note on sea monsters. Jón said he did not write more about them because he had not read much about them. He had indeed seen many of them, but they all died in the extremely cold winter of 1602 (Guðmundsson 1924: 5).

The best-known part is a thorough description of whales in the ocean around Iceland, real as well as mythical. While this text is to some extent based on the 13th-century Norwegian *King's Mirror*, Jón added much to that since he had caught whales himself and was very knowledgeable about them. The mythical monster-whales, such as "rauðkembingur" and "hrosshvalur," he writes, are extremely dangerous to humans. He also describes the attributes and uses of a number of coastal species such as seals, polar-bears, birds, insects, seaweeds, shells and conches, worms and insects (Guðmundsson 1924: 5–26). The descriptions and classifications are apparently his own.

Jón's writings often include moral dimensions, and relate to human society. At the beginning of his work on the "natures" of Iceland, he describes the utopian dwellings of semi-giants or trolls who came from remote districts in Northern Norway and settled in the interior of Iceland, in the hidden Demonvalleys: "They knew how to open the earth and rocks, how to close them again, and how to walk in and out," Jón says, and he continues:

> Such old leaders chose to live in such hideouts, caves or hills, to be free from attacks by the inhabitants of the country. Otherwise they could not be at ease with their magic stones, mass of silver and other metals from the earth, with the good intoxicating grapes and mineral springs that naïve people have found both in ancient and recent times and which truly cannot be denied"
>
> GUÐMUNDSSON 1924: 1–2

In this fascinating description, Jón uses the word "bernskur" or naïve with a positive connotation. The naïve person is able to see the hidden qualities in life, those connected to the mineral springs and magical stones. Jón's literary output as a whole can be interpreted as an ongoing inquiry into the natural world of which humans and even semi-humans like elves and trolls are a part. He conceived of nature as complex and partly out of reach for humans, in the sense that humans will never grasp and fully understand it. In Tim Ingold's terms, this is an open world in which creation is on-going (Ingold 2011: 117). This is in full accordance with the medieval meaning of the word nature. Rather than framing nature, he led an interrogative dialogue with it as if studying "the composition of Nature" (von Uexküll 2010:171). Again this stands in sharp contrast to Ole Worm's contemporaneous attempts to frame nature with his Wunderkammer. Jón occasionally describes the correspondence between the microcosm and the macrocosm of the whole world: God's spirit was in the microcosm of the bezoar, and he was in nature as a whole. Jón would never have thought of objectifying and dominating nature. His writings are relational; in their attempts to attain harmony between his readings and experiences of nature, they have the "texture of the lifeworld" (Ingold 2011: 70). Like in Spinoza's radical philosophy, God is conceived not an anthropomorphized figure with plans and purposes, but as both being "in" nature and *being* nature (Spinoza 2002: 217–243, Nadler 2013a, 2013b). Both positions essentially resist the framing of nature as object which was in the ascendance at the time. Jón was a

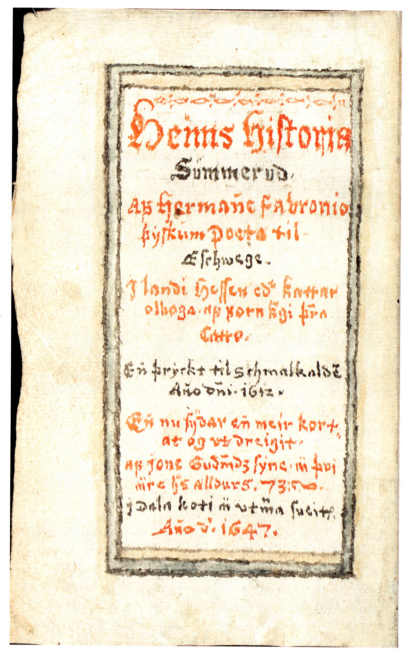

FIGURE 5.5 *Title page of paper manuscript "The world's history summarised by Hermann Fabronius ... still more shortened by Jón Guðmundsson." Written with a shaking hand in 1647, this is Jón lærði's last preserved manuscript.*
© THE ÁRNI MAGNÚSSON INSTITUTE, REYKJAVÍK AM 201 8VO FROM 1647. PHOTOGRAPH BY JÓHANNA ÓLAFSDÓTTIR.

believer and his faith had Catholic traits, but he did not believe in the authoritarian Lutheran God who underwrote the worldly powers and the centralizing tendencies in society.

In the eyes of the Church, Jón's heresy lay in attributing human and spiritual qualities to earthly beings. The dualism between flesh and spirit was among the most important premises for the dualism between humans and nature which developed from the 17th century onwards, along with a mechanistic, Cartesian rationalism. This conceptually closed rationalism, setting free will over a nature that is there to be manipulated and dominated, still prevails in western cultures today. The world of Jón lærði, where nature is not-yet-framed but complex, non-mechanistic, contextual, holistic, a dialogical Other which affords free will the opportunity to seek unity with God as Nature, stands as a reminder that it does not have to be this way.

Bibliography

Manuscripts

27 long poems. Lbs. 2131 4to (National and University Library of Iceland).
Tíðfordríf. AM 727 II 4to (The Árni Magnússon Institute for Icelandic Studies).
Fjandafæla. Sthm. Papp. 8:o nr 17 (The Royal Library in Stockholm).

Primary Sources

Guðmundsson, Jón. 1924. "Ein stutt undirrétting um Íslands aðskiljanlegu náttúrur" in *Jón Guðmundsson and His Natural History of* Iceland (ed. Halldór Hermannsson) (Islandica 15). Ithaca: Cornell University Library.
Hauksbók. 1892–1896. Ed. Eiríkur Jónsson and Finnur Jónsson. Copenhagen: Kongelige nordiske oldskrift-selskab.
Pétursson, Einar G. 1998. *Eddurit Jóns Guðmundssonar lærða* I–II. Reykjavík: Stofnun Árna Magnússonar á Íslandi.

Secondary Sources

Crosby, Alfred W. 1997. *The Measure of Reality. Quantification and Western Society, 1250–1600.* New York, NY: Cambridge University Press.
Deleuze, Gilles and Guattari, Félix. 1987. *A Thousand Plateaus. Capitalism and Schizophrenia* (tr. and foreword by Brian Massumi). Minneapolis and London: University of Minnesota Press.
Driscoll, Matthew James. 2010. 'The words on the page: Thoughts on Philology, old and new' in Judy Quinn and Emily Lethbridge (ed.) *Creating the medieval saga: Versions, variability, and editorial interpretations of Old Norse saga literature* (The Viking Collection, Vol. 18). Odense: Syddansk Universitetsforlag, 87–104.

Ezell, Margaret J.M. 1999. *Social Authorship and the Advent of Print*. Baltimore, MD: The Johns Hopkins University Press.

Hafstein, Valdimar Tr. 2003. 'Bodies of Knowledge. Ole Worm & Collecting in Late Renaissance Scandinavia' in *Ethnologia Europaea* 33(1): 5–20.

Hreinsson, Viðar. 1996. 'Tvær heimsmyndir á 17. öld. Snorra Edda í túlkun Jóns Guðmundssonar lærða' in Tómasson, Sverrir (ed.) *Guðamjöður og arnarleir. Safn ritgerða um eddulist*. Reykjavík: Háskólaútgáfan: 117–163.

Ingold, Tim. 2011. *Being Alive. Essays on movement, knowledge and description*. London and New York, NY: Routledge.

Isidore of Seville. 2006. *The Etymologies of Isidore of Seville*. Translated with introduction and notes by Stephen A. Barney, W.J. Lewis, J.A. Beach, and Oliver Berghoff. Cambridge UK: Cambridge University Press.

Jakobsson, Sverrir. 2007. 'Hauksbók and the Construction of an Icelandic World View' in *Saga-Book* XXXI, Viking Society for Northern Research, University College London: 22–38.

Karlsson, Stefán. 1983. 'Inngangur' in Stefán Karlsson (ed) *Guðmundar sögur biskups* I. *Ævi Guðmundar biskups. Guðmundar saga A* (Editiones Arnamagnæane, Series B, vol. 6). Copenhagen: C.A. Reitzels forlag: XV–CCII.

Lotman, Juri 1990. *Universe of the Mind: A Semiotic Theory of Culture*. London: I.B. Tauris.

McInerny, Ralph and O'Callaghan, John, "Saint Thomas Aquinas," in *The Stanford Encyclopedia of Philosophy* (Summer 2014 Edition), Edward N. Zalta (ed.). On line at: http://plato.stanford.edu/archives/sum2014/entries/aquinas/ (consulted 04.04.2016).

Merchant, Carolyn. 1989. *The Death of Nature. Women, Ecology and the Scientific Revolution*. San Francisco: Harper.

Merrian-Webster. "Nature." Online at: http://www.merriam-webster.com/ (consulted 04.04.2016).

Nadler, Steven. 2013a. "Spinoza," in *The Stanford Encyclopedia of Philosophy* (Fall 2013 Edition), Edward N. Zalta (ed.). On line at: http://plato.stanford.edu/archives/fall2013/entries/spinoza/ (consulted 04.04.2016).

Nadler, Steven. 2013b. "Why Spinoza was excommunicated" in *Humanities* 34 (5). On line at: http://www.neh.gov/humanities/2013/septemberoctober/feature/why-spinoza-was-excommunicated (consulted 04.04.2016).

Ordbog over det norrøne prosasprog. On line at: http://dataonp.ad.sc.ku.dk/ wordlist _d_adv.html (searchword "náttúra," consulted 25.04.2014).

Ritmálssafn. On line at: http://www.arnastofnun.is/page/gagnasofn_ritmalssafn (searchword "náttúra," consulted 20.04.2014).

Schepelern, H.D. 1971. *Museum Wormianum. Dets Forudsætninger og Tilblivelse* Odense: Wormianum.

Shackelford, Jole. 1999. 'Documenting the factual and the artifactual. Ole Worm and public knowledge' in *Endeavour* 23(2): 65–71.

Spinoza, Baruch. 2002. *Spinoza. Complete Works*. Translated by Samuel Shirley, edited with introduction and notes by Michael L. Morgan. Indianapolis: Hacket.

Springborg, Peter. 1977. 'Antiqvæ historiæ lepores – om renæssancen i den islandske håndskriftproduktion I 1600 tallet' in *Gardar* VIII: 53–89).

von Uexküll, Jakob. 2010. *A Foray into the Worlds of Animals and Humans* with *A Theory of Meaning*. Translated by Joseph D. O'Neil, with an introduction by Dorion Sagan and an afterword by Geoffrey Winthrop-Young. Minneapolis: University of Minnesota Press.

CHAPTER 6

Reframing Sacred Natural Sites as National Monuments in Estonia: Shifts in Nature-Culture Interactions

Ott Heinapuu

Abstract

The article will discuss sacred natural sites as a traditional mode of framing nature within vernacular religion and landscape management, especially after extant traditional natural sites of worship and taboo have been reframed as national monuments to exemplify beliefs rooted in Romantic-era narratives about Estonian history. Sacred natural sites in Estonia offer an example of interplay between, on the one hand, vernacular traditions on sacred landscapes that have been passed on orally and by custom and, on the other hand, invented traditions consolidating a national identity. By now, invented traditions originating in the civil religion have become parts of the vernacular religion and are replacing the portion of vernacular oral traditions that are not perceived as relevant. In the process of nation-building, local lore has been codified and crystallised, subordinated to the national canon, supplanted by the national standard or forgotten.

1   Introduction

Sacred natural sites are defined as 'areas of land or water having special spiritual significance to peoples and communities' according to guidelines for protected area managers developed in co-operation between the UNESCO and the International Union for Conservation of Nature (Wild and McLeod 2008: xi). While the guidelines emphasise that it is a working definition, the concept of sacred natural site is useful as an umbrella term that includes both the various vernacular types and categories of such sites – each of which may have specific defining features inherent in the tradition of the community in question – as well as unique sites that defy categorisation.

Sacred natural sites are best characterised with the help of the concept of vernacular religion or 'religion as it is lived' (Primiano 1995) because the traditional customs and beliefs associated with such sites form an integral part of 'individuals' sometimes wonderfully unique, sometimes wonderfully ordinary religious lives' as they are 'actually lived' (Primiano 1995: 41). They do not belong to any single distinct institutional teaching or authoritative fount of religious ritual. If one tried to pin the Estonian sacred natural site traditions down by origin, it would result in speculation about the relationships of non-Christian and pre-Christian elements, as well as Catholic ones, along with internationally known magical practices within current religious practice.

Sacred natural sites in general do not fit the general Western way of framing nature very well as such sites inhabit an ambiguous position somewhere between generally accepted implicit notions of 'culture' and 'nature' (cultural vs natural landscapes), 'tangible' and 'intangible' heritage.

As purely natural phenomena, sacred natural sites may lack any specific scientific value in regard to natural diversity, and usually have no specific criteria for identification that could be defined by means of the natural sciences. The heritage to be protected in sacred sites could rather be perceived supernatural entities than natural ones; understandably, naturalists of a materialist bent can't be expected to share belief in supernatural phenomena. This complicates protecting these sites on the merits of their uniqueness as natural monuments. On the other hand, cultural heritage in practice often stands for monuments of architecture or spectacular buildings. Thus a 19th-century neoclassical noble mansion fits better into the model of a monument than a communal gathering site, a healing site or a grove of trees associated with funerary rites. Furthermore, when it comes to monuments important to European civilization, the Parthenon of Athens, as a spectacular piece of engineering and art, is better known than the oak grove of Dodona (as invoked by Achilles in the *Iliad*, 16.231–235). Moreover, the Parthenon, lit by electric light in the darkness, also thrones over nearby sacred natural sites like the Cave of Pan below on the slope of the Acropolis and the pond within the Erechtheion that marks the spot of Poseidon's defeat at the hands of Athena – although these mythologically important sites of worship no doubt motivated the political decision to add another grand temple for worship on the hill (see Burkert 1985: 85–87).

The Japanese Shinto tradition may present the best-known set of sacred natural sites to the Western reader and the sanctity of Mount Fuji is well acknowledged. Yet, depictions of these tend to focus on Shinto temple architecture and red *torii* gates that mark the boundary of profane and sacred landscape rather than natural sites where Japanese gods have been known to dwell before temples and other infrastructure for worship have been built (e.g. Okada and Ujitoko 1958 as an example published in Japan).

Sacred natural sites typically are known parochially among close-knit communities who lack the kind of written tradition which could grant them the accolade as historical monuments. Thus it is hardly surprising that sacred natural sites can acquire more central cultural significance in postcolonial or anticolonial situations where the architectural heritage is construed as foreign. That is exactly the case of Estonia, where the pre-20th-century upper-class architectural tradition was associated with the German-speaking nobility and successive foreign German, Danish, Swedish, Polish and Russian administrative regimes.

Estonian sacred natural sites have functioned in this manner in a traditional culture with no written tradition in a mostly agrarian setting. The customs maintaining the sacredness of such sites emphasize local social cohesion and the relations of the human community with non-human supernatural beings and forces, reinforcing these links or drawing on them at times of crisis or illness or at calendar holidays. An example of this is the communal celebration of Midsummer (June 23) with a bonfire on the sacred hill Hiiemägi in Paluküla that has been observed well into the 20th century (Kõivupuu 2011: 185). Other annually recurring customs have been historically observed, revived, reinvented or invented on other traditional sacred natural sites. In the 21st century, personal healing rituals at healing stones or springs of water deemed to have healing properties are more common than communal festivals at sacred natural sites.

The 19th-century Estonian nationalist search for the distinct Estonian heritage concentrated on the pre-Christian past that also marked hallowed political independence prior to the 13th-century conquest of Livonia in the Baltic Crusade. In the absence of ancient temples, sacred natural sites form a part of this putative distinct national heritage that has been incorporated into the Estonian civil religion, or the system of values hallowed by the national community as a whole.

I think sacred natural sites provide important insights that help understand the relationships and interactions between culture and nature more generally. In turn, the treatment and status of sacred natural sites in the Estonian culture offers an interesting case of how these interactions have transformed in the quite rapid modernisation of society into a nation-state. This experience might also provide valuable lessons about conservation, heritage management as well as municipal planning and zoning that could be useful elsewhere.

In the following, I will introduce the main features of Estonian civil religion so as to give a context for understanding the perception of sacred natural sites introduced in the 19th century. Then I will proceed to the central part of the essay, eliciting and discussing four types of treating inherited vernacular landscape traditions in modern society. It has to be admitted that the author has a background in the study of folklore and therefore tends to be partial to the vernacular tradition and critical of the Romantic agenda.

FIGURE 6.1 *Hiiemägi, a sacred hill in the village of Paluküla; the sign posted at the foot of the hill reads 'Kõnnumaa landscape conservation area' and displays the emblem of the Estonian national nature conservation system.*
PHOTOGRAPH BY MARKO VAINU, CC BY-SA 3.0

2   Estonian Civil Religion as a Framework for Perceiving Sacred Natural Sites

I understand civil religion to be, after Robert N. Bellah, 'a collection of beliefs, symbols, and rituals with respect to sacred things and institutionalized in a collectivity' (Bellah 1967) or a phenomenon providing a 'set of values, symbols and rituals upon which the spiritual unity and social cohesion of nation' can be built (Ferrari 2010: 749). Since the founding of an independent republic in 1918, the Estonian constitution has supported the development of a society with broadly secular institutions and, consequently, a civil religion of a secular type. The secularisation of society was underscored during the five decades of Soviet rule. Since 1992, the state has maintained a predominantly neutral and secular relationship towards institutional religions while most Estonians do not belong formally to any religious organization (see Kiviorg 2010). According to the 2011 census data, 54 percent of the population over 15 years of age 'do not feel an affiliation to any religion' while only 29 percent say they do (14 per cent refused to answer; Population and Housing Census 2013).

However, Romantic-era narratives about the Estonian nation and its history – including narratives of ancient indigenous nature worship – play a strong role in Estonian civil religion. The Estonian civil religion is mainly of a secular nature. In Silvio Ferrari's typology, this corresponds to the French type of civil religion (*laïcité*) which sacralizes secular concepts and symbols 'that become the axis around which political and civil society is organized' (Ferrari 2010: 751). Ferrari contrasts the secular type of civil religion to the Abrahamic non-denominational (American) type that espouses the separation of church and state but recognises the helpful public role that religion can play, having built a civil religion based on the values of Judaism and Christianity with no preference to a single denomination, and the Italian or denominational type that raises to the rank of civil religion the values of the religious denomination of the majority (in Italy's case, Catholicism; Ferrari 2010: 753–757). The focal concept of the Estonian civil religion is the nation as defined on an ethnic and historical basis. This distinguishes the Estonian variety of *laïcité* from its French precursor, which is founded on universal and egalitarian values of political organisation. According to the preamble of the 1992 constitution, the Estonian state – while founded on the principles of liberty, justice and the rule of law – must 'guarantee the preservation of the Estonian nation, language and culture through the ages' (Constitution of the Republic of Estonia). According to the constitutional scholar Lauri Mälksoo, this compels the Estonian state to seek an equilibrium between, on the one hand, the Herderian concept of nations as defined on the basis of ethnic groups and, on the other hand, the Kantian universal principles of the republic (Mälksoo 2009). The cited passage of the constitution is often used by different interest groups to justify claims that the government should allocate more resources to supporting the arts ('culture') or safeguarding ethnic Estonian heritage ('preservation').

Institutional civil religion as supported by politicians and the public at large in Estonia has perpetuated elements of the 19th-century rhetoric from the era of when the traditions of the modern Estonian nation were invented. Modern Estonian national identity has been founded on myths created within the sphere of Romantic literary culture and is based on the 'imagined community' of the Estonian nation in the sense of Benedict Anderson (2006). The spatial signs of such an identity – which, following Eric Hobsbawm (1983), can be plausibly described as based on an invented tradition – are inevitably different from those of small rural communities with a predominantly oral culture that originally used sacred natural sites. Prime examples of sacred oak groves belonging to this new Romantic imagery can be found in the Estonian national epic *Kalevipoeg*, published as a popular edition first in 1862. The epic describes the original home of the demigod Kalev, father of the hero Kalevipoeg: 'In the north there stood a house,/ Sturdy farmstead built on rocks,/ Close to Taara's sacred oak groves,/ Half still hidden by the forest,/ Th'other half right in the clearing' (Kreutzwald 2011: 31). At a later point, the epic has the hero build a hill fort and city in Tartu, '[b]y the banks of Mother River,/ Shelter for the grove of Taara' (Kreutzwald 2011: 246–247), and, finally, the hero Kalevipoeg '[r]ode on the back of his war-horse/ Swift t'wards Taara's sacred grove,/ Where his troops were being gathered' (Kreutzwald 2011: 465).

Creating a modern Estonian national identity since the first half of the 19th century has meant constructing a common history for the nation as a whole and creating a common standard language to replace local dialects. It has also extended to such areas as forming a canonical understanding of what the standard folk costumes of Estonians in every single parish should be like (see Nõmmela 2010). In turn, this dominant discourse of Estonian national identity serves as a guide for understanding many features of traditional agrarian Estonian culture for most people living in an Estonian-language environment. This is especially evident in the case of sacred natural sites.

3   Modes of Reframing Sacred Natural Sites in Estonia

19th-century antiquarian and nationalist thinking focussed on the Estonian history before and during the Baltic Crusade when the Estonians, Livonians and Latvians were Christianised. Therefore it was the pre-Christian era before the 13th century that came to be defined as the golden age of the Estonian nation in the Romantic invented tradition of Estonianness. All non-Christian and unofficial religious elements of local traditions came to be identified with pre-Christian relics. This also led to hugely successful popular campaigns where, in an early instance of 'crowd-sourcing,' people were asked to collect and report local lore and landscape traditions that, in a Western European context, would be characteristic of mediaeval landscapes (Valk 2007: 201–202). These campaigns and the archives they produced have contributed to the resurgence of interest in the archaic traditions in the 19th and 20th centuries. However, in the processes of transferring the recorded lore into civil religion during the nation-building process, the texts describing natural sacred sites and the traditions associated with the sites have undergone many substantial changes. Local lore and traditions have often been either (a) codified and crystallised (as in lists of historic and natural monuments), or (b) subordinated to the general national canon (by associating traditional sites with national historical narratives as pre-Christian relics), (c) supplanted by the national standard (e.g. by planting new oak groves) or (d) forgotten in the process of cultural renewal. Each of these transformations is explained below.

3.1 *Codifying and Crystallising*

Codification and crystallisation in the context of sacred sites have meant compiling national lists of natural and historic monuments to be protected, the merits of which must not be underestimated (cf. Lowenthal 1985: 185–259). Giving a site the status of a monument may certainly support the vernacular traditions related to it; and, similarly, the continuation of traditional vernacular practices in sacred natural sites has doubtless been supported by the national discourse on sacred sites. But on the other hand, a fixed list of sites assigns great symbolic value to the sites included and condemns the rest to relative obscurity; the existence of a definitive list contrasts to the vernacular dynamic where sacred sites can be taken into use or abandoned over time.

It is difficult to estimate the total number of traditional sacred natural sites in Estonia that were used by the mainly agrarian oral society. According to researchers' estimates, there are about 2800 traditional sacred natural sites attested for in the archives. These include 800 complex sites, that is, land areas such as holy groves with possibly several foci of ritual activity that would be considered a sacred natural site each (Kütt, Remmel and Kaasik 2009).

However, after recent fieldwork that has revealed oral tradition about sites unknown in prior archive material, it has been hypothesized that over 4000 sites deemed sacred in the 19th century could yet be described in detail (Ajalooliste 2014: 3). Probably a handful of sacred natural sites in Estonia have been in religious use since before the 13th-century Baltic Crusade and remain so (Metssalu 2011), and a number of sites used for worship and healing in the 19th-century agrarian society retain such traditional practices.

Nearly 500 sites have the status of a national monument, with 447 sites officially declared cultural monuments subject to heritage protection, and 50 protected as natural objects (Kõivupuu 2009: 224). This would mean that roughly one in eight traditional sacred natural sites has the official status of a national monument. Getting sites de-listed (in case of the physical destruction or severe disfigurement of the landscape) is easier than getting sites listed because government institutions tend to be wary of additional costs that may be accrued from fulfilling statutory duties in administering a larger set of monuments.

Gro B. Ween and Lars Risan, speaking about the canon of World Heritage, describe this method of codifying and crystallising as the colonial mode of heritage, characterized by regimes of auditing, mapping and loss (Ween and

Risan 2014: 64–65). A very similar mode of thinking about sacred natural sites has been widely adopted in Estonia.

According to Ween and Risan (2014: 64), the regimes of auditing rely on the bureaucratic exercises of counting and ordering, classification and list making and reporting. It is exactly these operations that are essential also for the canon of national monuments in the production of Estonian national heritage. The National Registry of Cultural Monuments registers information on the location, protection status as well as information on inspections and studies of the monument. Monuments are regularly inspected and every subset (such as archaeological monuments) has an Inspector-General at the National Heritage Board whose duties include drawing up assessments on the cultural value of objects that could be listed or delisted; local inspectors are charged with overseeing monuments in each county, including regular inspections.

A fixed list of monuments interferes with the traditional ecology of landscape management by cultivating the notion that all sacred sites have been listed, thus precluding the creation of new sacred sites and the abandonment of old ones. In the traditional sense, supernatural creatures may inhabit a variety of places, some of which are unknown to the human population and may yet be 'discovered.' By contrast, an approach concentrating on auditing and mapping sites that have to be previously known and the existence of a definitive official list may inspire false confidence that the list is exhaustive.

In Estonian practice, in addition to listing, archaeological as well as natural monuments have been marked in the landscape with metal signs that give the monument's name or generic designation (for example 'sacrificial stone,' 'cult stone,' 'burial mound') and sometimes annotated with additional information. Among those listed as archaeological monuments are about 1300 cup-marked stones that have been presumed by archaeologists to be prehistoric cult sites but usually had no continued vernacular religious tradition. A cup-marked stone has one or several mainly round-bottomed small cup-marks with the diameter of usually 4 to 7 cm. and a depth of 0.5–2 cm. chipped into it; offering stones used in the past few centuries sometimes but not always have one or two larger offering pits (Tvauri 1999: 113). Alongside cup-marked stones protected as monuments, signs identifying them as 'cult stones' (*kultusekivi*) have been erected. This has caused the extension of some vernacular practices of giving offerings to such stones. According to the observations of the researcher Jüri Metssalu, the cup-marked stone at Rehe in the Hõreda village of Juuru parish in northern Estonia started receiving offerings of coins after a sign detailing archaeological information was erected: this is evident as Estonia adopted the euro in 2011 and offerings are in euro coins.

FIGURE 6.2 *A cup-marked stone signposted as a 'cult stone' in Vana-Vinni village, Lääne-Viru county (cultural heritage monument no. 10659); the sign reads: 'Archaeological monument'; 'Cult stone'; 'Under state protection' and displays a logo formerly used by the National Heritage Board.*
PHOTO BY JULIA KAAS, CC BY-SA 3.0

The regime of mapping, by determining the visibility of particular sites to authorities, has immediate practical consequences (Ween and Risan 2014: 64). Once a traditional site is off the map, municipal planning processes will no longer have to take it into account. In the case of listed and mapped sites, planning processes need only heed the mapped boundaries of sites while remaining free to violate any taboos that have applied in prior vernacular religion. In Estonia, this has led to court disputes in the 21st century in which local authorities have been challenged by groups who oppose plans to develop sacred natural sites in ways that would not be allowed in the vernacular tradition but might be permissible under current law (that is, in cases where the legal protection regime of monuments falls short of local expectations rooted in tradition).

The regime of loss (Ween and Risan 2014: 65) is already evident in the examples above: in public discussions, the sacred natural sites of Estonia are generally perceived as something that is about to be lost and thus must be conserved. Various parties in discussions disagree on the extent of inevitable and preventable loss, but depictions of a living, vibrant, and continuing tradition are rare.

Romantic grief and nostalgia for pre-Christian ancient times as expressed by writers in the 19th century have been made into a resource of politics and forming policy (cf. Yusoff 2011). This discourse is particularly effective in Estonian national media when groups focussed on preserving vernacular traditions need to rally support for their cause or demand action from the authorities.

3.2 *Subordination to the National Canon*

By associating traditional sacred natural sites with national historical narratives as supposed pre-Christian relics, local traditions have been subordinated to the national canon of history. In the national canon, non-Christian vernacular traditions are assumed to date from before the 13th century. According to Marek Tamm, the first focal point of the common narrative of the Estonian national history has been the conquest of Livonia and Estonia by German and Danish crusaders in what is known internationally as the Baltic Crusade and locally as the ancient struggle for independence; the second focal point of history was the reversal of the crusade's result, or the Estonian War for Independence that secured the independence of the Republic of Estonia, declared in 1918 (Tamm 2012: 55–64).

The linkage of sacred natural sites with pre-conquest history still has legal and regulatory relevance: in the national heritage protection system, sacred natural sites have usually been protected as archaeological monuments, which in turn stand for sites used in the 13th century or earlier. (However, a draft law unveiled by the Ministry of Culture in March 2015 introduces sacred natural sites as a distinct subset of monuments.)

However, relying on archaeological evidence to prove the ancient use of a sacred natural site is fraught with uncertainty. Tiina Äikäs has argued that the absence of artefacts does not necessarily disprove the use of a sacred natural site as such, as taboos may prohibit leaving traces of human activity at the site even if the sites are used for worship (Äikäs 2011). This is the case in Japanese sacred mountains that according to the Shinto religion used to be off limit for people (Lindström 2007: 226). Sacred places significant in the religious experience have not necessarily been the spaces where ritual activities were performed. 'Olympus has played such a role. It was the place where gods lived, not where cult activities were,' argue Szczepanik and Wadyl (2014: 2). The absence of archaeological findings in such cases may show that taboos have been observed.

The other avenue to official protection is protecting the sacred sites on their merits as natural monuments, which is not always unproblematic either, as sites perceived as sacred need not have outstanding biological properties but, as argued above, values that can be understood in cultural terms only.

In the case of a number of Estonian traditional sacred natural sites, vernacular agrarian folklore has become hybridised with the Romantic-era nationalist discourse where vernacular motifs in local legends and experiences coexist with Romantic motifs of literary provenance, thus blurring historically different ways of framing landscapes into each other.

It is quite common that former healing, festive, or worship sites are interpreted mostly through the frame of archaeological or natural monuments as representative of the pre-Christian past. For example, the agrarian tradition known from the 19th and 20th centuries associated Paka hill in the Rapla parish in northern Estonia with the giant diabolical figure Vanapagan, ghosts and monks. On the basis of a vague reference from the mediaeval Chronicle of Livonia (*'intraverunt provinciam Harionensem, que est in media Estonia, ubi et omnes gentes circumiacentes quolibet anno ad placitandum in Raigele convenire solebant,'* (Henricus 1982: 172), 'they entered the province of Harrien, which is in the midst of Estonia. There every year all the people round about were accustomed to assemble at Raela to make decisions' (Henricus Lettus 2003: 156, dated August 15, 1216)), it has been identified as the meeting site of ancient Estonian elders – with supernatural visible or auditory encounters of those ancient elders appearing in the repertoire of local folklore where previously Catholic monks had been seen or heard (Metssalu 2008).

The national canon of history includes the assertions that 'the sacred tree of the ancient Estonians was the oak' and that 'the sacred sites of the ancient Estonians were sacred oak groves' that refer to the era before the Baltic Crusade. Statements claiming the sanctity of the oak as a species for Estonians can be found in a general knowledge Estonian encyclopedia in the entry on the oak species *Quercus robur* ('The oak was considered sacred by the Estonians'; Tamm 1975: 469) and on the website of the Government Office dedicated to the centenary celebrations of the Republic of Estonia ('The oak has been a sacred tree of the Estonians through the ages'; Eesti 100 tamme). More curiously, a similar assertion ('The oak was the Estonians' sacred tree,' Henricus 1982: 200) appears as the caption to an illustration in the Estonian and Latin scholarly edition of the Chronicle of Livonia, although the text of the chronicle itself does not discuss Estonians' holy trees in detail.

In public discourse, such assertions have overshadowed all other types of sacred natural sites as 'true ancient Estonian' ones after becoming dominant. This has happened early on in Estonian-language national culture: collectors of folklore from the late 19th century onwards, drawing on the Romantic literary tradition, have woven references to worship in 'the sacred oak groves of the ancient Estonians' into local oral legends they were supposed to be faithfully recording in writing. Take, for example, a part of a text sent into the folklore archives in 1939, after one generation of people had been brought up within the school system of the new Republic of Estonia:

> Near the village of Võuküla on the bank of the Võhandu River, there was a sacred hill. On the hill there grew great old oaks and lindens. There was a sacrificial stone in the middle of the hill. People used to worship gods on the hill and sacrifice at the sacrificial stone.
> REMMEL 2011: 22

Public discourse about sacred natural sites in Estonia also nearly always includes similar Romantic-tinged images of ancient sanctuaries. Thus, motifs from the formative writings of the 19th-century Estonian national awakening, and the ideology it engendered, left their marks on the vernacular religion.

The mythologemes emphasizing the oak and oak groves mostly echo the prevailing literary and scholarly discourse of the 19th century. As Estonia is situated at the northern limit of the distribution of the oak (*Quercus robur*), oak groves are rare in actual landscapes. Botanically, groves with a majority of oaks do not occur as fully natural phenomena in the hemiboreal conditions of Estonia: oak groves are managed, semi-natural plant communities like planted parks or wooded meadows used for pasturing and other economic activities that ill suit the usual prohibitions of sacred sites (see Leibak 2007: 174–176). While there are some sacred oak groves in Estonia, these are few and far between, which leads one to think that the dominance of the symbol is of literary provenance and depends more on examples from classical antiquity and Romantic Germany than Estonian local tradition. There are, of course, single oak trees that have been considered sacred. In the data collated by Fred Puss (1995: 6) there are 347 sacred trees, out of which 85, or roughly a quarter, are oaks. However, one should note that the majority of sacred trees are not oaks even by this reckoning. Traditionally, a sacred tree in Estonia may be of any species, and Romantic literary influences have boosted the incidence of oaks in recorded tradition.

Influentially, Jacob Grimm said in his *Deutsche Mythologie* that the oak is first and foremost among the sacred trees of the Germans (Grimm 1876: 542–543), and noted the association of the Greek, Roman and Germanic thunder gods Zeus, Jupiter and Donar or Thor with the oak. Such developments in comparative Indo-European mythology have left their mark on the Estonian popular mythology of today – the Estonian nation-builders in the 19th and 20th centuries also associated the putative Estonian head god Taara with the oak and with Thor. It is also relevant that in the German-speaking world, St Boniface (who, according to his *Vita*, felled a sacred oak dedicated to the thunder god of the Hessians) is more popular and better known than St Martin of Tours, whose legend includes felling a sacred fir in Gaul, spreading the motif of the oak as the preeminent sacred tree.

In the spread of the idea that the species of the sacred tree is crucial, one could see the effect of 19th-century naturalists' preoccupation with species over ecosystems. In the literary discourse, it is the species of the holy tree that is of the primary importance and not, as in the vernacular tradition, the individual characteristics of the sacred tree or its position in the intricate web of interrelations in the landscape and society. Thus, something that is now popularly perceived as an inherent peculiarity of Estonian mythology and landscape – the sacred oak grove – looks more like an offshoot of common European culture planted in the 19th century.

3.3 *Supplantation*

Supplantation by the national standard means that a vernacular element of culture becomes extinct and is replaced by a functionally similar phenomenon introduced from the national culture. An example from the last two decades is a revived tendency to plant new oak groves supposedly in emulation of ancient Estonian sanctuaries. Such initiatives often have political or official support, as in a government campaign to plant a grove of a hundred oaks in at least in every county for the 100th anniversary of the republic in 2018. To quote a press release by the Government Office:

> Another project to kick off next year is the laying out of parks of one hundred oak trees using trees grown from oak acorns gathered by pupils of basic schools and upper secondary schools in fall 2013. In the year of Estonia's centenary, these will be planted in parks of one hundred trees in local government units in order to create oak groves that symbolize eternity, dignity and wisdom. The project will be carried out in conjunction with the State Forest Management Center.
>
> EESTI VABARIIK VALMISTUB 2012

Initially, a new oak grove was planned into every one of Estonia's over 200 municipalities but the extent of the initiative has been scaled down.

The first similar initiatives of planting new oak groves in emulation of ancient sanctuaries date from the 1930s but the current wave seems to have started at the most recent turn of the century when President Arnold Rüütel floated the idea that a man-made national sanctuary, the Song Festival Grounds in the capital Tallinn, should be given an additional layer of sanctity by planting a sacred oak grove there. The national Song Festival, held every five years, has been one of the most important ceremonies of the civil religion of the Estonian nation for nearly 150 years, having at its peak drawn nearly a quarter of ethnic Estonians to the festival grounds. Although a version of the idea of planting a sacred grove near the festival grounds has received the backing of the Tallinn city government, it has not been implemented.

Elected municipal officials from around the capital have since 2005 gathered to plant young oak trees in the village of Loo in what is called the Sacred Grove of Freedom on every Midsummer. Similarly, in Estonia's second city by population, Tartu, the city government has founded a municipal oak grove where every mayor and honorary citizen of the city plants an oak tree. In the earliest versions of this idea in 2007, the site was explicitly called 'the oak grove of Taara' after the thunder god of Romantic literature. All these initiatives implicitly assume that the species of the plants will grant the site the purported sanctity, supplanting a modern view on sacred sites for the traditional one.

3.4 *Forgetting*

Despite the fact that some traditional sacred natural sites retain old practices and others have been reframed as national monuments of historic or natural value, many such sites in Estonia are in fact disappearing from cultural memory in the processes of cultural renewal in the context of urbanisation, thus demonstrating the fluid and ephemeral nature of oral vernacular tradition. Those sites that remain in communal memory in turn are more and more often associated with narratives from the literary tradition promoted by the common memory of the nation that spread by means of national school curricula, media and literature as well as different art forms. I believe this process of forgetting to be of a more structural and radical nature than the rotation of shrines in traditional societies as outlined by Jack Goody (1977: 30) as whole categories of sacred sites and ecologies of tradition have been or are being forgotten and abandoned in great numbers. This amounts to a fundamental shift in perceiving landscapes.

4 Conclusion

Differently framed sacred natural sites in Estonia remain relevant on different levels of social organization. Sacred natural sites within the traditional frame of vernacular religion are relevant in the small village or family communities that may include perceived supernatural entities (such as the dead ancestors or nature spirits). Traditions related to these sites reinforce communal cohesion, as in communal Midsummer celebrations with a bonfire where the village community convenes. Formerly, in the agrarian society of the 19th century, these sites were also relevant in the categories of everyday livelihood and prosperity (e.g in determining whether livestock prosper) but this is less the case now. However, common knowledge persists that sacred natural sites can help provide remedies for ill health or diseases, or provide luck generally.

Within the frame of civil religion, sacred natural sites are relevant in contexts that underscore Estonian national cohesion and continuity within the invented tradition that has been extended to the pre-Christian era of ancient independence. In this frame, ancestors can be seen as the collective historical body of ancestors of the nation rather than concrete personal ancestors. This may be manifested in the government-mandated school curriculum and on official festive occasions. Signifiers used for conveying these meanings need not be present in the landscape and the sites may also be either imagined (lost oak groves of yore) or manufactured (new oak groves to be planted) but traditional sacred sites are now also often linked to the invented traditions surrounding the Estonian national identity. Traditional sacred natural sites with no such semiotic support are likely to be forgotten and fall out of the bounds of current culture.

Bibliography

Äikäs, Tiina. 2011. 'From Fell Tops to Standing Stones: Sacred Landscapes in Northern Finland' in *Archaeologica Baltica* 15: 16–22.

'Ajalooliste looduslike pühapaikade piiritlemise ja kaitse korraldamise alused. Eelnõu' 2014. Tartu: Tartu Ülikooli looduslike pühapaikade keskus. On line at: http://www.flaj.ut.ee/sites/default/files/www_ut/kaitsemetoodika_270204.pdf (consulted 12.01.2015).

Anderson, Benedict. 2006. *Imagined Communities. Reflections on the Origin and Spread of Nationalism.* London, New York: Verso.

Bellah, Robert N. 1967. 'Civil Religion in America' in *Dædalus* 96(1): 1–21.

Burkert, Walter. 1985. *Greek Religion*. Translated by John Raffan. Cambridge, MA: Harvard University Press.

'The Constitution of the Republic of Estonia.' On line at: https://www.riigiteataja.ee/en/eli/ee/rhvv/act/530102013003/consolide (consulted 15.01.2015).

'Eesti 100 tamme.' On line at https://riigikantselei.ee/et/valitsuse-toetamine/eesti-vabariik-100/eesti-100-tamme (consulted 15.10.2015).

'Tamm' 1975 in Eesti Nõukogude Entsüklopeedia 7. Tallinn: Valgus: 469.

'Eesti Vabariik valmistub 95. sünnipäevaks ning 100. aastapäevaks,' December 12, 2012. On line at http://www.bns.ee/topic/638/news/44698566/?id=146266 (consulted 11.01.2015).

Ferrari, Silvio. 2010. 'Civil Religions: Models and Perspectives' in *The George Washington International Law Review* 41(4): 749–763.

Goody, Jack. 1977. *The Domestication of the Savage Mind*. Cambridge: Cambridge University Press.

Grimm, Jacob. 1876. *Deutsche Mythologie*. Vol. II. Berlin: F. Dümmler.

Henricus de Lettis. 1982. *Heinrici Chronicon Livoniae. Henriku Liivimaa kroonika* (tr. Richard Kleis, ed. Enn Tarvel). Tallinn: Eesti Raamat.

Henricus Lettus. 2003. *The Chronicle of Henry of Livonia* (tr. James A. Brundage). New York: Columbia University Press.

Hobsbawm, Eric. 1983. 'Introduction: Inventing Traditions' in Hobsbawm, Eric and Terence Ranger (eds) *The Invention of Tradition*. Cambridge: Cambridge University Press: 1–14.

Kiviorg, Merilin. 2010. 'Religion and the Secular State in Estonia' in Javier Martínez-Torrón and W. Cole Durham (eds) *Religion and the Secular State. La religion et l'État laïque*. Provo, Utah: International Center for Law and Religion Studies: 261–272. On line at: http://www.iclrs.org/content/blurb/files/Estonia.pdf (consulted 12.01.2015).

Kõivupuu, Marju. 2009. 'Natural Sacred Places in Landscape: an Estonian Model' in: Sigurd Bergmann, P.M. Scott, Maria Jansdotter Samuelsson and Heinrich Bedford-Strohm (eds) *Nature, Space and the Sacred. Transdisciplinary perspectives*. Farnham: Ashgate Publishing: 223–234.

Kõivupuu, Marju. 2011. *101 Eesti pühapaika*. Tallinn: Varrak.

Kreutzwald, Friedrich Reinhold. 2011. *Kalevipoeg* (tr. Triinu Kartus). Tartu and Tallinn: Eesti Kirjandusmuuseum, Kunst.

Kütt, Auli, Mari-Ann Remmel and Ahto Kaasik. 2009. *Ajaloolised looduslikud pühapaigad Lahemaa rahvuspargi Kuusalu kihelkonna osas. Ekspertiis*. Tartu: Hiite Maja, Taarausuliste ja Maausuliste Maavalla Koda.

Leibak, Eerik. 2007. 'Hiied kui loodusobjektid' in Ahto Kaasik and Heiki Valk (eds). *Looduslikud pühapaigad: väärtused ja kaitse*. Tartu: Maavalla Koda, Tartu Ülikool, Õpetatud Eesti Selts: 173–182.

Lindström, Kati. 2007. 'From Experiential to Chronometric Seasonality – the Establishment of Seasons as a National Symbol in Modern Japan' in Hannes Palang, Helen Sooväli, and Anu Printsmann (eds) *Seasonal Landscapes*. Berlin: Springer: 215–224.

Lowenthal, David. 1985. *The Past is a Foreign Country*. Cambridge: Cambridge University Press.

Mälksoo, Lauri. 2009. 'Põhiseaduspatriotism – kas ka Eesti jaoks?' in *Vikerkaar* 24 (10–11): 83–94.

Metssalu, Jüri. 2008. 'Ajalookirjutuse mõjust kohapärimusele Raikküla näitel ehk Katse tuvastada maa-alune tee munkadest muistsete vanemateni' in Kalmre, Eda and Ergo-Hart Västrik (eds). *Kes kõlbab, seda kõneldakse. Pühendusteos Mall Hiiemäele.* (Commentationes Archivi Traditionum Popularium Estoniae 25). Tartu: Eesti Kirjandusmuuseumi Teaduskirjastus: 323–359.

Metssalu, Jüri. 2011, 'Ulmu allikas' in Oja, Mare (ed.) *Eesti kultuuriloo õppematerjal. I. Raplamaa.* Tallinn: Eesti Ajaloo- ja Ühiskonnaõpetajate Selts: 20.

Nõmmela, Marleen. 2010. 'The State, the Museum and the Ethnographer in Constructing National Heritage: Defining Estonian National Costumes in the 1930s' in *Journal of Ethnology and Folkloristics* 4(1): 49–61.

Okada, Yoneo and Sadatoshi Ujitoko. 1958. *Nihon no jinja yo matsuri. Shinto shrines and festivals.* Jinja Honcho, Kokugakuin University, Institute for Japanese Culture and Classics.

Population and Housing Census. 2013. Statistical Database, Statistics Estonia: Table PC0451. On line at: http://pub.stat.ee/px-web.2001/I_Databas/Population_Census/databasetree.asp (consulted 17.02.2015).

Primiano, Leonard. 1995. 'Vernacular Religion and the Search for Method in Religious Folklife' in *Western Folklore* 54: 37–56.

Puss, Fred. 1995. *Puudega seotud pärimused ja traditsioonid Eesti rahvakultuuris.* Tartu: Tartu Ülikool.

Remmel, Mari-Ann. 2011. '"Püha" mõiste ja kivid meie maastikul' in Hiiemäe, Mall (ed.) *Pühad kivid Eestimaal.* Tallinn: Tammerraamat: 19–24.

Szczepanik, Paweł and Sławomir Wadyl. 2014. 'A Comparative Analysis of Early Medieval North-West Slavonic and West Baltic Sacred Landscapes: an Introduction to the Problems' in *Networks and Neighbours* 2(1): 1–19.

Tamm, Marek. 2013. *Monumentaalne Eesti.* Tallinn: Kultuurileht.

Tvauri, Andres. 1999. 'Cup-Marked Stones in Estonia' in *Folklore* 11: 113–169.

Valk, Heiki. 2007. 'Choosing Holy Places' in Ralph Haeussler and Anthony C. King (eds). *Continuity and Innovation in Religion in the Roman West.* Vol. 1. (JRA supplement volume 67.1). Portsmouth, RI: Journal of Roman Archaeology: 201–212.

Ween, Gro B. and Lars Risan. 2014. 'Exploring Heritage Lives: Indigenous Peoples in World Heritage Sites' in Herdis Hølleland and Steinar Solheim (eds) *Between dream and reality: Debating the impact of World Heritage Listing.* Oslo: Reprosentralen: 61–72. Special issue of *Primitive tider.*

Wild, Robert and Christian McLeod (eds). 2008. *Sacred Natural Sites: Guidelines for Protected Area Managers.* Gland: IUCN.

Yussof, Kathryn. 2011. 'Aesthetics of Loss: Biodiversity, Banal Violence and Biotic Subjects' in *Transactions of the Institute of British Geographers* 37(4): 578–592.

CHAPTER 7

Animals in Norwegian Political Party Programs: A Critical Reading

Morten Tønnessen

Abstract

Inspired by Arran Stibbe and drawing on ecolinguistics, corpus linguistics and Critical Discourse Analysis, this chapter presents a simple linguistic study of mentions of animals in Norwegian political party programs for the parliamentary term 2013–2017. The study is likely symptomatic of quite common attitudes to animals not only in Norway but also in a range of other countries. It documents a near-universal anthropocentric bias in Norwegian political party programs, with the Green Party as the only possible exception. This bias is particularly visible in the vocabulary constituted by occurrences of the morphemes "fisk" [fish] and "rein" [reindeer]. Rather than being framed as sentient beings, these animals are almost exclusively referred to in terms of economic resources that are to be managed by the authorities.

1   Introduction

When people think about Norway, they might think about a spot of wild, "real" nature on the outskirts of Europe – a somewhat exotic, sparsely populated country in an otherwise heavily populated continent. Some years back the household I was part of, located close to Oslo, Norway's capital, housed an asylum seeker from the Middle East. He once asked us how far North Norway was – and when we told him that the North Pole was the last stop on the

---

*   This work has been carried out thanks to the support of the research project "Animals in Changing Environments: Cultural Mediation and Semiotic Analysis" (EEA Norway Grants/Norway Financial Mechanism 2009–2014 under project contract no EMP151) and Partaking in The Green house: A Cross-Disciplinary Environmental Humanities Initiative at University of Stavanger. The analysis described in this paper was conducted for the Norwegian Animal Ethics Conference (see http://dyreetikkonferansen.no) 2013, on behalf of Minding Animals Norway (see http://mindinganimals.no) and representing University of Stavanger. I would like to thank participants at Minding Animals Norway's 3rd research seminar (Oslo, August 2013), the "Framing Nature" conference in Tartu in April–May 2014, and Minding Animals Conference 3 (Delhi, January 2015) for useful feedback on earlier drafts of this paper.

metropolitan subway, he had to pause to think for a few seconds before he realized that we were just joking with him. Norwegians, however (as most locals, it appears), tend to think about their land as *cultivated* land, not as wilderness.

Before I proceed, I must acknowledge that personally, I think that, in order to function satisfactorily, environmental ethics must be supplemented by animal ethics, and *visa versa*. In other words, I believe that clearheaded and respectful treatment of ecosystems and other larger ecological entities, such as species, must be complemented with clearheaded and respectful treatment of individual animals. Bereft of such a complementarity, any of these "green" approaches to nature will necessarily fail to achieve the high moral standards we should expect of them. This is a value stand, and expresses one of my "deepest intuitions" in Arne Næss' sense. This chapter is not the right venue for providing detailed justification of that value stand (however, see Tønnessen, 2016), but at the very least it should be mentioned.

Now, since Norway is a country that is often associated with nature and wilderness, one might perhaps expect that Norway would be particularly "green," or progressive, in its dealings with animals. Despite Norwegians' self-image as progressives in everything from peace-making to greenery, that is not necessarily the case (as it happens, Norway has over the last few years taken part in various wars of aggression, and is, as a considerable producer of oil and gas, one of Europe's biggest polluters). In the eyes of animal rights-inclined environmentalists internationally, Norway is notorious for its history with regard to whaling and seal hunting. In Norway, such practices have often been regarded as "traditions" and/or sensible ways of utilizing the resources of nature. In this perspective, *not* to make use of a given resource is equivalent with making resources go to waste. Within the framework of a predominating *economic discourse*, which we will hear more about later on in this study, that simply does not make sense. As this chapter will show, the economic discourse and the *management discourse* often dominate Norwegian political discourses on animals. This is symptomatic of a world view in which animals are primarily seen as potential economic resources (economic discourse), or alternatively as possible sources of conflicts (management discourse).[1]

Inspired by Stibbe 2012 and drawing on ecolinguistics, corpus linguistics and Critical Discourse Analysis, this chapter presents a simple linguistic study of mentions of animals in Norwegian political party programs for the

---

1 The animal discourse at large could further be said to include a more specifically scientific animal discourse and an animal welfare discourse, among several other discourses. In each case, the focus, or perspective, of the discourse frames how animals are seen.

parliamentary term 2013–2017 (Tønnessen 2013). The corpus consists of 12 programs, representing Norway's nine biggest political parties. This is because three of the parties operate with two programs, one focused on principles and the other on more practical questions.

The study is divided into two parts: a word frequency study,[2] involving 23 entries with altogether 28 search terms (including "dyr" [animal], "dyreetikk" [animal ethics], "dyrevelferd" [animal welfare], "fisk" [fish], "fugl" [bird], "rovdyr" [predator(s)] and a number of common animals) and a morpheme occurrence study. The latter results in complete overviews over the vocabulary applied in these political programs containing the morphemes "dyr" [animal], "rein" [reindeer] and "fisk" [fish].

The analysis includes programs of the following parties for the period 2013–2017:

- AP: Arbeiderpartiet [Labour party] (Arbeiderpartiet 2013)
- FrP: Fremskrittspartiet [the Progress Party]* (Fremskrittspartiet 2013a, 2013b)
- H: Høyre [the Conservative Party]* (Høyre 2013)
- KrF: Kristelig Folkeparti [Christian Democrats]** (Kristelig Folkeparti 2013)
- MDG: Miljøpartiet De Grønne [the Green Party] (Miljøpartiet De Grønne 2013a, 2013b)
- R: Rødt [the Red Party] (Rødt 2010, 2012)
- SP: Senterpartiet [the Centre Party] (Senterpartiet 2013)
- SV: Sosialistisk Venstreparti [the Socialist Left Party] (Sosialistisk Venstreparti 2013)
- V: Venstre [the Social-Liberal Party]** (Venstre 2013)

* in government
** allied with the government via a cooperation agreement

---

2   In this chapter I have chosen to analyse the frequency of selected search terms in form of number of mentions per program/party. This gives a rough idea about the profile and vocabulary of each party. I could instead have chosen to examine the frequency of these terms as number of occurrences per 1.000 words in each program – i.e., relative to the number of words in each program. For my current purposes, however, a simpler study will do. More detailed data can easily be aggregated from the corpus examined in this chapter (with programs ranging in length from 62 to 134 pages, except for programs of principles which range from 9 to 14 pages). Such data would be of much more interest in a broader, comparative study. Comparative studies – with comparison of the mentions of animals in political party programs across countries, and/or over time – would certainly be of interest.

Of the nine parties surveyed, AP/Labour is the biggest in terms of votes (31% of the vote in 2013) and number of seats in parliament, ahead of H/the Conservative Party (27%) and FrP/the Progress Party (16%). The rest are fairly small with 4–6% of the vote, except for MDG/the Green Party which, with 2,8%, only got one seat – its first ever – in parliament, and Rødt/the Red Party, which got 1,1% and no seat. While AP/Labour is social democratic and counted as left-wing along with SV/the Socialist Left Party and Rødt/the Red Party, H/the Conservative Party and FrP/the Progress Party are right-wing. The remaining four parties are in the political center (including MDG/the Green Party, which presents itself as being neither left nor right but "ahead" of the others).

The findings of the second part of the analysis show that the three mentioned morphemes – "dyr" [animal], "rein" [reindeer] and "fisk" [fish] – are often included in wordings that imply a systematic omission of basic aspects of animal life and behavior. In particular, the morphemes "fisk" [fish] and "rein" [reindeer] are predominantly, in fact almost exclusively, to be found in conceptual structures that constitute an objectification of animals, usually by reducing them to economic resources. This observation is consistent with one of the findings of the first part of the study, namely that "fisk" [fish], which is economically important in Norway, is mentioned some 300 times altogether in the corpus, whereas "fugl" [bird] is mentioned only three times. Even when applied as a word, "fisk" [fish] rarely refers to fish as living, sentient beings, but most often to fish products and governmental management of fisheries.

There are a few instances of statements connecting animal welfare and the like to the fishy vocabulary, but there is otherwise little correlation between the positive statements about animal ethics etc. on the one hand, and the use of language whenever animals are mentioned elsewhere in the party programs, on the other. The analysis thus shows that taken in their entirety, the word choices made in formulating the parties' policies reveal a deep-seated anthropocentrism which stands in direct contrast to the good intentions, officially shared by several of the analyzed parties, of getting animal ethics higher up on the political agenda.

2 Norwegian Discourses and Animals

The titles of the twelve programs are indicative of the variation in how political parties' programs are composed or conceived of in Norway. Some of the titles include the party name and/or the timespan of the parliamentary period, others not. The parties have different ideas about what to call a program. The Progress Party has a "prinsipprogram" [program of principles] (Fremskrittspartiet

2013a) and a "handlingsprogram" [action program] (Fremskrittspartiet 2013b), whereas both the Green Party and the Red Party have a program of principles (Miljøpartiet De Grønne 2013a, Rødt 2010) and an "arbeidsprogram" [working program] (Miljøpartiet De Grønne 2013b, Rødt 2012). The Socialist Left Party (2013) has a working program only, while Labour simply has a "program" (Arbeiderpartiet 2013). The Conservative Party and the Social-Liberal Party, on their side, have neither of the above but instead a "stortingsvalgprogram" (parliamentary election program) (Høyre 2013, Venstre 2013). Finally, the Christian-Democrats have a "politisk program" [political program] (sic!) (Kristelig Folkeparti 2013), and the Centre Party has a "prinsipp- og handlingsprogram" [program of principles and action program] (Senterpartiet 2013).

Four of the titles of political party programs involve political slogans (emphasis added):

>Labour: *"Vi tar Norge videre"*
>[We take Norway further]
>ARBEIDERPARTIET 2013

>The Conservative Party: *"Nye ideer, bedre løsninger"*
>[New ideas, better solutions]
>HØYRE 2013

>The Social-Liberal Party: *"Frihet. Fremtid. Fellesskap"*
>[Freedom. Future. Community]
>VENSTRE 2013

>The Socialist Left-Party: *Del godene!*
>[Share the goods!]
>SOSIALISTISK VENSTREPARTI 2013

While the book of which this chapter is a part addresses the topic of framing nature, this chapter deals with framing (i.e. representing, contextualizing) animals as resources and sentient beings/subjects respectively. For Alexander and Stibbe, it is crucial that "[o]nly when research explores the implications of language contact or linguistic diversity for human behavior and the consequent impact on real, physical ecosystems does it become 'ecolinguistics'" (2014: 108). Do representations always have such effects? The term "animal representation" could prove to be helpful here. But "[g]iven that [...] 'animal representations' means human representations of animals," as Tønnessen and Tüür write, this topic "is not identical with 'animal representations' understood in a wider sense":

Consider, for instance, the prospective topic of animals' representations of humans (i.e., 'human representations' from the point of view of some animal), thus encapsulating the ways in which we humans are collectively or individually represented by certain figures in the Umwelten of various animals. These perceptions, too, are in a sense anthropogenic.[3] (2014: 17)

Whatever capability an animal might have, it is evident that humans predominate in representing animals in written and other texts. Some discourses can justifiably be labeled as "*destructive discourses*," if they "potentially construct inhumane and ecologically damaging relationships between humans and animals" (Stibbe 2012: 6).[4]

Discourse analysis comes in many forms, ranging from broad to narrow conceptions of the field. In the words of Norman Fairclough, some versions "limit themselves to identifying the presence and forms of combination of recurrent and relatively stable and durable 'discourses' in texts, whereas others carry ou[t] various forms of detailed linguistic analysis [...] and/or detailed analysis of other semiotic features of texts" (2005: 916). In a somewhat similar vein, Alexander and Stibbe claim that "[d]iscourses consist of clusters of linguistic (and other semiotic) features used by groups in speaking about the world, which come together to produce specific models of reality. These models or shaping devices enable humans to construct relationships with the real world" (2014: 105). The political, write Fairclough and Fairclough, "is a socially constructed institutional order. Its very fabric gives people reasons for action" (2013: 339).

As we shall see in this study, how we speak of animals matters. How we speak of animals e.g. in political party programs is telling of our worldviews, our attitudes, our priorities. And what is more, it also matters what we omit to say about animals – or whether we mention them at all (for example, cows/cattle are not at all mentioned in Norwegian party programs, despite their central role in actual Norwegian ecology). When we speak about situations in

---

3 Some might object that animals do not truly form representations, since they lack symbolic capacities. However, I and many with me think that several animals (e.g. cats; cf. Tønnessen 2009a) do have symbolic capacities, and furthermore that more rudimentary representations can be formed even without symbolic capacities.

4 For instance, "animal industry discourses use the pronoun *it* to refer to animals, use expressions that represent animals as machines, use the passive to hide the agent of killing, and use a range of other features that combine together to model a world where animals are constructed as objects" (ibid: 5). As we see here, *representing* animals often gives us the power to place them in the world, so to speak, and thus potentially to dominate over them.

which animals in actual fact, in material reality, appear, and are affected by our actions, and neglect to mention them – to see them, as it were – in our representations of that situation, this is also telling of our relations to these animals.

Norway, a country where the social-democratic Labour Party (Arbeiderpartiet) has been the largest party for practically all of the post-WWII period, stands out in some animal welfare issues. According to Martinsen, the aforementioned Norwegian traditions of seal hunting and whaling "have contributed negatively to developing understanding of and interest in animal ethics in Norway" (2013: 116, my translation). It is conceivable that Norwegians in general have a more instrumental relation to nature than many other Europeans. If that is true, David Abram's dictum that "our organic attunement to the local earth is thwarted by our ever-increasing intercourse with our own signs" (1996: 267) and claim that we have become "oblivious to the presence of other animals" (137) might be even more relevant in Norway than in many other countries.

Ellefsen (2013) finds that Norwegian discourses on animal welfare are characterized much more by respectable rhetorics than by real commitments. §3 in the Norwegian Animal Welfare Act (Dyrevelferdsloven) starts out with a quite radical statement (my translation): "Animals have an intrinsic value independently of the utility value they may have for humans." Already the next sentence, however, introduces *Realpolitik*-style pragmatics: "Animals shall be treated well and protected against the danger of unnecessary stress and strains." The implicit question is: In what cases is it *necessary* to subject animals to stress and strains? In what cases is this justified? Illustratively, when the law was being prepared, Lars Peder Brekk of the Centre Party, then the Minister of Agriculture and food, assured industry representatives that the wording related to the intrinsic value of animals would not lead to any practical changes (sic!), but was only intended to have symbolic value (ibid). With such clear-sighted politicians, one can only conclude (echoing Mühlhauser 2000: 250) that in many cases "green discourse [...] has become a substitute for green practice."

In contrast to the infamous Norwegian whaling, Norway is also the country where deep ecology emerged in the work of philosopher Arne Næss (1912–2009). So what exactly is the Norwegian attitude to nature, and to animals? A survey I conducted in 2006, with 37 Norwegian respondents that were environmentalists, politicians, scholars and industry representatives, found that "most respondents were generally eager to attribute value to a whole range of human and natural entities" (Tønnessen 2009b). For example, "[a]round 9 out of 10 attributed value to 'all of' 'individual human beings,' 'nature' and 'species'" – but 3 out of 10 reported that they "attributed value only to 'some' [...] 'individuals of other species.'" Briefly told: Environmentalism has traditionally had a stronger foothold in Norway than animal protection.

3 Word/Morpheme Frequency Study

Almost all of the mentions of animals in Norwegian political party programs occur in the more practical programs, not in the programs of principles. Table 7.1 shows how many times selected morphemes/words are mentioned in the programs of principles of FrP/the Progress Party, MDG/the Green Party and R/the Red Party.

All in all, only three of the search entries occur in any of the programs of principles. The morpheme "dyr" [animal] appears only in the program of principles of MDG/the Green Party, the words "dyreetikk, dyreetisk" only in the program of principles of FrP/the Progress Party, and the morpheme "fisk" [fish] only in R/the Red Party's program of principles. The remaining 20 search entries are not mentioned by any of these three parties in their programs of principles. Otherwise noticeable terms such as "rein" [reindeer] and "rovdyr" [predator] are among the omitted morphemes. While it might be understandable that such specific terms do not occur in the Norwegian programs of principles, it is perhaps more surprising that the generic term "dyr" [animal] is only mentioned in one program of principles. With the exception of MDG/the Green Party, animals do not appear to be foundationally important in the outlook of the Norwegian parties.

Table 7.2 shows how many times each of the nine parties mention words containing the morpheme "dyr" [animal] in their programs. On average each party mentions "dyr" [animal] 35 times, but there is considerable variation.

Of the three big parties, which account for a combined total of almost three quarters of the vote, two (AP/Labour and H/the Conservative Party – the two

TABLE 7.1 *Mentions of animals in programs of principles*

Selected morphemes/words	FrP/the progress party	MDG/the green party	R/the red party
Dyr [animal]	0	5	0
Dyreetikk, Dyreetisk [animal ethics, animal ethical]	1	0	0
Fisk [fish]	0	0	4
Kjøtt [meat]	0	0	0
Rein [reindeer]	0	0	0
Rovdyr [predator]	0	0	0

TABLE 7.2   *Ranking of parties by the number of occurrences of "dyr" [animal]*

Party	Number of mentions	Percentage of total
1. MDG/the Green Party	93	30%
2. V/the Social-Liberal Party	44	14%
3. KrF/Christian Democrats	41	13%
4. FrP/the Progress Party, SP/the Centre Party	40	13%
6. SV/the Socialist Left Party	27	9%
7. AP/Labour	14	4%
8. R/the Red Party	8	3%
9. H/the Conservative Party	6	2%
Total	313	
Average	35	11%
Median	40	13%

biggest parties) mention animals less than average, while FrP/the Progress Party mention animals slightly more frequently than the average. Apart from FrP/the Progress Party, all parties that mention animals more frequently than the average are in the political centre. The three left-wing parties all underperform, as it were, with a combined share of the total mentions of animals of only 16% (or 16 mentions per party on average). In comparison, the parties in the political centre accounts for 70% of all mentions of animals, and right-wing parties for 15%.

Table 7.3 shows how many times each of the nine parties mention the morpheme "rovdyr" [predator] in their programs. On average, each party mentions "rovdyr" eight times.

This keyword, the most widely used subcategory of "dyr" [animals], is mentioned most often by two parties in the political centre (SP/the Centre Party and KrF/Christian Democrats), one right-wing party (FrP/the Progress Party) and one left-wing party (AP/Labour). The two top parties, which are both placed in the political centre, account for more than half of all mentions of predators. All in all, the centre accounts for 64% of all mentions of predators, left-wing parties 21% and right-wing parties 15%.

Table 7.4 gives an overview of all search terms included in this study – how many times they are mentioned by all nine parties combined, and what party mentions each term most times.

TABLE 7.3 *Ranking of parties by the number of occurrences of "rovdyr" [predator]*

Party	Number of mentions	Percentage of total
1. SP/the Centre Party	25	33%
2. KrF/Christian Democrats	16	21%
3. FrP/the Progress Party	10	13%
4. AP/Labour	8	11%
5. SV/the Socialist Left Party	5	7%
6. MDG/the Green Party	4	5%
7. R/the Red Party, V/the Social-Liberal Party	3	4%
9. H/the Conservative Party	1	1%
Total	75	
Average	8	11%
Median	5	7%

TABLE 7.4 *Numbers of mentions by search term*

Search term	Total no. of mentions	Most mentioned
Bjørn [bear]	10	Krf/Christian Democrats: 4 (40%)
Dyr [animal]	313	MDG/the Green Party: 93 (30%)
Dyreetikk [animal ethics], dyreetisk [animal ethical]	3	R/the Red Party, FrP/the Progress Party, SV/the Socialist Left Party: 1 (33%)
Dyrevelferd [animal welfare]	49	MDG/the Green Party: 15 (31%)
Dyrevern [animal protection]	12	MDG/the Green Party: 8 (75%)
Dyrevelferdsloven [the Animal welfare law]	2	MDG/the Green Party, R/the Red Party: 1 (50%)
Fisk [fish]	314	V/the Social-Liberal Party: 54 (17%)
Flått [tic]	0	
Fugl [bird]	3	KrF [Christian Democrats], SP [the Centre Party], SV [the Socialist Left Party]: 1 (33%)

Search term	Total no. of mentions	Most mentioned
Gaupe [lynx]	9	KrF [Christian Democrats]: 3 (33%)
Gris [pig], svin [pork]	4	AP/Labour, MDG/the Green Party, R/the Red Party, V/the Social-Liberal Party: 1 (25%)
Hjort [deer]	0	
Hund [dog]	8	FrP/the Progress Party: 4 (50%)
Hval [whale]	1	MDG/the Green Party: 1 (100%)
Høns [hens], fjørfe [poultry], kylling [chicken]	3	MDG/the Green Party: 2 (67%)
Kjæledyr [pet]	1	MDG/the Green Party: 1 (100%)
Kjøtt [Meat]	18	MDG/the Green Party: 9 (50%)
Ku [cow], kyr [cattle]	0	
Pelsdyr [fur animal]	17	MDG/the Green Party: 5 (29%)
Rein [reindeer]	69	MDG/the Green Party: 13 (19%)
Rovdyr [predator, carnivore]	75	SP/the Centre Party 25 (33%)
Sau [sheep]	4	V/the Social-Liberal Party: 2 (50%)
Ulv [wolf]	14	KrF/Christian Democrats: 7 (50%)

MDG/the Green Party is the only party that mentions "hval" [whale] or "kjæledyr" [pet]. "Flått" [tic] is not mentioned by any party – despite the annual (often summertime) front pages in the tabloids. Neither is "hjort" [deer], a common game species. MDG/the Green Party is the one party that mentions 10 out of 23 search items most frequently. KrF/Christian Democrats comes in second place, topping 4 of the 23 search items – largely because of its interest in predators, followed by V/the Social-Liberal Party, topping 3 search items. Altogether parties in the political centre top 19 search items (either alone or along with other parties), versus 4 for left-wing parties and 2 for right-wing parties. Remarkably, no left-wing party tops any search item alone, and only one search item is topped by a right-wing party alone ("hund" [dog], topped by FrP/the Progress Party). In comparison, no less than 15 search items are topped by a party in the political centre alone.

H/the Conservative party, the leading government party, does not excel on any keyword. Norway's biggest party, AP/Labour, does not fare much better, topping only "gris" [pig], "svin" [pork] along with three other parties, with one mention each. But actually, AP/Labour does not refer to pigs as animals; instead, they make mention of "grisgrendte strøk" [literally: "pig-villaged areas"], a Norwegian expression that designates rural areas that are sparsely populated by people (places where you find pigs and little else). "Pelsdyr" [fur animals], which is mentioned most often by MDG/the Green Party, V/the Social-Liberal Party and SV/the Socialist Left Party, are not mentioned at all in the programs of H/the Conservative Party and SP/the Centre Party, which in political discourse have traditionally designated themselves as the primary defenders of the industry. One would think that the reason was that these parties do not want any debate, any political discourse, on the fur animal industry, because they are defenders of *status quo*.[5]

Quite remarkably, no party makes any mention of "ku" [cow], "kuer" [cattle], while "høns" [hens], "fjørfe" [poultry], "kylling" [chicken] is mentioned only by two parties (total number of mentions: 3) and "sau" [sheep] only by three parties (total number of mentions: 4). In other words, the most common livestock are hardly mentioned in the party programs. "Hund" [dog] fares somewhat better, with a total of 7 mentions divided by four parties. FrP/the Progress Party, the dog party above any other, refers to "servicehunder" [service dogs], "politihunder" [police dogs], "narkotikahunder" [narcotics dogs] and "jakthunder" [hunting dogs]. In all these cases, FrP/the Progress Party refers to dogs that have been trained to serve specific human needs – and the mentions of dogs are curiously often related to the maintaining of law and order.

Interestingly, "kjøtt" [meat] is mentioned by a majority of the nine parties – but only by six of the smaller parties, including the meat-critical Green Party, which stands for half of the instances. "Kjøtt" [meat] is not mentioned at all by SP/the Centre Party, FrP/the Progress Party or H/the Conservative Party, and is only mentioned by AP/Labour in the following peculiar programmatic statement (my translation): "Reindeer meat is an Arctic delicacy [...]." This implies that the three main parties, as well as the traditional farmers' party, do not at all articulate meat's role in Norwegian society – which is thus significantly under-communicated.

As Chouliaraki and Fairclough claim, "a major issue which can be addressed through discourse analysis is how certain simplifying and complexity-reducing construals of complex realities may come to have constructive effects upon

---

5 However, in the last program period (2009–2013), Høyre's program did include statements on fur farming. In light of this, the omission of statements on fur farming in the 2013–2017 program can be interpreted as allowing party members to make up their own minds in a question that was previously subjected to an official party line.

those complex realities, transforming them in particular ways and directions" (2010: 1216). What we observe in the context of mentions of animals in Norwegian political party programs is that a whole range of common animals, whether wild or domesticated, are either marginalized or totally neglected in the official political discourse. This is a significant finding in our simple study, given that "[w]hat is deeply embedded in or even hidden by certain linguistic choices is what a critical analysis of ecological texts sets out to unearth" (Alexander and Stibbe 2014: 105).

As we saw in Table 7.4, "fisk" [fish], in contrast to all these neglected animals, is mentioned a total of 314 times in Norwegian political party programs. This is of course not coincidental. Fish products happen to be Norway's second-biggest export product, second only to the export of oil and gas. In the morpheme occurrence study we will come to learn that even though fish at the face of it are mentioned very often in the party programs, they are not therefore framed as sentient beings.

4 Morpheme Occurrence Study

My analysis shows how morphemes such as "dyr" [animal], "fisk" [fish] and "rein" [reindeer] are very often included in wordings that imply a systematic omission of essential aspects of animal life and behavior. Particularly the morphemes "fisk" [fish] and "rein" [reindeer] occur predominantly in conceptual structures that represent an objectification of animals, usually by reducing them to economic resource. In the analyzed party programs, even the word "fisk" [fish] rarely refers to fish as living, sentient beings, but rather to fish products and resources. As for reindeer, these are economically important only regionally, in the North, where reindeer herding is of fundamental interest to the Sami people. Given this connection with Sami interests, and thus policies concerning indigenous rights and land use, it is nevertheless a hot political topic.

All nine parties mention "fisk" [fish] at least 18 times. In comparison, "dyr" [animal] is mentioned only 6 times by H/the Conservative Party and only 8 times by R/the Red Party. As a matter of fact, several parties mention "fisk" [fish] more often than "dyr" [animal]: AP/Labour (23/14), H/the Conservative Party (18/6), R/the Red Party (36/8), SV/the Socialist Left Party (42/27) and V/ the Social-Liberal Party (54/44). This can be interpreted in different ways: e.g., a prioritization of fish themes can signal the predominance of the economic discourse, proven interest in Northern or coastal Norway, etc. Here, too, MDG/ the Green Party stands out, as the only party that mentions "dyr" [animal] more than twice as much as "fisk" [fish] (93/41).

Quite surprisingly, the term "fiskerettigheter" [fish rights] is actually used in AP/Labour's program – but as it turns out, the word does not refer to the rights of fish, but rather to people's right to fish (fishing rights).[6] The word "fisk" [fish] is in KrF/Christian Democrats' program mentioned in connection with "fersk fisk" [fresh fish], but this refers to the freshness of dead fish as a product, and the importance of getting it as quickly as possible to the market.

The conclusion remains that fish are predominantly framed as an economic resource. And this does not appear to be a solely Norwegian phenomenon. In a reading of the mentions of fish and fisheries in the Millennium Ecosystems Assessment (2005), Stibbe observes that "[a]nalysis of the affected participant of the process of 'harm' in the Report reveals that it is overwhelmingly humans who are represented as affected. […] Where the affected participant is not human, it is most often 'ecosystem services' and, in one case, 'marine resources,' both of which express the nonhuman world only in terms of provisions for humans" (2012: 89).

Table 7.5 below shows the occurrences of the morpheme "fisk" [fish] in the program of H/the Conservative Party. As we see, the economic discourse and the management discourse predominate, while even the animal discourse, which may be of a more generic nature, is marginal.

Overall, the anthropocentric bias in Norwegian political party programs is particularly visible in the mentions of "fisk" [fish] and "rein" [reindeer]. In these cases, even the vocabulary of MDG/the Green Party is dominated by the economic discourse and management discourse. In the working program of MDG/the Green Party, fishing is discussed in conventional terms, in an anthropocentric industry perspective. Nevertheless, it includes claims that fish resources can be better utilized, and statements such as these (my translation): "Fish farming also constitutes a significant animal welfare issue"; "fish can feel pain." In the latter case, fish are actually explicitly characterized as living beings endowed with sentience.

"Rein" [reindeer] is mentioned only a few times, but here too a link to ethics is established, in the following statement (my translation): "Reindeer husbandry must […] be organized so that the interests of […] animal welfare is safeguarded." Below, in Table 7.6, we see the occurrences of the morpheme "rein" [reindeer] in the program of SV/the Socialist Left Party, another party that is generally conceived of as a rather green party.

Once more, we observe that the economic discourse and the management discourse predominate.

---

6 For an account on fish and fishing in nature writing, see Tüür 2014.

ANIMALS IN NORWEGIAN POLITICAL PARTY PROGRAMS 117

TABLE 7.5   *Morpheme occurrence – H/the conservative party, "fisk" [fish]*

Word	Discourse
Fisk [fish]	Animal/economic discourse
Fiske [fishing]	Economic discourse
Fiskeflåte [fishing fleet]	Economic discourse
Fiskekvote [fishing quota]	Management discourse
Fiske- og oppdrettsressursene [the fish and aquaculture resources]	Economic discourse
Fiske- og rekreasjonsområder [fishing and recreation areas]	Management discourse
Fiskeprodukter [fish products]	Economic discourse
Fiskeri [fishery]	Economic discourse
Fiskeriforvaltning [fishery management]	Management discourse
Fiskerinæring [fishery business]	Economic discourse
Fiskeri- og havbruksnæring [fishery and aquaculture business]	Economic discourse
Fiskeri- og kystdepartement [Ministry of fishery and coast]	Management discourse
Råfisklov [raw fish act]	Management discourse
Turistfiske [tourist fishing]	Management discourse
Villfiskbestand [wild fish population]	Animal/management discourse

TABLE 7.6   *Morpheme occurrence – SV/the socialist left party, "rein" [reindeer]*

Word	Discourse
Reindrift [reindeer husbandry]	Economic/management discourse
Reindriftsnæring [reindeer business]	Economic discourse
Reineier [reindeer owner]	Economic discourse
Reintall [number of reindeer]	Management discourse
Villrein [wild reindeer]	Animal discourse

Table 7.7 shows the occurrences of the morpheme "dyr" [animal] in the program of AP/Labour. As we saw in Table 7.2, AP/Labour mentions "dyr" [animal] only 14 times in its program, and accounts for only 4% of all mentions. In consequence, the party's vocabulary is not especially developed.

TABLE 7.7 *Morpheme occurrence – AP/Labour, "dyr" [animal]*

Word	Discourse
Dyr [animal]	Animal discourse
Dyrevelferd [animal welfare]	Animal welfare discourse
Pelsdyrnæring [Fur animal business]	Economic discourse
Rovdyrforvaltning [predator management]	Management/predator discourse
Rovdyrpolitikk [predator policy]	Management/predator discourse
Rovdyrstamme [predator population]	Management/predator discourse

TABLE 7.8 *Morpheme occurrence – SP/the centre party, "dyr" [animal]*

Word	Discourse
Beitedyr [grazing animals]	Economic discourse
Dyr [animal]	Animal discourse
Dyreart [animal species]	Animal discourse
Dyrehelse [animal health]	Animal/economic/animal welfare discourse
Dyreholder [animal owner/keeper]	Economic discourse
Dyrevelferd [animal welfare]	Animal welfare discourse
Rovdyr [predator]	Predator discourse
Rovdyrangrep [predator attack]	Predator/management discourse
Rovdyrbestand [predator population]	Predator/management discourse
Rovdyrforlik [predator settlement]	Predator/management discourse
Rovdyrpolitikk [predator policies]	Predator/management discourse
Rovdyrproblematikk [predator topics]	Predator/management discourse
Rovdyrtetthet [density of predators]	Predator/management discourse
Skadedyr [vermin]	Management/economic discourse

Due to its emphasis on predators (cf. Table 7.3, where AP/Labour ranks around the average), AP/Labour's program is characterized by the Management discourse more than any other discourse. The program of SP/the Centre Party is even more characterized by a predator focus – see Table 7.8.

Here we see the predator discourse and the management discourse prevailing over discourses of secondary importance, such as the animal discourse and (remarkably) the economic discourse.[7] In contrast, MDG/the Green Party's mentions of animals are, seen as a whole, both richer and more characterized by the animal welfare discourse and the more foundational animal discourse (see Table 7.9). In MDG/the Green Party's programs, the animal welfare discourse and the Animal discourse is as significant as the economic discourse (all three involve eight–nine occurring words).[8] A hallmark of MDG/the Green Party is thus that it is the only party in parliament that to some extent escapes the otherwise universal anthropocentric bias in Norwegian political party programs.

TABLE 7.9   Morpheme occurrence – MDG/the green party, "dyr" [animal]

Word	Discourse
Dyr [animal]	Animal discourse
Dyrefôr [animal feed]	Economic discourse
Dyreforsøk [animal experiment]	Animal welfare discourse
Dyregenetiske ressurser [animal-genetic resources]	Animal discourse
Dyrehold [animal husbandry]	Animal discourse
Dyremishandling [cruelty to animals]	Animal welfare discourse
Dyrerase [animal race]	Animal discourse
Dyretetthet [density of animals]	Management discourse
Dyretilsyn [supervision with animals]	Management discourse
Dyretransport [transport of animals]	Management discourse
Dyrevelferd [animal welfare]	Animal welfare discourse
Dyrevelferdsloven [the Animal Welfare Act]	Animal welfare/management discourse
Dyrevelferdstiltak [animal welfare measures]	Animal welfare discourse
Dyrevern [animal protection]	Animal welfare discourse
Dyrevernforsvarlig [justifiable with regard to animal protection]	Animal welfare discourse
Dyrevernhensyn [animal protection consideration]	Animal welfare discourse
Dyrevernproblem [animal ethics problem]	Animal welfare discourse

7   One would think that the party generally conceived of as the farmers' party would be more focused on economic discourse and on the farm animals that the predators are perceived as threatening.
8   Somewhat surprisingly, judging by the animal-related vocabulary applied, the economic discourse appears to be more developed in MDG/the Green Party's programs than in SP/the Centre Party's program.

TABLE 7.9 *Morpheme occurrence – MDG/the green party, "dyr" [animal] (cont.)*

Word	Discourse
Familiedyr [family animal]	Animal discourse
Havpattedyr [marine mammal]	Animal discourse
Husdyr [livestock]	Economic discourse
Husdyrgjødsel [livestock manure]	Economic discourse
Husdyrnæring [livestock business]	Economic discourse
Husdyrslag [kind of livestock]	Economic discourse
Kjæledyr [pet]	Human–animal relations discourse
Landbruksdyr [animal in agriculture]	Economic discourse
Pelsdyr [fur animal]	Economic discourse
Pelsdyrnæring [fur animal business]	Economic discourse
Pelsdyroppdrett [breeding of fur animal]	Economic discourse
Rovdyr [predator]	Predator discourse
Rovdyrart [predator species]	Predator discourse
Rådyrkalv [roe deer calf]	Animal discourse

5   Concluding Remarks

As Sørensen and Torfing succinctly state, "[t]he political values and preferences of the government – that is supposed to incarnate the will of the people – are translated into more or less detailed laws and regulations that are implemented and enforced by publicly employed bureaucrats" (2005: 201). Unfortunately, the legal protection animals enjoy tends to be weaker the more specific the law or regulation in question is. This is likely the case on an international level, across countries. While the Norwegian Animal welfare act acknowledges all animals' intrinsic value, as we have seen, the Norwegian "Forskrift om hold av høns og kalkun" [Regulation on the keeping of chickens and turkeys] thus says that a farmer can keep up to nine laying hens kept in free stall per m², and that a farmer can similarly keep up to 33 kg of broiler chickens per m². This is how intrinsic value and human utility are balanced in practice, in today's Norwegian reality.

"Achieving a significant measure of dominance," observe Chouliaraki and Fairclough, is "one precondition for discourses coming to be operationalized, 'put into practice,' dialectically transformed into new ways [of] acting and interacting, new identities, new material realities" (2010: 1216). The animal welfare discourse and other variations of animal protection discourses have gotten off the ground in Norway, but they are still marginal, both in terms of discursive power and, relatedly, of actual influence.

Bibliography

Primary Sources[9]

Arbeiderpartiet 2013. Vi tar Norge videre. Arbeiderpartiets program 2013–2017 [We take Norway further. Labour's program 2013–2017]. On line at: http://arbeiderpartiet.no/Media/Images/Grafikk/Vi-tar-Norge-videre-Arbeiderpartiets-partiprogram-2013-2017 (consulted 13.08.2013). 88 pp.

Fremskrittspartiet 2013a. Prinsipprogram for perioden 2013–2017 [Program of principles for the period 2013–2017]. On line at: https://www.frp.no/~/media/files/politiske-dokumenter/prinsipprogram-2013-2017.pdf?la=nb-no (consulted 13.08.2013). 14 pp.

Fremskrittspartiet 2013b. Handlingsprogram for perioden 2013–2017 [Action program for the period 2013–2017]. On line at: https://www.frp.no/~/media/files/politiske-dokumenter/handlingsprogram-2013-2017.pdf?la=nb-no (consulted 13.08.2013). 86 pp.

Høyre 2013. Nye ideer, bedre løsninger. Høyres stortingsvalgprogram 2013–2017 [New ideas, better solutions. The Conservative Party's parliamentary election program 2013–2017]. On line at: http://www.hoyre.no/www/politikk/hoyres_programmer/hoyres_stortingsvalgprogram_2013-2017/Her+finner+du+PDF-versjonen+av+Stortingsvalgprogrammet+2013-17.d25-T2drW1m.ips (consulted 13.08.2013). 104 pp.

Kristelig Folkeparti 2013. Politisk program 2013–2017 [Political program 2013–2017]. On line at: http://krf.no/politikk/politiske-dokumenter/politisk-program/ (consulted 13.08.2013). 119 pp.

Miljøpartiet De Grønne 2013a. Prinsipprogram [Program of principles]. On line at: https://www.mdg.no/content/uploads/2013/06/MDG_Prinsipprogram_web.pdf (consulted 13.08.2013). 9 pp.

Miljøpartiet De Grønne 2013b. Arbeidsprogram 2013–2017 [Working program 2013–2017]. On line at: https://www.mdg.no/content/uploads/2013/06/MDG_Arbeidsprogram_web.pdf (consulted 13.08.2013). 71 pp.

Rødt 2010. Prinsipprogram [Program of principles]. On line at: rødt.no/politikk/prinsipprogram/ (consulted 13.08.2013). Ratified 2010.

---

9 Year of ratification is provided where information is available, unless the political program was ratified in 2013 (the election year). Number of pages is provided in case of PDF documents.

Rødt 2012. Arbeidsprogram [Working program]. On line at: rødt.no/politikk/arbeids program/ (consulted 13.08.2013). Ratified 2012.

Senterpartiet 2013. Senterpartiets prinsipp- og handlingsprogram 2013–2017 [The Centre Party's program of principles and action program 2013–2017]. On line at: http://www.senterpartiet.no/getfile.php/Bildegalleri/Fellesfiler/PHP%202013-2017%20-%20Trykkformat%2017x24.pdf (consulted 13.08.2013). 62 pp.

Sosialistisk Venstreparti 2013. Del godene! Arbeidsprogram for Sosialistisk Venstreparti 2013–2017 [Share the goods! Working program for the Socialist Left Party 2013–2017]. On line at: https://www.sv.no/wp-content/uploads/2013/12/Arbeidsprogram_for_SV_2013_til_2017.pdf (consulted 13.08.2013). 134 pp.

Venstre 2013. Frihet. Fremtid. Fellesskap. Venstres stortingsvalgprogram 2013–2017 [Freedom. Future. Community. The Social-Liberal Party's parliamentary election program 2013–2017]. On line at: http://www.venstre.no/assets/stortingsvalgprogram_2013_web.pdf (consulted 13.08.2013). 112 pp.

Secondary Sources

Abram, David. 1996. *The spell of the sensuous*. New York: Vintage.

Alexander, Richard and Arran Stibbe. 2014. 'From the analysis of ecological discourse to the ecological analysis of discourse.' *Language Sciences* 41: 104–110.

Chouliaraki, Lilie and Norman Fairclough. 2010. 'Critical discourse analysis in organizational studies: Towards an integrationist methodology.' *Journal of Management Studies* 47(6): 1213–1218.

Ellefsen, Rune. 2013. *Med lov til å pine: Om bruk og beskyttelse av dyr*. Oslo: Inspirator Forlag/Fritt Forlag.

Fairclough, Norman. 2005. 'Discourse analysis in organization studies: The case for critical realism.' *Organization Studies* 26(6): 915–939.

Fairclough, Isabela and Norman Fairclough. 2013. 'Argument, deliberation, dialectic and the nature of the political: A CDA perspective.' *Political Studies Review* 11: 336–344.

Martinsen, Siri. 2013. 'Hvordan enkelte tradisjoner i bruk har formet norsk tenkning om dyrs verdi [How certain utility-related traditions have formed Norwegian thinking on animals' value].' In Ragnhild Sollund, Guri Larsen and Morten Tønnessen (eds), *Hvem er villest i landet her? Råskap mot dyr og natur i Antropocen, menneskets tidsalder* [Who is the wildest one in the country here? Brutality against animals and nature in the Anthropocene, the era of mankind]. Oslo: Spartacus/Scandinavian Academic Press: 99–120.

Millennium Ecosystems Assessment. 2005. *Ecosystems and human well-being: Synthesis*. Washington, DC: Island Press.

Mühlhauser, Peter. 2000. 'Bleached language on unbleached paper. The language of ecotourism.' In B. Ketteman and H. Penz (eds) *ECOnstructing Language, Nature and*

Society. The Ecolinguistic project Revisited. Essays in Honour of Alwin Fill. Tübingen: Stauffenburg Verlag: 241–251.

Sørensen, Eva and Jacob Torfing. 2005. 'Network governance and post-liberal democracy.' *Administrative Theory & Praxis* 27(2): 197–237.

Stibbe, Arran. 2012. *Animals Erased: Discourse, Ecology, and Reconnection with the Natural World.* Middletown, CT: Wesleyan University Press.

Tønnessen, Morten. 2009a. 'Abstraction, cruelty and other aspects of animal play (Exemplified by the playfulness of Muki and Maluca).' *Sign Systems Studies* 37(3/4): 558–579.

Tønnessen, Morten. 2009b. 'The nature view held by environmentalists: Attitudes in the Norwegian environmental establishment.' IOP Conference Series: Earth and Environmental Science, volume 6 (doi: 10.1088/1755-1307/6/7/572037). 2 pp.

Tønnessen, Morten. 2013. Analyse av partiprogrammer for 2013–2017 [Analysis of political party programs for 2013–2017]. Conducted for Dyreetikkonferansen [the Norwegian Animal Ethics Conference] 2013. Oslo 2013: Dyreetikkonferansen. DOI: 10.13140/2.1.3693.1203. 21 pp.

Tønnessen, Morten. 'The Semiotics of Predation and The Umwelten of Large Predators' in Timo Maran, Morten Tønnessen, and Silver Rattasepp (eds) *Animal Umwelts in a changing world – Semiotic studies of human-animal relations.* Tartu: Tartu University Press, 2016: 150–181.

Tønnessen, Morten and Kadri Tüür. 2014. 'The semiotics of animal representations: Introduction' in Kadri Tüür and Morten Tønnessen (eds) *The Semiotics of Animal Representations* (Nature, Culture and Literature 10). Amsterdam: Rodopi: 7–30.

Tüür, Kadri. 2014. 'Like a fish out of water: Literary representations of fish.' In Kadri Tüür and Morten Tønnessen (eds) *The Semiotics of Animal Representations* (Nature, Culture and Literature 10). Amsterdam: Rodopi: 263–288.

CHAPTER 8

Chemical Unknowns: Preliminary Outline for an Environmental History of Fear

Michael Egan

Abstract

We live in a Toxic Century. While we cannot see it, each of us is a walking, breathing artifact of humanity's toxic trespasses into nature. Sociological findings suggest that toxic chemicals scare human beings in new and special ways. This has more to do with what we do not know about their danger than what we do know, and those unknowns strike at the epicentre of how fear is individually and culturally manifested. The method through which persistent organic pollutants assault human and environmental health, the manner in which they proliferated after World War II, and the unanticipated consequences of their spread are key characteristics of this new landscape of fear. Persistent organic pollutants contaminate rather than merely damage; their pollution penetrates human tissue indirectly rather than attacking the surface in a more straightforward manner; and the threat from exposure is not acute, but rather slow, chronic, and enduring. That we lack a full understanding of the hazards they pose and have little control over their environmental mobility distinguishes chemical toxins. As a result, a culture of fear associated with new toxins is an explicit and unmistakable feature of the post-World War II world.

This paper examines the rise of toxic fear in the American 1980s, a decade punctuated by a series of environmental crises and explicit fears about chemical pollution, both within the United States and internationally. I examine the politics of uncertainty and point to the 1980s as a watershed moment in our contemporary understanding of toxic fear.

> This is a special way of being afraid.
> PHILIP LARKIN, "Aubade"

1   Introduction

Over the past decade, the environmental humanities have opened new avenues of inter- and multidisciplinary inquiry, which promise important and novel contributions to environmental scholarship, the contexts of which ought in turn to help to produce richer and more nuanced environmental policies. Because the modern physical environment (and our understandings of it) is such a complex web of social and ecological interactions, its comprehension defies traditional disciplinary boundaries. It makes sense to peer over the walls that have long divided disciplinary methodologies to see what we have in common – and to see what we might learn from our colleagues "down the hall." As an unrepentant historian, I do not mean to begin by denigrating traditional, disciplinary scholarship, but rather to welcome new methods of engaging with it. This essay constitutes a cautious foray in that direction. In preparing a history of toxic fear in the American 1980s, I found that my research and reading took me on a fantastical tour of history, literature, psychology, sociology, philosophy, media studies, art, toxicology, and chemistry (and many more disciplines, besides). This sometimes irreverent interdisciplinary romp permitted questions and analyses that likely would not have crossed my radar had I concentrated exclusively on historical sources.

Toxic fear is distinct from other kinds of fear. Toxic contaminants – real and imagined – provoke fear "in new and special ways," writes sociologist Kai Erikson in *A New Species of Trouble* (144). They "elicit an uncanny fear in us." That is because chemicals contaminate rather than merely damage. Their poisons penetrate human tissue indirectly rather than attacking the surface in a more straightforward manner. The threat from chemical exposure is not acute, but rather slow, chronic, and enduring. The emotions these threats inspire are critical to understanding the contemporary environmental narrative, and they demand new frameworks for engaging with environment and society. Historian Joanna Bourke argues that fear is the dominant emotion in modern society (2005). It is an explicit feature of modern malaise. In modernity, degenerative disease outpaced contagion as the primary catalyst for our reflections on personal vulnerability and mortality. The more we aged – and the longer we degenerated – the more the social and cultural relationships with life and death changed. As a result, individuals and societies expressed markedly different responses to fear and well-being.

This transformation of what scares us is especially apparent in new threats to human health, such as the proliferation of toxic chemicals in the environment. Indeed, toxic fear occupies a distinctive place within the taxonomy of this most dominant of modern emotions. Erikson shows that people in general find toxic substances a good deal more threatening than natural or technological hazards that do not involve toxicity, even when that fear is drastically exaggerated compared with the real threat (Erikson 1994: 139–157). Invisible carcinogens and poorly understood endocrine disruptors pose new problems and introduce new landscapes for individual and public anxieties consistent with the more latent promulgations of modern fear. To better understand the widespread nature of chemical pollution and the social unrest it has produced, it would be valuable to put toxicity, fear, and toxic discourse under the microscope. If toxicity and fear are omnipresent components of the modern world, understanding their relationship might offer novel and critical perspectives on how publics respond to environmental risk and how scholars might engage with environmental decision making processes, past and present, especially as they relate to tensions between experts and publics.[1]

2   Toxic Fear in Time and Place

Toxic fear plays on traditional fears of the unknown, but chemical pollution is more than simply a new iteration of that longstanding narrative. Rather, it reflects a new discourse, born out of industrial modernity on the one hand, and a crucial chemical chapter of a broader history of unanticipated consequences. The hazards are generated by human industry and their risks are misunderstood until it is too late to escape from them. Toxic fear's point of origin is clearly located in the aftermath of World War II. Euphoria at war's end was quickly mitigated by Cold War tensions and the prospects of the Atomic Age (Weart 2012; Boyer 1994; Rose 2001). Aboveground nuclear weapons testing reminded Americans that lasting peace remained elusive. Subsequent discoveries about the hazards of radioactive fallout changed the nature of Cold War risk and risk assessment and dramatically altered the scope of environmental activism (Egan 2007: 47–78).

At the same time, myriad chemicals developed before and during World War II escaped the manufacturing plants and their military applications and entered into the marketplace, though they did not break down in nature and presented serious health and ecological problems. DDT, PCBs, thalidomide, PVC plastics, and countless synthetic fertilizers, herbicides, and pesticides – the products of the petrochemical industry – spread chlorinated hydrocarbons and other dangerous materials through every conceivable environment. Rachel Carson's *Silent Spring*, in 1962, helped to usher in an age of ecological awareness, both in the United States and internationally. At the heart of this

---

[1]   One underlying theme in my analysis of toxic fear – and attempts to explain both rational and irrational chemical anxieties – stems from Ulrich Beck's critique of risk management experts, who seemed to show contempt for public perceptions of risk (1992). In this vein, the study of toxic fear seeks to reconcile for risk experts the mechanisms that drives public fear.

new awareness was the stark realization that human actions were imperiling the natural foundations that made civilization possible. Environmentalism's mandate was expanded – beyond efforts to curtail human trespasses into nature – to include recognition that the human body was an ecological landscape under threat. This defense of human health certainly galvanized social anxieties about pollution and the invisible contaminants that were now omnipresent.

For the most part, this story is known and has been told before. And while the culture of fear that this story provoked is implicit in its telling – most especially in the popular response to environmental threats in the guise of the first Earth Day, the international significance of the 1972 UN Conference on Humans and the Environment in Stockholm, and the burgeoning of numerous environmental organizations and their growing memberships – little work has been done to investigate the emotional and cultural impact of this fear. Similarly, the American 1980s constitute a rich and untapped venue for exploring these questions. That environmental fears received noticeably more media attention in the 1980s than they did in the "environmental" decades of the 1960s and 1970s is indicative of the perfect storm that coalesced as scientific knowledge pertaining to environmental pollution matured, even while popular scientific literacy declined.[2] Further, a panoply of environmental crises altered the nature of environmental awareness. Whereas concerns about nuclear fallout and pesticides during the early 1960s ushered in a popular environmental consciousness, its 1980s offspring appeared fractured (Rodgers 2011). Americans could celebrate a singular "environmental crisis" at the first Earth Day in April 1970. A decade later that vocabulary had ebbed.[3] According to a variety of different metrics, more Americans were more afraid of environmental threats. If environmental crisis was in decline, chemophobia – the fear of chemicals – was very distinctly on the rise.

The 1980s also mark the ascendancy of neo-liberalism and conservative politics, both of which constituted a departure from the last elements of the Great Society. In their place, free trade and smaller government trusted the market to direct the flows of goods and services. One might go so far as to suggest that

---

[2] This claim is based on some very simple tracking of language trends in *New York Times* databases. Much to my surprise, "toxic" and "fear" appeared in newspaper articles and editorials with growing regularity in the 1980s, far outpacing the 1960s and 1970s. For a summary of these findings and some brief analysis see Egan 2014.

[3] A google ngram search for "environmental crisis" corroborates the results of a search across numerous American newspapers: reference to "environmental crisis" dropped considerably in frequency during the late 1970s and only reemerged in the 1990s.

the 1980s were to the Right what the 1960s had been for the Left. Expanding liberalism and deregulation replaced welfare nets and government controls. Social problems became individual problems: their solutions required individual fixes. The onus moved from government and government agencies to a public that had abdicated environmental oversight and the necessary scientific literacy to experts no longer equipped for the job. If uncertainty excited toxic fears, then it was certainly aided by deregulation and the curtailing of government agencies tasked with monitoring environmental health. In the absence of funding, fewer tests were conducted and more public questions and concerns about local water and air quality went unanswered. Deregulation in American federal politics seemed an almost knee-jerk reaction to the decade of extensive environmental regulation that had preceded it. In the late 1960s and throughout the 1970s, American environmental policy expanded dramatically, implementing strong controls on how air, soil, and water could be used as sinks for industrial waste (Hays 1987). This legislation culminated with the Comprehensive Environmental Response, Compensation, and Liability Act, signed into law in December 1980. The famous "Superfund" constituted tacit acknowledgment that chemical pollution posed real and present dangers to Americans and their neighborhoods. In the ensuing decade, however, deregulation limited federal agencies' capacity to measure and define the extent of a myriad of environmental risks.

3   The Language of Toxic Fear

In his essay on "Toxic Discourse," Lawrence Buell observes that the discourse of toxicity has not received extensive attention, largely because discourse might be perceived as a low priority when individual and public health is in immediate jeopardy (Buell 1998).[4] It is a fair point, but perhaps historical inquiry can mitigate the macabre nature of examining toxicity, fear, and toxic discourse by inserting temporal distance. An historical perspective – trying to situate the emergence of toxic fear in context – might provide the right resolution for investigating how that discourse has become all-consuming. It is manifest not just in contemporary concerns about air and water quality or individual pollution sources, but also in mainstream conversations about healthful living and food consumption.

---

4   On the immediacy of disaster, Buell writes: "Not even most humanistic intellectuals might agree with Emerson's dictum that the most abstract truth is the most practical" (640).

It is important to stress at the outset that uncertainty-driven social malaise produces much of the anxiety present in toxic discourse. On the cultural significance of uncertainty, Buell argues that while "toxic discourse rests on anxieties about environmental poisoning for which there is copious historical evidence, it is plainly a discourse of allegation rather than of proof" (659). In my previous research on mercury pollution and nuclear fallout, it appears as though uncertainty – manifested by inconclusive science, political inaction, and obfuscation from critics – provoked widespread fear toward the chemical and nuclear industries (Egan 2007; Egan 2013). Many of these fears are fully justified, but the historical record suggests that toxic fear is not especially judicious or selective. Irrational fear is grounded in a curious knowledge deficit that points toward the aforementioned shift away from popular scientific literacy during the second half of the twentieth century. But it also is a distinct product of the way in which toxic chemicals infiltrate bodies. Their invisibility – the manner in which their attack on cells and genes happens without our awareness – is alarming. So, too, is the latency associated with carcinogens and endocrine disruptors. That exposure does not constitute a direct or immediate threat, but one that manifests itself years or decades later, contributes to fears drawn from uncertainty.

At the same time, invisibility and uncertainty also provoked disagreement and vitriolic debate. Toxic discourse was contentious at best. Where some people expressed concern, others dismissed anxieties out of hand. In a caustic response to a 1987 Environmental Protection Agency warning about chloroform – a suspected carcinogen – in the water, a Washington Post op-ed article mocked: "anyone with an ounce of foresight would have realized some time ago that showering would eventually be found by researchers from the EPA to be dangerous, and bought a gas mask to be prepared" (*Washington Post* 1987). The chemist David Mog fired back in a letter to the editor that such farcical dismissal of chemical risks did untold damage: "Understanding, which reduces fear and guides action," he wrote, "is needed to confront difficult realities and break the paralysis that 'chemophobia' brings on society" (Mog 1987). The role of responsible journalism, he intoned, was to spread information, not just to add to the noise. Mog's reference to chemophobia was not singular during the decade. Indeed, the term gained currency over the course of the 1980s (see fig. 8.1). The changing vocabulary, which included more regular reference to toxicity from the 1970s into the 1980s, was one indicator of a rising culture of fear associated with human-made toxins. Chemical contamination was an explicit and unmistakable feature of the last quarter of the twentieth century's cultural and environmental landscapes. The discourse and rhetoric give some

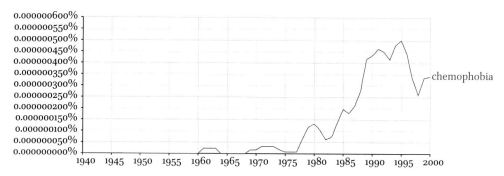

FIGURE 8.1 *Google Ngram for "chemophobia."*

credence to the psychological theory that situational factors are prime drivers of human behaviour (Mischel 1968).

In addition to tracing an evolving toxic lexicon, the challenge to historians and other environmental humanists interested in examining the relationship between emotions and the environment involves articulating effective metrics. How does one measure fear – or even recognize it in the past? In short form, I offer four avenues of inquiry: media saturation, disaster insurance trends, perceptions of psychological stress, and cancer cluster reporting.

(1) Perhaps the "easiest" metric – from which the language of fear is primarily drawn – is the media's impact. In *The Culture of Fear*, sociologist Barry Glassner claims that during the final quarter of the twentieth century Americans became increasingly inept at independently evaluating risk, due in large part to the manner in which media and politicians manipulated public dialogue (2009). The media, he argues, scaled new heights of sensationalism to generate readers and viewers. This was evident not only in shrill headlines, but also in the confusion fostered by such op-ed pieces as *The Washington Post*'s mockery of chemophobia.

(2) In 1980 the insurance industry defined a catastrophe as an event that caused $1 million in insured losses. The previous year, there had been 54 catastrophes in the United States, which resulted in more than $1.68 billion in insured losses. This was the highest amount claimed in a single year up to that point. 1980 was worse. In Washington State, Mount St. Helens erupted; floods washed out parts of California and the Southwest; and an increased number of tornadoes ripped across the country. "It's like living in a disaster movie," a member of the Insurance Information Institute told The New York Times. Another trend, noted by insurance experts, was

that "people seem more concerned about man-made disasters" (Charle 1980). In-depth examination of insurance trends and habits over time and across space – especially as they pertain to chemical contaminants – might help in taking the emotional pulse of communities.

(3) The psychological impact of technological disaster has also left numerous semiotic traces that historians interested in toxic fear might pursue. Psychological distress can be measured in multiple ways. While studies have shown that the citizens of Love Canal – the site of a particularly famous contamination of entire community in the late 1970s – did not seem to suffer from increased rates of cancer than the average American public, indications of mental health upset and suicides were higher (Gensburg et al. 2009). These can be linked to the uncertain fears associated with the potential harm, but they are also a consequence of the aftermath of the incident. Drawing on the previous theme of insurance, many homeowner policies were forfeited while the rapid evacuation resulted in burglary and looting of abandoned homes.

Furthermore, after the near-disaster at Three Mile Island, where the central Pennsylvania nuclear reactor threatened to melt down, the US Court of Appeals for the District of Columbia, which handled federal agencies, ruled that the Nuclear Regulatory Committee would need to carry out a new kind of environmental assessment on subsequent construction projects. The new assessment was designed to review the "psychological stress" felt by residents neighbouring nuclear sites. "We cannot believe that the psychological aftermath of the March 1979 accident falls outside the broad scope of the National Environmental Protection Act," the majority opinion argued (*New York Times* 1982). It was an unprecedented ruling, but it marked the spirit of the era. Into the 1980s, the most commonly observed negative health effect of the Three Mile Island accident was what physicians and public health experts referred to as "mental stress" (*New York Times* 1988; Hartsrough and Savitsky 1984). In a 1982 New York Times piece that treated environmental contamination, the science writer Maya Pines deliberated on how toxins, more broadly, constituted a "psychological time bomb" (Pines 1982).

(4) One manifestation of that psychological time bomb was the growing fear of cancer clusters across the United States. During the 1980s, the Centers for Disease Control and state health agencies experienced a growing number of phone calls from citizens and physicians reporting cancer incidence in their neighbourhoods (DiPerna 1984). Much of the information was incomplete or inaccurate, which made ascertaining the statistical improbability of the number of cases difficult. But the message

was clear: Americans were convinced that environmental factors were giving them cancer. Cancer clusters emerged in small towns such as Woburn, MA and in industrial corridors. But the epidemiological task of identifying environmentally caused cancer clusters only took shape in conjunction with the 1980s fears of cancer being reported (Nash 2007).

To these methods of evaluating toxic fear, we might add specific historical events and the actions taken by communities and officials in response to an apparent environmental threat. Case studies lack a clear a method for quantifying toxic fear, but they help to ground analyses in time and place, especially as their frequency appears to increase. And during the 1980s, there were ample case studies across the United States, from Hardeman County, Tennessee where Velsicol poisoned local water supplies, to Times Beach, Missouri, where a community was evacuated after dioxin contaminated the entire town. Indeed, across the United States, communities small and large experienced countless local instances of environmental contamination, many of which provoked fear and uncertainty regarding their short- and long-term risks. Collectively, they marked the shift from a singular environmental crisis to punctuated environmental crises that occurred on smaller scales – and frequently outside the spotlight of national news coverage.

4 Complicating the Narrative

Bourke makes the intriguing observation that fear expanded its influence with the increase of scientific knowledge and the concomitant decline of religious faith.[5] But perhaps the 1980s constitutes such a fascinating period for analyzing toxic fear because of the apparent retreat of science and scientific authority. A growing American distrust of science and scientists had been festering since the end of World War II and the rise of nuclear fears during the Cold War. By 1980, a move to the right resulted in the Reagan Administration's rampant deregulation across a number of government agencies designed to inform and protect public health. Deregulation – especially as it undermined the Environmental Protection Agency, the Department of the Interior, and the Food and Drug Administration – generated greater public uncertainty and confusion over what was safe and what was dangerous.

---

5 Wolf Lepenies makes the opposite argument in a nineteenth-century context, where science was seen as combatting fears of the unknown (1989). I am grateful to the editors for pointing out this essay to me.

Indeed, the uncertainty works both ways. In 1989, the Natural Resources Defense Council published a damning report that raised alarm bells about the use of daminozide on apples. Daminozide, known commercially as Alar, was a chemical growth regulator that helped to keep apples from falling before they were ripe. Earlier in the 1980s, the discovery of daminozide found in apple juice and applesauce raised concerns about its health to humans. In the 1989 report, the NRDC urged the Environmental Protection Agency to ban daminozide, and provided scientific evidence suggesting that the chemical was 240 times more carcinogenic than the EPA standards allowed. The report was followed by a mainstream media campaign fronted by the actress Meryl Streep on CBS's 60 Minutes and growing, nationwide awareness. According to one account, state troopers chased a school bus after a desperate call from a mother hoping to intercept and confiscate the apple in her child's lunch (American Council on Science and Health: 1999). School administrators had apples and apple products summarily destroyed. Apple markets rotted overnight.

By June, the EPA decided to act, banning daminozide on the basis that "long-term exposure" posed "unacceptable risks to public health." After the ban, apple growers in Washington State filed a libel suit against the NRDC and CBS, claiming that the public outrage against daminozide was spurred by media propaganda capitalizing on toxic fears. Indeed, their $100 million lawsuit criticized the faulty science upon which the ban was based. The story is muddier than this. The science and the publicity campaign do provoke some questions about their credibility, but it would be wrong to exonerate daminozide completely. Nevertheless, it is clear that the public reaction forced the EPA into action, not a more objective evaluation of the research. Impassioned rhetoric sealed daminozide's fate. In many respects, the accuracy of claims on either side of the debate – and there is a worthwhile debate – is less interesting here than the fear that the campaign provoked. As effective as it was, it warrants noting that the American public was well primed to respond negatively to any polysyllabic chemical name based on the litany of historical events in which chemicals from strontium-90 in nuclear fallout to DDT had poisoned people and landscapes. Growing fears over the latency of carcinogens and the emerging understanding of hormone-disrupting chemicals exacerbated hyperbole on both sides of the daminozide debate and others like it across the United States.

5   Conclusion

This study has concentrated on the American example. Time and place matter. Daniel T. Rodgers (2011) describes the fragmenting of American cultural norms during the final quarter of the twentieth century. The social, moral, and economic boundaries that defined previous American generations lost concrete definition, creating a certain ambivalence that trades on a new chapter of American exceptionalism. This is a distinctly American cultural transformation. But we should not underestimate the historical impact of globalization. The shift from environmental crisis to environmental crises was a global phenomenon. Chernobyl, Bhopal, the Sandoz Rhine spill, Mad Cow Disease, and countless smaller incidents the world over received worldwide attention and provoked further environmental anxieties. So, too, was the economic transition to neoliberalism, as zealously taken up in the United Kingdom, Canada, Germany, New Zealand, and other developed countries as in the United States. Deregulation and social fears surrounding the uncertainties pertaining to toxic threats were not exclusively American. Nor did chemical threats or anxieties adhere to national boundaries. It would be entirely possible to think about toxic fear through a transnational perspective. Before such synthetic work could be undertaken, however, the first task might involve identifying national differences and peculiarities.

By way of conclusion, allow me to offer some questions for further inquiry. Investigations of toxic fear have the potential to become exceptionally sprawling in scope. I have not dwelled on *Silent Spring*, the environmental dystopian literature emerging concurrently with the rise of the toxic century, or the growing interest in the history of the future, particularly as it relates to anticipatory fear, action, and reaction. New work, for example, on fourth generation carcinogenesis in lab studies raises some alarming issues surrounding DES and the persistence of hazardous chemicals, but it also threatens to transform our understanding of how genetics and evolution actually work (Walker and Haven 1997).[6] That, in itself, offers a critical lens for thinking about toxic fear. But to the questions:

(1) The first question involves asking whether toxic fear has a cultural geography and if we can scale it across varying interpretations of regionalism? The short answer is: of course it does and of course we can. But where do the distinctions lie and to what extent can we identify or articulate universal elements of a toxic fear? To what extent are insurance decisions and reports of feared cancer clusters expressions of the same kind of toxic fear? The beginning of this investigation involves returning to traditional discourses on industrialization and the kinds of post-materialist impulses that drove environmental concern

---

6 I am grateful to Nancy Langston for pointing me in this direction.

after World War II. But post-material priorities in the developed world do not alone explain or justify the heightened presence of toxic fear.

(2) Can we classify fear by race, class, and/or gender? Such a query should want to move beyond environmental justice or subaltern frameworks to examine the active production of fear and how it is manifested, but these categories remain useful. Ulrich Beck (1992, 36) observes that while "poverty is hierarchic, smog is democratic." This overlooks the grossly unequal distribution of environmental hazards, and it ignores the authority attributed to victims in toxic discourse (Buell 1989). At the same time, though, toxic fear's anticipatory nature has a far greater reach than simply those most susceptible to environmental harm. More to the point, subaltern disparities represent one of the most obvious and important grounds for interdisciplinary cooperation between historians and cultural studies scholars.

(3) How does fear evolve over the course of the post-World War II period, and especially through the 1980s? Or: how do we historicize the expanding historical legacy of the human relationship with toxic substances in the environment? In essence, this is a disciplinary question that hearkens back to examining methods of developing metrics for identifying fear in the first place. But scholars must be cognizant of the fact that toxic fear cannot be a static entity. It evolves in social and cultural context over time and manifests itself differently in different places.

(4) Have we become too afraid of chemicals? This is the other side of the uncertainty question. What do we know and how can we best assess and act upon chemical risk? How do we distinguish between known knowns, known unknowns, and unknown unknowns? Put more ominously, how does a generic fear of all chemicals serve or concentrate specific forms of power and authority? I raise this last question because ignorance would appear to be an all-too-prevalent foil to fear, and a benign expression of not knowing the risks. In the presence of uncertainty or ignorance, we rarely find actors working with good or complete knowledge.[7]

On some level, this last question begs for analysis of the precautionary principle, which plays out as a regulatory tool, a scientific form of measurement,

---

[7] This final point invites merging an environmental history of fear with recent studies in agnotology. See, as a starting point, Proctor and Schiebinger 2008; Michaels 2008; Oreskes and Conway 2010; Markowitz and Rosner 2002.

and a cultural reference point. But this seems like the easy way out, historically and discursively. Perhaps more interesting is to inquire about excessive fear as an expression of the dystopian modernism as laid out by Henri Lefebvre, where the planet and its peoples are recruited into "the capitalist 'trinity'" of land-capital-labor, and disassociated in "abstract space" (Lefebvre 1991: 282). In lacking connection to place, community, and culture, our modern malaise is a product of social disruptions. Add, too, a deficit of accessible scientific knowledge, and fear becomes an understandable default in the face of toxic uncertainties.

Concluding with a series of open-ended questions is not especially satisfactory, but while the history of fear has received considerable attention in recent years, the examination of fear through an environmental lens is quite distinctly the road less travelled. This essay is more a reflection from the trailhead than an exposition of research results. And while my interest has explicitly concentrated on historicizing the problem to toxic fear, it would appear that this inquiry might benefit from a multidisciplinary investigation conducted by scholars across the environmental humanities. Historians might help to situate toxic fear in its historical context, but cultural fears demand so much more than the historical lens. Indeed, our appreciation of the complexities inherent in environmental scholarship – the overlapping layers of science, policy, economics, society, and culture – would likely enjoy even further complication and richer understanding at the juncture where environment and emotions meet.

Bibliography

"An Unhappy Anniversary: The Alar 'Scare' Ten Years Later," American Council on Science and Health (1 February 1999), 1–4. On line at: http://acsh.org/1999/02/an-unhappy-anniversary-the-alar-scare-ten-years-later/ (consulted 01.04.2016).
Beck, Ulrich. 1992. *Risk Society: Towards a New Modernity*. London: SAGE Publications.
Bourke, Joanna. 2005. *Fear: A Cultural History*. London: Virago Press.
Boyer, Paul. 1994. *By the Bomb's Early Light: American Thought and Culture at the Dawn of the Atomic Age*. Chapel Hill: University of North Carolina Press.
Buell, Lawrence. 1998. "Toxic Discourse," *Critical Inquiry* 24, 639–665.
Charle, Suzanne. 1980. "And Now a Spate of Catastrophes Hits Homeowner," *New York Times*, 22 June 1980, R1.
"Cancer Clusters Prompt U.S. Study," *New York Times* (5 February 1988), A11.

"Court Rules 'Psychological Stress' Must be Weighed at Three Mile Island," *New York Times* (15 May 1982), 1.

DiPerna, Paula. 1984. "Leukemia Strikes a Small Town," *New York Times* Saturday Magazine, 2 December 1984, 100–108.

Egan, Michael. 2007. *Barry Commoner and the Science of Survival: The Remaking of American Environmentalism*. Cambridge, MA: MIT Press.

Egan, Michael. 2013. "Communicating Knowledge: The Swedish Mercury Group and Vernacular Science, 1965–1972," in *New Natures: Joining Environmental History with Science and Technology Studies*, edited by Dolly Jørgensen, Finn Arne Jørgensen, and Sara B. Pritchard. Pittsburgh: University of Pittsburgh Press, 103–117.

Egan, Michael 2014. "The 80s Almost Killed Me: Toxic Fear in America." On line at: http://eganhistory.com/2014/10/31/the-80s-almost-killed-me-toxic-fear-in-america/ (consulted 02.04.2016).

Erikson, Kai. 1994. *A New Species of Trouble: Explorations in Disaster, Trauma, and Community*. New York: W.W. Norton.

Gensburg, Lenore J. et al. 2009. "Mortality Among Former Love Canal Residents," *Environmental Health Perspectives* 117 (February), 209–216.

Glassner, Barry. 2009. *The Culture of Fear*. New York: Basic Books.

Hartsough, Don M. and Jeffrey C. Savitsky. 1984. "Three Mile Island: Psychology and Environmental Policy at a Crossroads," *American Psychologist* 39 (October), 1113–1122.

Hays, Samuel P. 1987. *Beauty, Health, and Permanence: Environmental Politics in the United States, 1955–1985*. New York: Cambridge University Press.

Lefebvre, Henri. 1991. *The Production of Space*. Translated by Donald Nicholson-Smith. Oxford: Blackwell Publishing.

Lepenies, Wolf. 1989. *Gefährliche Wahlverwandschaften*. Leipzig: Reclam.

Markowitz, Gerald & David Rosner. 2002. *Deceit and Denial: The Deadly Politics of Industrial Pollution*. Berkeley: University of California Press.

Michaels, David. 2008. *Doubt is Their Product: How Industry's Assault on Science Threatens Your Health*. New York: Oxford University Press.

Mischel, Walter. 1968. *Personality and Assessment*. New York: Wiley & Sons.

Mog, David M. 1987. "The Paralysis of Chemophobia," *Washington Post* (14 March 1987), A21.

Nash, Linda. 2007. *Inescapable Ecologies: A History of Environment, Disease, and Knowledge*. Berkeley: University of California Press.

Oreskes, Naomi and Erik M. Conway. 2010. *Merchants of Doubt: How a Handful of Scientists Obscured the Truth on Issues from Tobacco Smoke to Global Warming*. London: Bloomsbury Press.

Pines, Maya, "Psychological Time Bombs," *New York Times* (13 June 1982), 10E.

Proctor, Robert N. and Londa Schiebinger (eds). 2008. *Agnotology: The Making and Unmaking of Ignorance.* Palo Alto: Stanford University Press.

Rodgers, Daniel T. 2011. *The Age of Fracture.* Cambridge, MA: Harvard University Press.

Rose, Kenneth D. 2001. *One Nation Underground: The Fallout Shelter in American Culture.* New York: New York University Press, 2001.

Walker, B.E. and M.I. Haven. 1997. "Intensity of Multigenerational Carcinogenesis from Diethylstilbestrol in Mice," *Carcinogenesis* 18 (April 1997), 791–793.

"A Healthy Life Style," *Washington Post* (5 March 1987), A26.

Weart, Spencer. 2012. *The Rise of Nuclear Fear.* Cambridge, MA: Harvard University Press.

CHAPTER 9

Czeching American Nature Images in the Work of Robinson Jeffers and John Steinbeck

Petr Kopecký

Abstract

This chapter addresses the reception of the works of two California authors, Robinson Jeffers and John Steinbeck, in communist Czechoslovakia (1948–1989), where they both enjoyed immense popularity. Its primary focus is on selected nature images, namely trees, rocks, and the ocean. I discuss the associations and meanings these images acquired after they were transplanted from the United States to communist Czechoslovakia through high-quality translations. The different political environment into which the literary texts were introduced affected their reading in ways that even the authors could hardly have anticipated. The new associations and interpretations, determined largely by ideological factors, thus receive considerable attention in the present study.

1   Introduction

The image of the United States of America (hereafter America) in Cold War era Czechoslovakia was subject to political supervision and censorship, which formed part of the official propaganda machine. America was portrayed as an epitome of the spoiled and decadent West. The systematic efforts to discredit and denigrate America were not only a concern of the state-controlled media. Artists and writers were also mobilized to fight against the corrupt America on the cultural front and to promote communist values (Svašek 1997: 386). Czechoslovakia was one of the Soviet satellites that deployed artists and

---

*   This text is a result of the project SGS8/FF/2014 "Paradise Lost: Transformations of the Image of California in Historical and Cultural Contexts" supported by the internal grant scheme of the University of Ostrava. It draws partially from research whose outcome was published as a separate chapter entitled "The Warm Reception of Robinson Jeffers in Communist Czechoslovakia" in *The Wild That Attracts Us: New Critical Essays on Robinson Jeffers* (University of New Mexico Press, 2015).

writers in this campaign. As the first communist president of Czechoslovakia Klement Gottwald asserted, artists should serve the state and the new world order as political propagandists (Svašek 1997: 387). No wonder the publication of American literature was a rather delicate matter in this intellectual climate. It took the ideological thaw of the late 1950s to change the climate that was utterly hostile to America. While the decade following the communist coup in 1948 saw only a handful of (pro-)communist writers (Howard Fast, Langston Hughes, etc.) on the shelves of bookstores, between 1958 and 1968 the firm grip of the censors loosened somewhat, and even some US authors who were not adherents of communism managed to get through the ideological filter. Two quintessential California writers, Robinson Jeffers and John Steinbeck, ranked among them.

While Steinbeck experienced his debut in Czechoslovakia in 1941 when the Czech translation of his *The Grapes of Wrath* became the book of the year,[1] Jeffers established his presence on the Czech literary scene in the 1960s. In this decade, both Jeffers and Steinbeck became immensely popular with readers in Czechoslovakia. By contrast, in their home country they had fallen out of favor with the critics owing to the rise of New Criticism as a prevalent stream in American literary scholarship. Even though the political criteria governing the publication of US authors in Czechoslovakia were less dogmatic in the 1960s, an ideological review still had to be written before a Czech translation was released. The books in question did not have to be openly pro-communist, but they had to manifest a palpable anti-American streak. It was not that difficult to interpret Jeffers and Steinbeck in this light. Thus, the prologs and afterwords to the Czech translations of their works often classified these authors as social critics who castigated American consumerism, commercialism and ruthless capitalism.

While the political background will be relevant throughout this essay, its main focus is on the nature-related images that appealed so much to the readers in Czechoslovakia. It will probe the symbolic value of key nature images and *topoi* in the writings of Jeffers and Steinbeck, namely rocks, trees, and the ocean. The different political landscape into which the texts were transplanted sometimes resulted in unexpected readings and interpretations. Nature images, which were commonly regarded as politically neutral and innocent by Czech critics and censors, acquire new associations. A closer look at the process of intercultural translation can thus yield useful insights about the limitations and ideological conditioning of nature imagery. The three selected

---

1   In the decade following the communist coup in 1948, Steinbeck's work was not published in Czech translation because of the critical tone of *A Russian Journal* (1948).

images figured prominently in the authors' repertoire. They also received the attention of Czech editors, translators and critics.

2   Nature Imagery

Nature-oriented literature was a genre of negligible importance in Cold War Czechoslovakia. The official writers usually celebrated the new socialist order, which was characterized by techno-optimism. The so-called socialist novel, a popular genre especially in the 1950s, panegyrized the achievements of the working class. The emphasis on social issues and the faith in technological progress were arguably similar to the way in which the New Deal was depicted in American letters of the 1930s. The communist era in Czechoslovakia was marked by heavy industrialization which degraded whole regions of the country. Nature was largely objectified, both by the state and the state-sponsored writers. Environmental issues were not open to public debate. Protesting the decimation of the environment was commonly categorized as a politically subversive act. Still there were many who refused to indulge in this "progressive" zeal and instead resorted to nature as their refuge from technocratic society. It was primarily this segment of the population with whom the works of Jeffers and Steinbeck resonated.

2.1   *Rock*
Rock imagery is one of the cornerstones of Jeffers' poetry. Thanks to the numerous afterwords by Kamil Bednář, Jeffers' Czech translator, the poet's already strong reputation was further boosted due to his remarkable construction of the Hawk Tower, which figures in a host of his verses. The tower was erected by the poet himself. He used boulders from the nearby beach to build the stone structure from which he observed the ocean as well as the night sky. Thanks to Bednář's afterwords, pictorial appendices and the titles he gave to his volumes of Jeffers' selected poetry translated into Czech, Jeffers' Hawk Tower acquired a metonymic dimension in the minds of Czech readers. It reminded them of the (ruins of) medieval castles that played a vital role in Czech Romantic literature. It is worth noting that the Hawk Tower is analyzed by a prominent Czech scholar, Daniela Hodrová, in her study of the role of towers in literature, *Poetika míst* (Poetics of Places, 1997). Hodrová maintains that a tower exemplifies a vertical axis that stands for spirituality. It is also used as a literary *topos* that evokes isolation, especially in Romantic literature where the "poet seeks refuge from worldly turmoil [in the tower]. In the tower, a lonely soul finds an ideal place for contemplation (of the world, the self, and God) and meditation"

(Hodrová 1997: 203; this and all subsequent translations from the Czech are by the author). In communist Czechoslovakia, the refuge took form of weekends spent at family cottages in the countryside. In a poem from 1960, Egon Bondy, a leading figure of underground literature in communist Czechoslovakia, laments the dire fate of creative spirits in the Soviet bloc using Jeffers as a self-fulfilled author:

> Robinson Jeffers could with his own hands
> from granite blocks fetched from the sea-shore
> build a house for his wife
> I can merely hoe the soil with state-organized brigades
> build a new dam that will feed
> dim light to a few village bulbs
> and high voltage to a new arms factory.
> (2009: 111)

This extract can also be read as an implicit criticism of the technocratism that underpinned the building of the socialist order. Bondy was troubled by the heedless exploitation of natural resources, primarily the extraction of materials such as sandstone and limestone which were turned into cement. Cement, in turn, became the staple building material of the new dams and factories which epitomized the megalomaniacal engineering projects of the period. It is worth pointing out that the "dam novel" was a recognizable subcategory of the so called "construction novel" which celebrated the construction zeal and accomplishments of the socialist order. The construction novel was a principal genre in the communist Czechoslovakia of the 1950s.[2]

Jeffers' poetic treatment of rocks and stones was dramatically different from the utilitarian position described above. The poet's geological erudition allowed him to picture this seemingly dead matter as a substance that is animate, fluid and dynamic: "I am heaping the bones of the old mother / To build us against the host of the air; / Granite the blood-heat of her youth / Held molten in hot darkness against the heart" (1988: 5). It is no surprise that the most representative volume of Jeffers' selected work in Czech translation, *Maják v bouři* (Lighthouse in a Storm), contains a thematic section that is dedicated to rocks and stones.

In Jeffers' verse, rocks are endowed with capacities commonly attributed to living creatures. However, they are set within a different time frame compared

---

[2] Both the construction novel and dam novel are explored by Daniela Hodrová in "Žánrový půdorys tzv. budovatelského románu" (1979).

to humans: "I / felt the changes in the veins / In the throat of the mountain, a grain in many centuries, we / have our own time, not yours; [...] I was / mankind also, a moving lichen, / On the cheek of the round stone" (1988: 177). In this poem, as in many others, Jeffers juxtaposes the transient life of man with the permanence and stability of stone whose lifetime is measured in eons. The philosophical implications of this statement are profound. Jeffers challenges the widely shared belief in the central role of humanity on the earth. This subversive notion resonated with many readers in communist Czechoslovakia because they rejected the arrogant official stance *vis-à-vis* nature that was commonly summed up by the slogan "We will command the wind and rain."

What also attracted Czech readers was Jeffers' treatment of prehistoric peoples, especially the Irish Celts. In the spiritual void of communist Czechoslovakia, pantheism had a great appeal. It was closely linked with the Celts who had inhabited the Czech lands in prehistoric times; the name of their tribe gave the name "Bohemia" to the largest section of the country. Therefore, it does not come as a surprise that Kamil Bednář included one thematic section in *Maják v bouři* that is inspired by the Jeffers' stay in Ireland. The poet reads and writes the Celtic nations primarily through stone imagery. It was arguably the nostalgia for a bygone era in which people were not yet insulated from the earth which captivated Czechoslovak readers who took pleasure in reading that "We'll be wishing ourselves back in the stone age" (1991: 470). And as Kamil Bednář aptly observes in his biography of Jeffers *Přátelství přes oceán* (Friendship Across the Ocean), the poet had the soul of Stone Age people (1971: 114).

Mystery and spirituality surrounding rocks and stones are some of the many features that Jeffers shares with John Steinbeck. Like Jeffers, Steinbeck was proud of his Irish ancestry and considered Ireland his second home (Benson 1984: 352). He also shared Jeffers' interest in Celtic mythology and prehistoric stone monuments. In his 1933 novel *To a God Unknown*, rocks are endowed with life and meanings that are characteristic of Jeffers' poetics. They connote permanence, stability and disregard for human designs. The mysterious rock at the center of a forest clearing is a crucial site in the novel. It is portrayed as a primeval fountain of life that has the potential to save the region which is in decline because of extreme drought. The protagonist of the novel, Joseph Wayne, loves the rock more than his family. He performs Paleolithic fertility rituals on the rock, which juts out of the land's surface. In the context of Steinbeck's gendered landscape, the moist rock can be interpreted as the earth's womb. At the same time, it stands for the deep knowledge of the place and lasting values. This facet of Steinbeck's novel struck a chord in the Czech psyche. It is not a coincidence that the rocks, or the "bones of the earth" as Steinbeck called them, had a tremendous appeal to those who sought refuge from the urbanizing society bound by ideological restraints. Rocks and rock formations were romanticized in literature but also became havens for the Czech offshoot of the "tramping" movement,[3] which enjoyed immense popularity in communist Czechoslovakia. In the cultural landscape of Central Europe, transformed by many centuries of human activity, the so-called rock towns, located in some of the best-preserved nature reserves in the country, became places where Czech tramps gathered. The intimate relationship with rocks, which played an important role in certain tramp ceremonies, was partly inspired by the exotic sceneries of the Wild West and shamanistic rites of its native population. It is not by chance that the authors of the authoritative *Slovník spisovatelů: Spojené státy americké* (The Dictionary of Writers: United States of America) claim that Steinbeck's best works are characterized by masterly represented relationship between man and rock (Vančura 1979: 604). On a more down-to-earth level, an extract from *To a God Unknown* was used to support an environmental cause, namely the preservation of a canyon of the Vltava River (Jonáš 2015). The fact that rocks figure prominently in the Czech imagination can be also illustrated by the accomplished geologist Václav Cílek, whose books on the memory of rocks and their essential role in the Czech landscape, both mental and physical, have become bestsellers.[4]

That Steinbeck perceived rocks and stones as animate entities is well demonstrated in the remarkable travelog *Sea of Cortez* (1941).[5] As the author himself claims, the book reveals the underlying ideas that support his worldview. His holistic view of life encompasses also rocks, generally regarded as inanimate objects: "[E]ach species is at once the point and the base of a pyramid … One merges into another, groups melt into ecological groups until the time when what we know as life meets and enters what we think of as non-life: barnacle and rock, rock and earth, earth and tree, tree and rain and air" (Steinbeck 1986: 256–257). This Romantic sensibility of the author, who sought to rediscover the fundamental unity of life and, in so doing, combined holistic science and what his wife Elaine called a "spiritual streak," evoked a strong emotional response

---

3 Although the word "tramp" entered the Czech language through the 1922 translation of Jack London's *The Road* (1907), the foundations of the movement had been laid in 1919. The first Czech tramps came from the ranks of Scout dissenters. The Czech tramps were critical of rapid urbanization and industrialization. In the communist era, tramping was more and more associated with the emphasis on environmental protection.

4 Cílek's most popular book is *Krajiny vnitřní a vnější* (Inner and Outer Landscapes, 2002). Geological imagination figures prominently in his recent books such as *Kameny domova* (Rocks of Home, 2011) and *Kameny a hvězdy* (Rocks and Stars, 2014).

5 The narrative part of the book, whose first edition contained a comprehensive scientific catalog, was published in 1951 as *The Log from the Sea of Cortez*.

in Czechoslovakia. Vladimír Procházka, the translator of the first six Czech editions of *The Grapes of Wrath*, saw Steinbeck as a "great spiritual support" in the difficult times of German occupation but also beyond it ("Afterword," 1963, 397). Ivan Martin Jirous, a leading dissident, artist and close friend of Václav Havel, read *The Grapes of Wrath* repeatedly while in prison in the 1970s. In this dispiriting environment, Jirous perceived Steinbeck's novel as "immensely strong ... the greatest experience" of his stay in prison (2005: 140).

In the communist era, that is to say, life was fragmented, heavily bureaucratized and subject to sterile mechanization. Spiritual life was systematically uprooted through the doctrine of so-called Scientific Atheism, a course every university student was obliged to take.

2.2 Tree

Translating Jeffers' poetry, which was permeated with scientific ideas and terms, was a challenging job for Kamil Bednář. As he states in *Přátelství přes oceán*, even botanists who were uninterested in poetry could enjoy reading Jeffers. But what attracts the botanist exasperates the translator (1971: 80). In the pre-internet era, Bednář had to write letters to his friend Melba Bennet enquiring about the Latin equivalents for the plant names in Jeffers' work. Besides that, he consulted experts from the Botanical Garden in Prague and scholars from the city's Charles University. Even these experts did not have the knowledge of certain species that were endemic to America. No wonder: in Czechoslovakia of that time, America was not only a *terra prohibita* but, to a certain degree, also a *terra incognita* regarding its natural characteristics.

It is not surprising that some endemic species were lost in Czech translation. Even the iconic redwood was tricky because the Czech word *sekvoj* associates the world's most voluminous trees, rather than the tallest ones, to the readers. Be that as it may, the redwoods were regarded as exotic and sublime trees because their monumentality was unparalleled in Central Europe. It is also worth mentioning the pantheistic reading of redwood groves that often appear in Jeffers' verse. To a Czech reader, they evoked a sacred place, a forest temple. If the frequent image of redwoods as overwhelming towers in *Ženy od mysu Sur* (The Women at Point Sur, 1965) had spiritual connotations, this was especially true for Czech readers:

> ...I know that I stand near
> God and speak for him.
> He brought me from the north; I was fifty years old, I am ageless.
> He gave me sap of redwoods to drink, towers of millennial
> Inexhaustible life....
>
> (1988: 302)

These sky-high trees, which Czechs could only admire in photo books and TV documentaries, represented a spiritual axis that linked the earth to higher spheres, to the realm of spirit and mystery. They represented an apt opposition to the towering chimneys which heralded the new era in Czechoslovakia.[6] Redwoods, similarly to rocks, had a spiritual meaning that was a critical factor in the reading of Jeffers in Czechoslovakia.

In his book on Jeffers, Kamil Bednář points out another characteristic feature of trees in Jeffers' work. He emphasizes that the poet planted roughly two thousand trees (mostly eucalyptus) to "protect his residence against the expanding civilization" (1971: 239). In *The Beginning and the End* (Sbohem, moře), Jeffers uses juxtaposition to bemoan the elimination of those trees. In a poem titled "Ghost," Jeffers' ghost confronts the future owner of the Tor House and the surrounding property.

> "I see you have played hell
> With the trees that I planted." "There has to be room for people," he answers. "My God," he says, "*That* still!"
> (1991: 465)

It is worth noting that even environmentally-minded Czech readers did not mind the fact that eucalyptus was not native to North America. In fact, the notion of a forest in communist Czechoslovakia had long been associated with the spruce monoculture that dominated the timber industry. This industrial forest was thus regarded as authentic by most people, even though deciduous trees had accounted for most of the woodlands prior to industrialization.

In Steinbeck's writing, trees often acquired symbolic and even philosophical meanings. Man's identification with a tree is used to convey a non-anthropocentric outlook in his *To a God Unknown*. Like the aforementioned rock in the novel, this oak tree invokes the Celtic pantheism that has a strong appeal in the Czech lands. The oak is more than a mere Romantic prop reflecting the mood of the protagonist Joseph Wayne. In fact, it influences the health of the protagonist as well as the land. It is significant that the tree, which serves a symbol of unity in the novel, is destroyed by Joseph's Puritan brother who epitomizes the frontier mentality.

---

6   When Jeffers was first published in Czechoslovakia, chimneys and factories were positive symbols in the official literature in the 1950s. Heavy industries were depicted heroically. For more, see the semiotic study on factories *Šťastný věk* (2008) by Vladimír Macura.

Steinbeck harshly criticizes the frontier mentality in his non-fiction, especially in *America and Americans* (1966). In his eyes, acts of savagery were perpetrated by white colonists, not the "savages" (i.e. Native Americans):

> I have often wondered at the savagery and thoughtlessness with which early settlers approached this rich continent [...]. They burned the forests [...] and ran a reckless scythe through the virgin and noble timber. Perhaps they felt that it was limitless and could never be exhausted and that a man could move on to wonders endlessly. (1994a: 377)

The writer rightly observes that the tree was perceived as a mere obstacle to the expansion of civilization. In the process of westering in America, trees were considered to be an inexhaustible resource standing in the way of the colonization of the continent. A few people reconsidered this exploitative approach once they hit the final frontier of the continent on the Pacific Coast. Steinbeck's perspective on American history struck a chord with readers in Czechoslovakia, who tended to favor wilderness and side with its wild inhabitants rather than its conquerors.[7] Their natural proclivity to support the subjugated was fostered by the official propaganda that condemned the destructive capitalist ethos. As has been demonstrated in the quote above, in Steinbeck's eyes the tree exemplifies a counterforce to the expansionistic and aggressive civilization, and this was a cause with which Czech readers sympathized. In the afterword to the 1966 Czech edition of *Toulavý autobus* (The Wayward Bus), Jaroslav Schejbal suggests that whether he travels by car, bus or on foot, Steinbeck does not perceive the environment as a mere coulisse, while journeying he can stop and admire the beauty of birds as well as trees (1966: 251). Similarly, in a 1965 review of *Toulky s Charleym* (Travels with Charley), Jaroslav Šimůnek emphasized Steinbeck's critique of the overmechanized American society and the importance of smelling "the grass and trees" (1965: 4).

The tree is also thematized in Steinbeck's masterpiece *The Grapes of Wrath* (1939). It stands for the interdependence between humans and the natural environment: "Can you live without the willow tree. Well, no, you can't. The willow tree is you" (1939: 20–21). In this often-cited passage, the willow tree obviously has a symbolic value. It is no coincidence that Steinbeck chose this tree; it was sacred to Celtic societies, where it represented (among other things)

---

7   For more on the idealized image of Native Americans in Czechoslovakia, see Don Sparling and Tomáš Pospíšil, "Thirteen Ways of Looking at America" (2001), and Petr Kopecký, "The Wild West through Czech Eyes: Cowboys and Indians in the Heart of Europe" (2006).

wisdom. It should be also noted that a tree was an unofficial emblem of the somewhat narrow version of the conservation movement in Czechoslovakia. For some time, the state even organized voluntary weekend "brigades" where young people planted (spruce) trees. This initiative was synonymous with the reductionist conception of conservation in communist Czechoslovakia. It follows that tree symbolism had an appeal to those who cared about the environment in communist Czechoslovakia, be they enthusiastic conservationists or ecophilosophically-minded intellectuals.

2.3   Ocean

Arguably, the ocean represented the most powerful symbol in Jeffers' poetry in the eyes of the Czech readership. That applies both to the physical and metaphysical dimension. This hypothesis is supported by the entry in *Slovník světových literárních děl* (The Dictionary of the World's Literary Works) which includes *Roan Stallion, Tamar and Other Poems* among the classics of world literature. Even more importantly, the editors list the ocean as one of the most potent symbols in the poet's writing, adding that it is "related to the notion of the permanency and inalterability of the material essence of the universe, the cyclical course of natural processes and the relative nature of the 'passing' of time" (Macura et al. 1988: 396).

The potential of the *topos* of ocean to allure Czech readers was as immense as the Pacific Ocean itself. First, Czechoslovakia was a landlocked country. Second, in the communist period, travelling abroad, especially out of the Eastern bloc, was subject to severe restrictions. Only the fortunate few could enjoy the beaches of the Adriatic and the Black Sea. Many others dreamt of the sea with a conch over their ear. The vast Pacific Ocean was beyond the imagination of Czechs who had lived their lives within a comparatively small area. As Kamil Bednář writes in the opening chapter of *Přátelství přes oceán*, "we lived so modestly here that we – at least most of us – could not imagine the sea" (1971: 8). He goes on to explain that his only direct encounter with the sea was a brief vacation with his parents on the Adriatic coast. Owing to this sole experience, the translator could at least partially envisage the Pacific Ocean. The sea remained a distant but crucial memory for him, "a phantom from childhood, a mystery of the Earth, life's cradle, the last unexplored territory, a wonderful realm of water, swelled by the Moon and affecting the life on the Earth, God knows how" (1971: 77). In another chapter of his biographical sketch of Jeffers, Bednář describes his notion of the ocean, which is the leitmotif of the whole book, in the following way: "The Pacific. The word sounds somewhat steely, it is the greatest ocean on the Earth. In our eyes, it represents the highest degree of freedom imaginable, it has an untamable nature, immense power and unearthly beauty" (1971: 21). In the context of the time in which Bednář's book on Jeffers was published (1971), these sentences could hardly be read without considering the restrictions in all spheres of life. These restrictions became particularly harsh following the suppression of the liberalization movement in Czechoslovakia by the troops of the Warsaw Pact in 1968. The political undertones can be also traced in another noteworthy statement that concerns the boundless Pacific Ocean. Whenever the translator invoked its image, he "could not have claustrophobia, a feeling of anxiety from confined spaces" (1971: 12).

On the one hand, the images of ocean associated stability and peace, in keeping with the ocean's name. On the other hand, the Pacific is often represented as a fierce element. Perhaps no other *topos* in Czech literature had such a capacity to provoke sublime emotions. In the Czech reviews of Jeffers' work, the Pacific figured as a prominent feature. The noted Czech critic Josef Fleischmann depicts the awe people experience when facing the ocean. Even though he does not deploy the expression 'sublime' in his review "Velký básník průhledného rozporu" (A Great Poet of Lucid Discrepancy), he conveys some of the ideas that have been explored in much greater depth by Robert Zaller's remarkable study *Robinson Jeffers and the American Sublime* (2012). Fleischmann portrays Jeffers' home region as a territory which attracts people who are eager "to sense the transience and insignificance in the infinite stream of the enduring elements" (1950: 4). Jeffers' vivid descriptions of the ocean charmed the critic, who had never been to the ocean himself. And they certainly captured and stirred the imagination of Czech readers. Their reading of the oceanic sublime in Jeffers' verses was thus different from that of American readers. Czechs' idea of the ocean was often just mediated; they could not relate it to their own real-life experience. Still they were fascinated by "the rush and trampling of water / And hoarse withdrawals, the endless ocean throwing his skirmish-lines against granite" (*CP* 3: 481).

The above-cited lines from Jeffers' late poem capture the moment at which the ocean waves clash with the coastal rocks. Kamil Bednář was mesmerized by poems that contained dramatic scenes, above all storms. He titled one volume of Jeffers' selected poems *Maják v bouři* (Lighthouse in a Storm). It was particularly the waves breaking against the cliffs that resonated with both Czech readers and critics. The dramatic force of these scenes is discussed by Fleischmann ("Velký básník průhledného rozporu"), Bednář (*Přátelství přes oceán*), as well as by Irena Dubská in her widely read travelog *Americký rok* (American Year, 1966). Dubská was one of the very few Czech scholars in the communist era who wrote on Jeffers' poetic rendering of the ocean after she experienced Big

Sur for herself. While she appreciates the magnificence of the Pacific Ocean, she is also daunted by its fierceness and hostility (1966: 170).

Steinbeck's conception of the ocean was largely shaped by two preeminent thinkers. Ed Ricketts, the author's closest friend, was a marine biologist whose holistic methods received full recognition only long after his death.[8] The other influential figure was the acclaimed mythologist Joseph Campbell, who spent much of 1930 in the company of Steinbeck and Ricketts in Monterey. It is thus no wonder that in Steinbeck's work the ocean carries associations of mystery, darkness and the unconscious. The ocean depths are analogous to the deep strata of the unconscious mind. The ocean is used as an archetypal symbol in several of Steinbeck's novels, most significantly in the Monterey trilogy (*Tortilla Flat, Cannery Row, Sweet Thursday*). While Danny in *Tortilla Flat* (1935) subconsciously turns his back on civilization and meditates by the dark deep waters of the ocean shortly before his death, the mysterious Chinaman in *Cannery Row* (1945) descended to the ocean at dusk where he "disappeared among the piles and steel posts which support the piers. No one saw him again until dawn" (1994b: 24). The Jungian elements in Steinbeck's fiction were all the more enthralling because Jungian psychology was deemed subversive by communist ideologues and its practice and dissemination was basically illegal.[9] Steinbeck ranked among the few writers published in communist Czechoslovakia who linked the depths of the Pacific with the depths of the human mind. Steinbeck was heavily influenced by Jung's theory of the collective subconscious. The representation of the oceanic depths was thus often inspired by depth psychology. The connection between the depths of the mind and the ocean was most explicitly expressed in *The Log from the Sea of Cortez* (1951):

> For the ocean, deep and black in the depths, is like the low dark levels of our minds in which the dream symbols incubate and sometimes rise up to sight like the Old Man of the Sea [...] We have thought often of this mass of sea-memory or sea-thought, which lives deep in the mind. If one ask for a description of the unconscious, even the answer-symbol will usually be in terms of a dark water into which the light descends only a short distance (1986: 36–37).

---

8   Ricketts coauthored a pioneering ecological study *Between Pacific Tides* (1939), which came to be one of the best-selling titles in the history of Stanford University Press.
9   Carl Gustav Jung's work became widely popular in Czechoslovakia following the Velvet Revolution in 1989.

In the 1930s and 1940s, in the prime of Steinbeck's literary career, the Pacific Ocean was still largely unexplored. In western culture, it was considered an untouched and primeval territory.[10] Steinbeck realized the imaginative potential of this unknown and enigmatic world. In some of his novels set in the inland California valleys (*To a God Unknown, East of Eden*), the vast expanse of water beyond the coastal mountain range conceals the greatest mysteries of life. As we read in *The Red Pony*, "Jody knew something was there, something very wonderful because it was not known, something secret and mysterious" (2000: 40). In the words of John Timmerman, the author *The Dramatic Landscape of Steinbeck's Short Stories*, the lure of the ocean dwelled in its "mystical transcendence, the power that lies beyond human understanding" (1990: 133). Needless to say, Czech readers were thirsty for intellectual and spiritual impulses that transcended their ordinary lives. They were also enchanted by phenomena beyond human understanding, which were eliminated from all spheres of life because they undermined the positivistic science that was widely promoted by the education system in communist Czechoslovakia. It is interesting to note that in the eyes of acclaimed Czech author Miroslav Holub, the mysterious nature of the Pacific was dissolved in the commercialized society in post-WWII America. In his widely read travelog *Anděl na kolečkách* (An Angel on Wheels, 1963), Holub visits the Monterey Peninsula and sadly states that the sterile and superficial industrial society had done away with the wildness and depth of this coastal region.

3 Conclusion

The selected images and *topoi* were undoubtedly perceived differently in the heart of Europe than in the land of their origin. They were also enticing due to their exotic character; this may be hard to understand even for today's Czech youth, who – unlike the generation of their parents and grandparents – are well-traveled. It is also important to emphasize that the landscape depicted in the works discussed here, especially in Jeffers' poems, was perceived as untrammeled and somewhat otherworldly amid the dull reality of totalitarian Czechoslovakia – which was, moreover, free of the topographical extremes that characterize California. As Kamil Bednář states, as a translator who had never been to "Jeffers Country" in person, he was left with the verse and photographs: "From a distance, eyes of love can see the essential. From nearby, they

---

10 See Gary Kroll, *America's Ocean Wilderness: A Cultural History of Twentieth-Century Exploration* (2008).

might be deceived by circumstantial ordinariness, which comes into the way of the extraordinary" (1971: 160). This observation seems to capture the manner in which the literary texts were approached in Czechoslovakia. The geographical distance and exoticism of the setting of Jeffers' and Steinbeck's texts made it possible for Czech readers to partially idealize the ultimate uncontaminated free world on the Pacific Coast.

The ideological dimension of the reception of the authors' writings was immensely important. Nature images took on new meanings once they were transplanted from America to Czechoslovakia. The images were charged with values and ideas that were systematically suppressed in the Soviet bloc, such as freedom, spirituality and human humility in the face of the grand scheme of nature. Czech readers did not read the rocks, trees and ocean as mere natural objects. Due to the political restraints and restrictions placed upon them, they perceived (and sometimes even invented) the levels beneath, behind and beyond these objects with a peculiar intensity, quite unlike that of American readers. The geographical distance meant that what could be ordinary to American readers was extraordinary, if not otherworldly to Czech readers. Living in a country where nature was controlled and commodified, Czech readers appreciated the fact that the California authors did not conceive of it merely as a backdrop. On the contrary, they filled the seemingly void natural objects with meanings, associations and even with life, which evoked bygone times to Czech readers. They were reminiscent especially of the Celtic heritage in the Czech lands. The industrial and economic progress made Jeffers, Steinbeck as well as many Czech readers turn back to Celts for inspiration. It was the filling of the "dead matter" (i.e. nature) with meaning and spirit that brought satisfaction to those Czech readers who did not come to terms with the fact that chimneys and factories became the celebrated symbols of the new communist era.

Bibliography

Bednář, Kamil. 1971. *Přátelství přes oceán*. Praha: Československý spisovatel.
Benson, Jackson J. 1984. *The True Adventures of John Steinbeck, Writer*. New York: The Viking Press.
Bondy, Egon. 2009. *Ve všední den i v neděli...: Výbor z básnického díla 1950–1994*. Edited by Milan Machovec. Praha: DharmaGaia.
Cílek, Václav. 2007. *Krajiny vnitřní a vnější*. Praha: Dokořán.
Cílek, Václav. 2011. *Kameny domova*. Praha: Krásná paní.
Cílek, Václav. 2014. *Kameny a hvězdy*. Praha: Dokořán.

Dubská, Irena. 1966. *Americký rok*. Praha: Československý spisovatel.

Fleischmann, Ivo. 1960. 'Velký básník průhledného rozporu' in *Literární noviny* 21:5.

Hodrová, Daniela. 1979. 'Žánrový půdorys tzv. budovatelského románu' in Hana Hrzalová and Radko Pytlík (eds) *Vztahy a cíle socialistických literatur*. Praha: ÚČSL: 121–141.

Hodrová, Daniela. 1997. 'Příběhy věže' in Daniela Hodrová, Zdeněk Hrbata, Marie Kubínová, Vladimír Macura (eds) *Poetika míst*. Praha: H&H.

Holub, Miroslav. 1963. *Anděl na kolečkách*. Praha: Československý spisovatel.

Jeffers, Robinson. 1963. *Sbohem, moře*. Translated by Kamil Bednář. Praha: Mladá fronta.

Jeffers, Robinson. 1983. *Maják v bouři*. Translated by Kamil Bednář. Praha: Ceskoslovenský spisovatel.

Jeffers, Robinson. 1988. *The Collected Poetry of Robinson Jeffers* (vol. 1). Stanford: Stanford University Press.

Jeffers, Robinson. 1991. *The Collected Poetry of Robinson Jeffers* (vol. 3). Stanford: Stanford University Press.

Jirous, Ivan M. 2005. *Magorovy dopisy*. Praha: Torst.

Jonáš, Jaroslav. 2015. 'S divočinou Vltavy' 16 October 2015, <http://www.s-divocinou-vltavy.estranky.cz/clanky/s-divocinou/slova-o-divocine/john-steinbeck--neznamemu-bohu--to-a-god-unknown-.html>.

Kopecký, Petr. 2006. 'The Wild West through Czech Eyes: Cowboys and Indians in the Heart of Europe' in Petr Kopecký, Stanislav Kolář, and Scot Guenter (eds) *Considering America from Inside and Out: A San José/Ostrava Dialogue Sharing Perspectives*. Ostrava: University of Ostrava: 70–80.

Kroll, Gary. 2008. *America's Ocean Wilderness: A Cultural History of Twentieth-Century Exploration*. Lawrence: University of Kansas Press.

Macura, Vladimír. 2008. *Šťastný věk*. Praha: Academia.

Macura, Vladimír et al. 1988. *Slovník světových literárních děl I*. Praha: Odeon.

Procházka, Vladimír. 1963. Afterword to *Hrozny hněvu* by John Steinbeck. Praha: Státní nakladatelství krásné literatury a umění: 397–406.

Ricketts, Edward and Jack Calvin. 1992. *Between Pacific Tides*. Stanford: Stanford University Press.

Schejbal, Jaroslav. 1966. Afterword to *Toulavý autobus* by John Steinbeck. Praha: Máj: 241–251.

Šimůnek, Jaroslav. 1965. 'Steinbeckova cesta Amerikou' in *Mladá fronta* (21 January 1965): 4.

Sparling, Don and Tomáš Pospíšil. 2001. 'Thirteen Ways of Looking at America' in *Brno Studies in English* 27: 73–84.

Steinbeck, John. 1939. *The Grapes of Wrath*. New York: Viking Press.

Steinbeck, John. 1948. *A Russian Journal*. New York: Viking Press.

Steinbeck, John. 1986. *The Log from the Sea of Cortez*. New York: Penguin.

Steinbeck, John. 1994a. *America and Americans and Selected Nonfiction*. New York: Penguin.
Steinbeck, John. 1994b. *Cannery Row*. New York: Penguin.
Steinbeck, John. 1995. *To a God Unknown*. New York: Penguin.
Steinbeck, John. 2000. *The Red Pony*. New York: Penguin.
Svašek, M. 1997. 'The Politics of Artistic Identity: the Czech Art World in the 1950s and 1960s' in *Contemporary European History* 6 (3): 383–403.
Timmerman, John H. 1990. *The Dramatic Landscape of Steinbeck's Short Stories*. Norman and London: University of Oklahoma Press.
Vančura, Zdeněk et al. 1979. *Slovník spisovatelů: Spojené státy americké*. Praha, Odeon.
Walker, Franklin. *The Sea Coast of Bohemia*. Santa Barbara: Peregrine Smith.
Zaller, Robert. 2012. *Robinson Jeffers and the American Sublime*. Stanford: Stanford University Press.

PART 3

Framing Nature on Screen

∴

CHAPTER 10

Black-and-White Telecasting? Water Pollution on Finnish and Estonian Television during the Cold War

Ottoaleksi Tähkäpää and Simo Laakkonen

Abstract

The Cold War era witnessed not only the rise of television as the leading mass media format throughout the industrialized world but also the surge of the environment as a major societal issue, both locally and internationally. According to the general consensus, television played an important role in initiating public discussion on and raising awareness of environmental issues in Western Europe, whereas in Eastern Europe, environmental protection is usually perceived as having been a top-down process subordinated to other political goals perceived as more pressing. Yet despite these prevailing preconceptions, surprisingly little is actually known about televised coverage of environmental issues on either side of the Iron Curtain. This comparative case study of Finnish and Estonian television aims to provide empirical evidence and novel perspectives on environmental television reporting in Eastern and Western Europe. When did environmental television reporting begin, how did it differ on either side of the Iron Curtain, and is the image such a juxtaposition yields as black-and-white as is commonly assumed?

1   Introduction

The Cold War never escalated into a full-blown military conflict between the Western and Eastern blocs. Instead, the Cold War was fought on multiple fronts, one of which was communications (Dennis et al. 1991: 7). Hence, the rise of television as the leading mass media format throughout the industrialized world, including both Eastern and Western Europe, ensured that the medium became a battleground in the competition for political power (Mickiewicz 1999, xi). In Estonia, this battle took literal form during the August 1991 *coup d'état*, when hardline communists in the Soviet Union attempted to overthrow Mikhail Gorbachev and stop the reforms he was championing. On August 20, Soviet troops reached the Tallinn television tower but failed to take possession of the 314-meter-high building due to the resistance of unarmed radio operators. The Estonian operators placed a matchbox between the elevator doors, jamming the elevators, and barricaded themselves into the communication center on the 22nd floor in order to maintain Estonia's links with the outside world during those critical days. The television tower takeover ultimately failed when it became clear that the attempted coup in Moscow had not succeeded (Laine 2014; Savisaar 2005).

This incident shows the concrete importance of television infrastructure during the Cold War. However, the media struggle was also fought on the terrain of language and images, over the hearts and minds of the people.[1] Environmental discourse naturally became a part of this struggle. We argue, however, that the environment played an ambivalent role in this showdown. On the one hand one, environmental issues were used to smear the opposing side. On the other hand, the environment was one of the few issues that connected nations on both sides of the Iron Curtain (Brain 2014; Räsänen & Laakkonen 2007a; Räsänen & Laakkonen 2008). Nevertheless, the overall environmental history of the Cold War, in general, and of the countries of the Socialist Bloc and of the developing world, in particular, is still poorly known today, despite the increasing availability of archival sources (McNeill and Unger 2013; Laakkonen & Tucker 2012; Pavlínek and Pickles 2000).

In this essay, we approach the role of environmental issues during the Cold War by zeroing in on two neighboring countries – the democratic Republic of Finland and the communist Estonian Soviet Socialist Republic (Estonian SSR). We focus on television broadcasting, exploring its history from the not-yet-examined environmental perspective. The methodological basis for our research is frame analysis: we examine how environmental problems were represented on Finnish and Estonian television. As David Deacon et al. have noted, "it is the content of what is contained that is of paramount importance" (2004: 160–161). Hence, by exploring actual program content, we aim to answer the following research questions: Was the environment addressed in television programs in democratic Finland and/or the Estonian SSR? And if broadcasting in both countries covered environmental issues, to what extent did broadcasts on environmental issues differ between the two countries? We ask these basic questions because, perhaps surprisingly, the environmental content of the most influential medium of the post-war era has remained, for all intents and purposes, unexplored. To our knowledge, only Monica Djerf-Pierre has studied environmental news reporting in the context of television, but her research

---

1 To learn more about cross-border radio broadcasting during the Cold War, see *Cold War History* 13(2) 2013; Johnson 2010.

was conducted from a rather quantitative point of view and focused primarily on the institutionalization of environmental reporting (Djerf-Pierre 1996; Djerf-Pierre 2013). In this regard, our research can be considered one of the first forays into the qualitative study of the environmental history of television.

Our study also falls under the rubric of the digital humanities, as it is based on digitized historical television programs broadcast by the Estonian and Finnish national television broadcasting companies, *Eesti Televisioon* and *Yleisradio* respectively. The source material for our study of Estonian reporting comes from the digital database of the Film Archives, a branch of the National Archives of Estonia (www.ra.ee), which enabled us to conduct direct online searches of the Estonian television programs database. In Finland, these searches were conducted by an employee working in the archives of the Finnish Broadcasting Company. In both instances, the searches were based on specific keywords, which in this case focused on water pollution issues, due to the exceedingly broad nature of "the environmental" as a concept. We focused on five themes that, in principle, emerged simultaneously in Eastern and Western Europe after World War II: radioactive fallout caused by nuclear weapons tests, marine oil pollution, toxic substances, industrial pollution, and discharge of nutrients.

Any programs covering the above-mentioned themes were included in the search except for news reports, which were excluded from the study altogether, as the Estonian television archives database, unlike its Finnish counterpart, did not include such materials. However, the number of omitted Finnish news reports strongly suggests that water pollution coverage was actually more comprehensive in both countries than this article proposes. The searches were restricted to the period 1955–1974, starting from the first national television broadcast in the Estonian SSR and ending at the signing of the so-called Helsinki Convention, that is, the Convention on the Protection of the Marine Environment of the Baltic Sea Area. This convention was signed in 1974 in Helsinki by all Baltic coastal states, including the Soviet Union, the Peoples' Republic of Poland, the German Democratic Republic (GDR), the Federal Republic of Germany (FDR), Denmark, Sweden, and Finland (Räsänen and Laakkonen 2007a; Räsänen and Laakkonen 2007b).

2   Geopolitical Background and the Two Television Systems

Like the Gulf of Finland that lies between Estonia and Finland, history has both joined and divided these two small nations. Both countries gained their independence from Imperial Russia during the First World War. A brief period of independence for both was, however, brutally truncated by the Second World

War. The Republic of Estonia was occupied by the Soviet Union first in 1939 and again in 1944, resulting in the establishment of an Estonian SSR subordinate to Moscow until the restoration of the Republic of Estonia in 1991 (Misiunas and Taagepera 1993: 15). The Soviet Union also attacked Finland in 1939, and a second war between the two countries broke out in 1941. However, Finland, unlike Estonia, managed to defend herself and maintain her independence, capitalist economic system, and parliamentary democracy. The Iron Curtain that descended upon Europe thus passed through the Baltic Sea, separating the two nations for almost fifty years, from 1944 to 1991. This Cold War bifurcation was also reflected in the different television systems adopted on the opposite shores of the Gulf of Finland; the Soviet-style totalitarian model was extended to the Estonian SSR, while Finland opted for a modification of the Scandinavian-style public service, combining it with private commercial television.

The Soviet Union had acknowledged the importance of television at an early juncture. The first experimental TV programs were broadcast as early as the 1930s, and in 1945 Moscow Television was the first in Europe to reintroduce transmission interrupted by the war (Roth-Ey 2011: 176; Paasilinna 1995, 93; Yurovsky and Boretsky 1966: 45–52). Soviet television was organized at the national, republic, regional and municipal levels. Two central television stations broadcast programming to all fifteen republics. Non-Russian republics had their own channels, accountable to Moscow, broadcasting in both Russian and the majority local language (Mickiewicz 1999, 24). The Estonian national television channel *Eesti Televisioon* (ETV) started regular television broadcasts in 1955, that is, three years earlier than regular telecasting started in Finland (http://news.err.ee/l/about_us). Three channels broadcasting programs in Russian – Soviet Central Television I, Soviet Central Television II and Leningrad TV – became available in Estonian SSR. Nevertheless, it was the fourth channel, Estonian-language ETV, which quickly became the most popular among Estonian audiences (Autti and Pantti 2013: 76). In 1972, about 88 percent of the 2,450 hours of programming on ETV was domestically produced, while in Finland the share of domestic programs was only about 60 percent. Almost all foreign television programs imported to the Estonian SSR originated from the Eastern bloc, mainly from the GDR and Czechoslovakia (Nordenstreng and Varis 1974: 13–14, 25). During the first years of broadcasting, Soviet television enjoyed relative freedom due to technological and institutional shortcomings in the Soviet system (Roth-Ey 2011: 212). Yet generally speaking, the Soviet television system was based, much like radio before it, on strict censorship and party control.

Some 85 kilometers north of Tallinn, Finnish decision-makers in Helsinki were considerably slower to embrace the potential of the emerging new medium. In terms of television broadcasting, Finland was initially at the receiving end. The first regular television programs transmitted in Finland in the mid-1950s came from the Soviet Union, as its broadcasts could be received in southeastern Finland. The threat of Soviet television expanding to Finland played a major role in pressuring Finnish politicians to speed up the nation's transition to the television era (Newcomb 2004: 1; Zilliacus 1981: 13; Sisättö 1981: 31). The national broadcasting company, *Yleisradio* (YLE), began transmitting regular television broadcasts in 1958. As in other Western European countries, YLE belonged to a centralized system that was under parliamentary oversight during the Cold War. In this period, YLE provided two channels for viewing audiences, broadcasting primarily in Finnish but also in Swedish, Finland's second official language. As YLE was a public service, the objective of the television programming policy was initially to provide unbiased and neutral reporting that tended to be superficial in nature, avoiding analysis and assessment (Kortti 2007: 118; Pernaa 2009: 27–31). Eventually, this was replaced by the more investigative, radical and opinionated "informative programming policy" of the late 1960s, which was in turn displaced by the more moderate and polyphonic period of "normalization" of the early 1970s (Newcomb 2004: 3–4; Salokangas 1996: 249, 261–265; Repo et al. 1967: 12–13). Regardless of this evolving programming policy, Finnish television adopted and sustained a careful stance when reporting on Soviet affairs, due to the proximity of the Soviet Union (Uskali 2003; Lounasmeri 2013).

Despite the divisions characteristic of the Cold War, the distinction between the media audiences separated by the Iron Curtain was not necessarily as rigid as is generally thought. In some cases, broadcasts from the opposite side of the Iron Curtain were eagerly consumed and even preferred over Soviet programs, which were widely perceived as unreliable. This was particularly the case in the Estonian SSR, which enjoyed a special relationship with Finland in this respect. Despite the existence of the Iron Curtain, geographical proximity and the kindred Finno-Ugric languages made it relatively easy for Estonians to follow Finnish radio (Mertelsmann 2012) and, later, television. With slight modifications, Estonian television sets were able to receive Finnish television broadcasts in northern parts of the country from 1958 onwards and more clearly and reliably after the erection of a new powerful TV transmitter near Helsinki in 1971 (Heli Pikk, interview). Also, perhaps surprisingly, there was official cooperation in terms of broadcasting. In 1966, the sole Finnish commercial television company, MTV, and ETV started production of a series of quiz shows entitled "Contest between Neighbors" (*Naapurivisa – Sõprusvõistlus*), shot by turns in both Tallinn and Helsinki and conducted in both Estonian and Finnish. The Finnish-Estonian show became highly successful, and for this reason was shut down by Moscow in 1970 (Intervjuu Hardi Tiidusega, 1988). It is no wonder Finnish programming enjoyed huge popularity on the other side of the Gulf of Finland, dwarfing Soviet broadcasts in popularity. Finnish television provided a "window to the West," and in this way, support for Estonian's struggle against communist rule (Kilmi 2009; Lepp and Pantti 2012: 77; Newcomb 2004: 5).

3   Water Pollution Issues on Finnish Television

Water pollution issues were covered on YLE's television channels throughout the research period, starting immediately in 1958, the first year of regular programming. The first two issues to feature were the radioactive fallout from nuclear weapons testing and marine oil pollution. Radioactive fallout was arguably the first truly global environmental concern to emerge after the Second World War (McCormick 1989: 51–55); considering the proximity of a Soviet testing site in the Arctic Ocean, it is no wonder that the issue figured prominently on Finnish television. In the late 1950s, coverage focused on reporting about the ongoing nuclear test ban negotiations being held by the opposing parties in the Cold War (1958b, 1958c). The test ban negotiations fell apart in 1961, leading the Soviet Union to once more accelerate its testing program, which climaxed in the detonation of the largest nuclear explosive in history, the 50–58 megaton "Tsar Bomb," in the Arctic in late October. These developments were reflected in television reporting, which now concentrated on soothing an alarmed public by showcasing the introduction and operation of the newly established national radiation monitoring system, while reporting that the radiation peaks had "only lasted for a few hours and were of harmless intensity" (1961c, 1961d). The Partial Test Ban Treaty prohibiting all atmospheric nuclear weapons testing was eventually signed in 1963. The treaty was celebrated on television as one of the watershed events of the year (1963a), marking the subsequent disappearance of the issue from Finnish television screens.

Finnish television coverage on marine oil pollution issues focused on major oil accidents; very few reports (1959a, 1959c) addressed the intentional discharge of waste oil, which was constant but difficult to document (Laakkonen and Lehmuskoski 2005). Reporting on marine oil accidents on Finnish television started in 1958, when an YLE camera crew documented the running aground of the Norwegian tanker *M/T Siranda* off the coast of southwestern Finland (1958a) and continued in the following years (1960, 1961b). Early reporting on marine oil accidents concentrated primarily on the incidents themselves and their immediate causes and consequences. A broader discussion concerning questions of responsibility, alternative solutions, and the role of the national oil company did not begin until after the *Torrey Canyon* disaster in England and three major domestic oil accidents in the late 1960s (1969a). Television coverage of marine oil pollution focused on the national oil company during the first half of the 1970s. The company's introduction of the first supertanker into the shallow waters of the Baltic Sea in 1970 provoked widespread opposition and fears of the "death" of the entire body of water (1970a, 1970l). The company's next major undertaking, a plan to build a new oil refinery near the oldest zoological field station in the Baltic Sea region, only served to fuel these fears and arouse opposition among the locals (1970m, 1971c, 1971d, 1971e, 1972c, 1973a; Kuisma 1997, 470–475, 479–484).

Consistent with reactions in other Finnish media, Rachel Carson's international bestseller *Silent Spring* failed to provoke any clear response on Finnish television (cf. Laurila 2007: 9; Suhonen 1994: 84). Despite a few programs referring to the plight and mass deaths of birds of prey (1961a, 1964b, 1965a), only one episode of a popularized science program dealing with the dangers of insecticides indicated awareness of Carson's work and the discussion it had stimulated, albeit neither was mentioned explicitly (1965b).[2] The turning point for the Finnish public debate on toxins came in spring 1967, when a current affairs program revealed that mercury levels had been detected in Finnish fish that exceeded the safety limits established by the World Health Organization (1967). The revelation was followed by a public uproar that resulted in a collapse in fish sales, after which the Minister of Agriculture requested that televised coverage of the mercury issue be dropped. The director of YLE repelled these attempts at censorship (Repo 1975: 218), and the issue was consistently covered on television in subsequent years, gaining fresh force from news of the Minamata mercury disaster in Japan, the subsequent clash between Finnish conservationists and health officials known as the "mercury war" (Nuorteva 1976), and the plight of mercury-poisoned seals (1968a, 1968b, 1968c, 1968d, 1970a, 1970d, 1970k, 1971f, 1972b, 1972d, 1972g, 1974b).

Industry, especially the chemical forest industry (the pulp and paper industries), was by far the biggest polluter of Finnish watercourses during the research period (Vesistönsuojelukomitean mietintö 1958: 9). Yet industrial discharge was seldom addressed in the media, especially in towns where companies wielded a strong grip on local newspapers (Louekari 1999: 194; Lahtinen 2005: 68–69). State-owned YLE did not have the same kind of restrictions as the local press, but nevertheless, industrial discharge remained practically

---

2 However, it should be noted that deliberate silence might have been one the reactions Carson's work provoked. Cf. Siiskonen 2002: 18–22.

uncovered until the late 1960s. A few exceptions to the rule exist, most noticeably a 20-minute documentary entitled *Why wastewaters?* broadcast in 1964. The program stated, among other things, that "[Finnish] industry in general approaches wastewater issues with the disdain of the ignorant," for which reason "Finland is gradually turning from the land of a thousand of lakes to the land of a thousand polluted lakes" (1964c). More systematic reporting on industrial water pollution gradually emerged during the mid-1960s. There were a few highly critical programs at the turn of the 1960s–1970s which demanded that the industry acknowledge the environmental damage it was causing and make more significant contributions to environmental protection (1969b, 1970l, 1970j, 1972a). However, it appears that large-scale industry in general and the wood-processing industry in particular got off relatively lightly in the Finnish public debate at the time, despite claims to the contrary (cf. Jensen-Eriksen 2007: 301–302; Nienstedt 1997: 116–121).

Discharges from agriculture, which is presently the biggest polluter of Finnish waterways and the Baltic Sea (Putkuri et al. 2013: 70; HELCOM 2012, 23), were relatively small in the 1950s–1970s. Agricultural nutrient loading, however, was growing rapidly as a result of increasing chemical fertilizer consumption (Niemelä 2008: 212), and the authorities had become aware of its detrimental impacts on waterways by the late 1950s (Vesistönsuojelukomitean mietintö 1958: 65; Leino-Kaukiainen 1999, 66). Curiously enough, the issue was not covered on television at all during the entire research period. This is probably due to the prevailing way of thinking, according to which discharge of nutrients into watercourses was considered a preferable rather than a harmful state of affairs. The thinking was that waterways could be "cultivated" like fields of grain, which meant that their output (i.e., fish stocks), could be increased through the addition of nutrients (Laakkonen and Parpola 2010: 88–89). This is exactly what farmers were instructed to do in a ten-minute educational film broadcast in 1959, *Did you know this about phosphorus?*: "So, go ahead, toss heaps of phosphorus into the water, and before you know it, our lakes will be splashing with fish tails!" (*Tiesittekö tämän fosforista?*, December 29, 1959). The exploitative attitudes towards nature started to become apparent, and discharge of nutrients into watercourses finally began to be regarded as a problem as the 1960s progressed (Laakkonen & Parpola 2010: 90–91). Nonetheless, agricultural pollution problems still did not feature on Finnish television screens. It appears that the problems Finnish agriculture faced at the time and the sympathy the journalists felt for small-time farmers struggling to make ends meet helped protect agriculture from public criticism (Reino Paasilinna, interview).

In addition to the above-mentioned themes, a more comprehensive understanding of water pollution issues and their interdependent relationships as well as their connections to overall degradation of the natural world gradually started to emerge during the 1960s. First, the deteriorating state of Finnish watercourses began to be perceived and represented as a single coherent problem from the early 1960s onwards (1963b, 1964a, 1964c), climaxing in reporting ahead of the signing of the Helsinki Convention by the seven coastal states in 1974 (1971b, 1972f, 1973b, 1974a). After the mid-1960s, water pollution as a whole began to be discussed in conjunction with other issues of degradation of the natural world, bearing witness to the emergence of the environment as a novel umbrella concept under which these various, previously separate issues were dealt with at the turn of the 1960s–1970s. In this respect, the pan-European Nature Conservation Year 1970 can be considered a peak year during which environmental issues, water pollution among them, were widely covered in broader current affairs programs, documentaries and children's programs (1970b, 1970c, 1970e, 1970f, 1970h, 1970i; cf. Suhonen 1994: 84–85). The initial optimism sparked by the dedicated year was, however, replaced by disillusionment as the decade progressed and television began questioning the adequacy of Finnish environmental protection, as can be deduced from program titles such as *Across the country: pollution* (1971h), *What is happening in our waters?* (1972e), *What if Finland becomes infected? Environmental protection 1* (1974d) and *Where will we find the drugs if Finland is infected? Environmental protection 2* (1974e). By 1974, environmental degradation was increasingly presented on Finnish television as endangering not only the well-being of humankind, but also the future of the entire globe (1971g, 1973c, 1973d, 1974c; cf. McCormick 1989: 67–87). Significantly, the then-president of Finland, Urho Kekkonen, stated in his New Year's speech in 1971 that he considered environmental pollution an even greater threat to humankind than the nuclear arms race (1971a).

4 Water Pollution Issues on Estonian Television

Programs broadcast on Estonian television differed considerably from Finnish programs. Some addressed problems such as urban floods caused by broken sewers, but these can hardly be said to be environmental programs (1964, 1965). Consequently, during the first decade of ETV, no programs concerning urban-industrial pollution were transmitted. Marine oil accidents were rare on the Estonian coast due to its depth, soft bottom and comparative ease of navigation. Nevertheless, not a single program reported on national or international oil accidents or spills, including the *Torrey Canyon* catastrophe. The peaceful use of atomic energy in power generation and icebreaking were presented, but not a single program from our source material addressed atom bomb tests anywhere in the world or the international negotiations to stop these tests (1957a, 1959). The Soviet Union was a major consumer of DDT and other agricultural toxins, but none of their environmental impacts were addressed on television. Like Finnish television, Estonian television did not regard the increasing use of artificial fertilizers as a problem for watercourses. Joint efforts to protect the Gulf of Finland from pollution had been initiated in 1968 between the Russian, Estonian and Finnish authorities (Räsänen and Laakkonen 2007a; Räsänen and Laakkonen 2007b). Yet neither this unique cooperation between Eastern and Western Europe during the Cold War nor the signing of the convention for the protection of the Baltic Sea in 1974 was addressed. In short, the environmental record of Soviet television was poor.

This does not, however, mean that there were not any environmental problems in Soviet Estonia that journalists were not aware of them, or that environmental pollution and degradation were completely neglected on television in Soviet Estonia. Convincing proof of this is a color documentary entitled *Nature and man* (*Loodus ja inimine*), which was shown on Estonian television in 1967. This Estonian-language documentary was directed by Mart Port and shot by Toivo Kuzmin. The documentary presented children playing at the seaside, landscape protection areas, smoking chimneys, a landscape of devastation created by the excavation of oil shale, hills of fly ash, saunas on the lakeside, polluted rivers, people fishing, and the biggest polluting chemical plants and forest industries in Soviet Estonia. The end of the film returned to the children playing at the seaside and people rowing on a lake. The visual idea of this documentary was to point out the contradiction between beautiful natural or rural landscapes and the landscapes created by the urban-industrial economy in Soviet Estonia.

This documentary showed that Estonian journalists had travelled through most of Estonia, filmed the worst polluters in the republic, and compiled an impressive overall picture of the state of the environment in Soviet Estonia. They showed all of the republic's major pollution sites except the radioactive waste dump at the seaside near Sillamäe, a closed atomic city that did not exist on maps. This documentary proves that Estonian journalists were perfectly aware of environmental problems in the country, that they were able to shoot relevant material, and that there was at least some freedom to address those problems.

However, ETV saw no successors to Port's outstanding documentary until the 1974 broadcast of *Water ways* (*Vee radadel*), another documentary directed by Kaupo Klooren. In the years that followed, this documentary was succeeded by several others that addressed the pollution of rivers and lakes in Soviet Estonia, such as *Water and Man* (1975a, 1975b, 1976). Programs directly addressing pollution and marine protection were not presented on television until the next decade (1983). Even then, such programs were produced in Russia, not Estonia. For Estonians, who lived by the sea, the sea remained a prohibited zone.

Yet even though Estonians lived in a totalitarian system, they had an alternative, Western source of information – cross-border watching. Soviet authorities were unable to block transmission from Finland, and two Finnish television channels (TV1, TV2) were available to 40 percent of the ethnic Estonians and 70 percent of the rest of the population (Mickiewicz 1988, 21; Paasilinna 1995, 160). By means of Finnish television, Estonians had access to environmental programs, which also featured Estonian experts and Soviet authorities who did not appear on ETV programming (1958a, 1959b, 1963a, 1968e, 1970l).

5   Conclusions

World War II divided the entire Baltic Sea Region into two distinctly different zones. This division was also evident on both sides of the Gulf of Finland. Estonia was subsumed by the totalitarian Soviet system, while Finland managed to preserve her capitalist economic and democratic political system. The countries' television broadcasting systems were divided accordingly. Finland adopted a Western broadcasting organization and technology, while Estonia was forced to adopt Soviet management and technical systems.

These divisions were further reflected in the environmental contents of each nation's programming. Finnish television addressed the water pollution issues caused by atom bomb tests, marine oil accidents, toxic substances, and industrial discharge, and also reported on international problems and protection initiatives. Hence, it is fairly safe to argue that the Finnish public was reasonably well-informed on the state of the aquatic environment relatively early on. In contrast, ETV showed only a couple of programs that covered national water pollution issues in the Estonian SSR. These programs did not address any international pollution issues.

These few exceptions showed that despite Soviet broadcasting policies, Estonian TV journalists were aware of water pollution problems in their country and wanted to address them at an early stage. And despite the fact that water pollution issues were covered on Finnish television relatively frequently and extensively, it should be noted that even in this democratic society, TV journalism faced a variety of restrictions affecting its environmental reporting. Based on our findings, it appears evident that programming policies in particular had a heavy influence on which environmental issues were covered on television, and how. Above all, the influential private forest industry was long protected from public criticism.

Yet in practice, environmental broadcasting in the region of the Gulf of Finland was not completely black-and-white, because in the end, almost half of all Estonians had access to Finnish television programs. Due to the long historical ties between the two nations, nearly all Estonians were able to understand at least something of the Finnish programs. Many Estonians actually became fluent in Finnish and were well informed of sociopolitical conditions in Finland. Despite the existence of the Iron Curtain, in many cases Estonians had access to Western environmental news, magazines and documentaries.

The beginnings of environmental reporting in both Eastern and Western Europe have long been unexplored. Our comparative study shows that environmental reporting started in Finnish television immediately after broadcasting commenced, even though the number of programs long remained modest. It has often been asserted that environmental issues were not addressed in public in the Soviet Union until the period of *glasnost,* or openness, in the late 1980s. Our study shows that this is actually not true, despite the fact that environmental programming was extremely rare on ETV until 1974, after which the number of environmentally themed shows gradually started to grow.

It can be argued that WWII and the subsequent Cold War framed two different socio-political realities for nations living around the Gulf of Finland. Nevertheless, the long historical ties between Estonians and Finns provided a common cultural frame that enabled cross-border exchange of information by means of television, even at the height of the Cold War. In terms of program content and popularity with audiences, the television tower in Helsinki won the war between the two towers. From an environmental point of view, the Gulf of Finland became one of the first places in Europe where the Iron Curtain was breached.

Bibliography

Primary Sources
Finnish Television

Kamerakierros 143, September 24, 1958a.
Kamerakierros 154, October 14, 1958b.

Kamerakierros 164, October 31, 1958c.
Kamerakierros 390, January 7, 1959a.
Kamerakierros 357, November 20, 1959b.
Aktuellt, November 11, 1959c.
Kamerakierros 357, November 20, 1959d.
Tiesittekö tämän fosforista?, December 29, 1959e.
Kamerakierros 399, January 20, 1960.
Kamerakierros 626, January 3, 1961a.
Finlandia-katsaus, November, 1961b.
Kamerakierros 835. Uutiset, November 3, 1961c.
Kamerakierros 838. Uutiset, November 7, 1961d.
Tapahtui vuonna 1963, December 31, 1963a.
Kun järvemme likaantuvat, May 14, 1963b.
Suojele vesiä, April 28, 1964a.
Hätähuuto viimeisten puolesta, May 29, 1964b.
Miksi likavesiä? October 1, 1964c.
Mustaa valkoisella, May 5, 1965a.
Tiedettä jokamiehelle: Elämänmyrkyt, June 10, 1965b.
Keskiviikko, May 5, 1967.
Silmätikku, May 7, 1968a.
Nous hauki puuhun laulamaan, September 3, 1968b.
Sju dagar, October 5, 1968c.
Me kysymme, October 21, 1968d.
Simätikku, June 12, 1968e.
Meriturvallisuus 1: Jos laineilla on öljyä, September 24, 1969a.
Me kysymme, October 18, 1969b.
Ajankohtainen kakkonen, January 17, 1970a.
Hyvää huomenta, February 2, 1970b.
Livsmiljö i fara, March 4, 1970c.
Ajankohtainen kakkonen, March 14, 1970d.
Barnförbjudet, March 18, 1970e.
Nuotta, April 21, 1970f.
Ajankuva, May 21, 1970g.
Jo viisi vuotta myöhemmin, September 9, 1970h.
Ajankohtainen kakkonen, October 10, 1970i.
Elintärkeät saasteet, October 15, 1970j.
Kamera kiertää, November 11, 1970k.
Jos vedet kuolevat, June 1, 1970l.
Zoom, November 20, 1970m.

Tasavallan presidentin uuden vuoden puhe, January 1, 1971a.
Itämeren saastuminen, January 27, 1971b.
Från dag till dag, February 6, 1971c.
Från dag till dag, February 10, 1971d.
Ylimäärä, April 14, 1971e.
Viisari, October 20, 1971f.
Sunnuntain vieras, November 21, 1971g.
Yli maan: saaste, November 26, 1971h.
Ajankohtainen kakkonen, June 6, 1972a.
I blixtbelysning, June 20, 1972b.
Zoom, June 22, 1972c.
Slagrutan, August 8, 1972d.
Mitä tapahtuu vesissämme?, August 21, 1972e.
Ajankohtainen kakkonen, November 11, 1972f.
Kamera kiertää, November 17, 1972g.
Ajankohtainen kakkonen, February 6, 1973a.
Uudenmaan aluevartti: Suomenlahti – Särkyneiden toiveitten lahti, February 17, 1973b.
Livsmiljö i fara, April 6, 1973c.
Livsmiljö i fara, April 13, 1973d.
A-Studio, March 15, 1974a.
Ajankohtainen kakkonen, March 26, 1974b.
Tulevaisuusshokki, May 29, 1974c.
Tulehtuuko Suomi? Ympäristönsuojelu 1, October 22, 1974d.
Mistä lääkkeet, jos Suomi tulehtuu? Ympäristönsuojelu 2, October 23, 1974e.

Estonian Television
Nõukogude Eesti nr. 13, Kunstiliste ja Kroonikafilmide Tallinna Kinostuudio, 1957a.
Turbamulla komposteerimine põlluväetiseks Märjamaa raj Tasuja kolhoosis, Tallinna Kinostuudio, 1957b.
Nõukogude Eesti nr. 42, Kunstiliste ja Kroonikafilmide Tallinna Kinostuudio, 1959.
Nõukogude Eesti nr. 27, Tallinnfilm, 1964.
Nõukogude Eesti nr. 4, 1965.
Naapurivisa. Sõprusvõistlus. 1966. Helsingis: https://arhiiv.err.ee/vaata/55588.
Loodus ja inimine, Tallinnfilm, 1967a.
Läänemeri-rahumeri, Tallinnfilm, 1967b.
Vee radadel, Eesti Maanparandusprojekt, 1974.
Vesi ja inimine, Eesti Maanparandusprojekt, 1975a.
Janu vee ääres, Tallinnfilm, 1975b.
Tagastatud väärtused, Tallinnfilm, 1976.
Mere saastamise vältimine, Tallinnfilm, 1983.

Interviews

Reino Paasilinna, former director of YLE, interviewed March 1, 2012 in Helsinki by Otto Tähkäpää.

Heli Pikk, director of the ERR radio and TV archives, e-mail interview February 22, 2015 by Simo Laakkonen.

Secondary Sources

Brain, Stephen. 2014. 'The Appeal of Appearing Green: Soviet-American Ideological Competition and Cold War Environmental Diplomacy.' *Cold War History* 16(4): 443–462.

Deacon, David, Michael Pickering, Peter Golding, and Graham Murdock. 2007. *Researching Communications: A Practical Guide to Methods in Media and Culture Analysis.* London: Hodder Education.

Dennis, Everette E., George Gerbner and Yassen N. Zassoursky (eds.). 1991. *Beyond the Cold War: Soviet and American Media Images.* London: Sage.

Djerf-Pierre, Monika. 2013. 'The Greening of the News. The institutionalization of "the environment" in television news reporting 1961–1973' in Djerf-Pierre, Monika and Ekström, Mats (eds.) *A History of Swedish Broadcasting. Communicative ethos, genres and institutional change.* Gothenburg: NORDICOM and University of Gothenburg: 283–306.

Djerf-Pierre, Monika. 1996. *Gröna nyheter. Miljöjournalistiken i televisionens nyhetssändningar 1961–1994.* Göteborg: Institutionen för journalistik och masskommunikation.

Elmgren, Ragnar. 2001. 'Understanding Human Impact on the Baltic Ecosystem: Changing Views in Recent Decades.' *Ambio* 30(4–5): 222–231.

HELCOM 2012. *The Fifth Baltic Sea Pollution Load Compilation (PLC-5) – an Executive Summary. Balt. Sea Environ. Proc. No. 128A.* HELCOM: Vantaa.

Intervjuu Hardi Tiidusega, 1988. Soomekeelne saade. Naapurivisa. ERR Arhiiv. Eesti Raadio 1988. Online at: https://arhiiv.err.ee/vaata/soomekeelne-saade-naapurivisa-intervjuu-hardi-tiidusega (consulted 02.04.2016).

Jensen-Eriksen, Niklas. 2007: *Läpimurto. Metsäteollisuuden kasvun, integraation ja kylmän sodan Euroopassa 1950–1973.* Helsinki: Suomalaisen Kirjallisuuden Seura.

Johnson, A. Ross 2010. *Radio Free Europe and Radio Liberty: The CIA years and Beyond.* Washington D.C. and Stanford: Woodrow Wilson Center Press and Stanford University Press.

Kortti, Jukka. 2007. *Näköradiosta digiboksiin. Suomalaisen television sosiokulttuurinen historia.* Helsinki: Gaudeamus.

Kilmi, Jaak. 2009. *Disco and Atomic War.* An Estonian documentary film produced by Icarus Films.

Kuisma, Markku. 1997. *Kylmä sota, kuuma öljy. Neste, Suomi ja kaksi Eurooppaa.* Porvoo: WSOY.

Laakkonen, Simo and Lehmuskoski, Antti. 2005. 'Musta meri. Öljyonnettomuuksien ympäristöhistoriaa Suomessa vuoteen 1969.' *Historiallinen aikakausikirja* 103(4): 381–396.

Laakkonen, Simo and Parpola, Antti. 2010. 'Rehevöitymiskäsitysten historiaa' in Bäck, Saara et al. (eds.) *Itämeren tulevaisuus*. Tampere: Gaudeamus: 82–99.

Laakkonen, Simo and Tucker, Richard. 2012. 'War and Natural Resource in History: Introduction' in Agnoletti, Mauro, and Corona, Gabriella (eds.) *Global Environment* 10: 8–15.

Lahtinen, Rauno. 2005. *Ympäristökeskustelua kaupungissa. Kaupunkiympäristö ja ympäristöasenteet Turussa 1890–1950*. Turku: Turun Yliopisto.

Laine, Timo. 2014. *Torakoita ja panssarivaunuja. Silminnäkijänä hajoavassa Neuvostoliitossa*. Kustannusosakeyhtiö Tammi: Helsinki.

Laurila, Sari. 2007. 'Itämeren ympäristötutkimus Suomessa ennen 1960-lukua.' *Historiallinen aikakausikirja* 105(1): 9–21.

Leino-Kaukiainen, Pirkko. 1999. 'Vesistöistä viemäreiksi. Vesiensuojelu Suomessa 1945–1970' in Laakkonen, Simo & Laurila, Sari and Rahikainen, Marjatta (eds.) *Harmaat aallot. Ympäristönsuojelun tulo Suomeen*. Helsinki: Suomen Historiallinen Seura: 33–67.

Lepp, Annika and Pantti, Mervi. 2013. 'Window to the West: Memories of Watching Finnish Television in Estonia During the Soviet Period.' *Journal of European Television History and Culture* 2(3): 77–87.

Louekari, Sami. 1999. '"Meidän saamaton Ateenamme." Ympäristöasenteet Jyväskylässä' in Laakkonen, Simo, Sari Laurila, and Marjatta Rahikainen (eds.) *Harmaat aallot. Ympäristönsuojelun tulo Suomeen*. Helsinki: Suomen Historiallinen Seura: 189–205.

Lounasmeri, Lotta. 2013. 'Through Rose or Blue and White Glasses? Decades of News about Soviet Union in the Finnish Press.' *Nordicom Review*, 34 (1): 105–123.

Lyytinen, Eino. 1996. 'Perustamisesta talvisotaan' in Lyytinen, Eino and Vihavainen, Timo (eds.) *Yleisradion historia. 1. osa, 1926–1949*. Helsinki: Yleisradio.

McCormick, John. 1989. *Reclaiming Paradise: The Global Environment Movement*. Bloomington and Indianapolis: Indiana University Press.

McNeill, John R. and Unger, Corinna R. 2013. *Environmental Histories of the Cold War*. Cambridge: Cambridge University Press.

Mertelsmann, Olaf. 2012. *Everyday Life in Stalinist Estonia* (Tartu Historical Studies vol. 2). Frankfurt am Main and New York: Peter Lang.

Mickiewicz, Ellen. 1988. *Split Signals: Television and Politics in Soviet Union*. New York: Oxford University Press.

Mickiewicz, Ellen. 1999. *Changing Channels: Television and the Changing Struggle for Power in Russia*. Durham and London: Duke University Press.

Misiunas, Romuald and Taagepera, Rein. 1993. *The Baltic States: The Years of Dependence, 1940–1990*. London, Berkeley, and Hurst: University of California Press.

Newcomb, Horace. 2004. 'Finland' in Newcomb, Horace (ed.) *Encyclopedia of Television* (2nd edition): 1–6. Online at: http://www.uta.fi/cmt/en/contact/staff/kaarlenordenstreng/publications/finland_rev1.pdf (consulted 02.04.2016).

Nienstedt, Sirje. 1997. *Ympäristöpolitiikan alku. Ympäristönsuojelun tulo Suomen valtakunnalliseen politiikkaan 1960- ja 1970-lukujen vaihteessa*. Turku: Turun yliopiston poliittisen historian laitos.

Niemelä, Jari. 2008. *Talonpoika toimessaan. Suomen maatalouden historia*. Helsinki: Suomalaisen Kirjallisuuden Seura.

Nordenstreng, Kaarle and Varis, Tapio. 1974: *Television traffic – a one-way street? A survey and analysis of the international flow of television programme material*. Paris: UNESCO.

Nuorteva, Pekka. 1976. *Elohopea Suomen luonnossa ja hallintokoneistossa*. Porvoo: Werner Söderström Osakeyhtiö.

Paasilinna, Reino. 1995. *Glasnost and Soviet television: A study of Soviet mass media and its role in society from 1985–1991*. Helsinki: YLE.

Paatero, Jussi and Hatakka, Juha. 2011. 'Ydinkokeiden vaikutukset ilmakehässä' in Paatero, Jussi and Ylikangas, Irma (eds.) *Ydinkokeista Fukushimaan – keinotekoinen radioaktiivisuus ympäristössä*. Ylöjärvi: Suojelu, pelastus ja turvallisuus ry: 23–28.

Pavlínek, Petr and Pickles, John. 2000. *Environmental Transitions: Transformation and Ecological Defense in Central and Eastern Europe*. London and New York: Routledge.

Pernaa, Ville. 2009: *Uutisista, hyvää iltaa. Ylen tv-uutiset ja yhteiskunta 1959–2009*. Hämeenlinna: Karttakeskus.

Putkuri, Eija, Matti Lindholm, and Aino Peltonen. 2014. *The state of the environment in Finland 2013*. Helsinki: SYKE Publications 1.

Rahvusarhiiv. Online at: www.ra.ee (consulted 02.04.2016).

Repo, Eino S. 1975. *Pihlajanmarjat. Muistelua vuosilta 1939–1969*. Helsinki: Weilin+Göös.

Repo, Eino S., Kari Ilmonen, N.B. Storbom, Mauno Tamminen, and Ville Zilliacus. 1967. *Yleisradion suunta. Yleisradiotoiminnan tehtävät ja tavoitteet*. Helsinki: Weilin+Göös.

Roth-Ey, Kristin. 2011. *Moscow Prime Time: How the Soviet Union Built the Media Empire That Lost the Cultural Cold War*. New York: Cornell University Press.

Räsänen, Tuomas and Simo Laakkonen. 2007a. 'Cold War and the Environment: The Role of Finland in International Environmental Politics in the Baltic Sea Region.' *Ambio* 36(2–3): 223–230a.

Räsänen, Tuomas and Simo Laakkonen. 2007b. 'Suomen ja Neuvostoliiton ympäristöyhteistyön alkuvaiheet.' *Historiallinen aikakauskirja* 1: 43–56b.

Räsänen, Tuomas and Simo Laakkonen. 2008. 'Institutionalization of an International Environmental Policy Regime: the Helsinki Convention, Finland and Cold War' in Joas, Marko, Detlef Jahn, and Kristine Kern (eds.) *Governing a Common Sea: Environmental Policies in the Baltic Sea Region*. London: Earthscan.

Räsänen, Tuomas. 2012. 'Converging Environmental Knowledge: Re-evaluating the Birth of Modern Environmentalism in Finland.' *Environment and History* 18(1): 159–181.

Salokangas, Raimo. 1996: *Yleisradion historia 2. osa. 1949–1996. Aikansa oloinen.* Porvoo: WSOY.

Savisaar, Edgar. 2005. *Viron vaaran vuodet.* Tammi: Helsinki.

Siiskonen, Harri. 2002: '*Silent Spring* and the Nordic Agricultural Magazines.' *Scandinavian Economic History Review* 50(1): 7–23.

Sisättö, Seppo. 1981. 'Televisio ja Suomen viestintäpolitiikka,' in Sinkko, Risto (ed.) *Televisio ja suomalainen.* Espoo: Weilin+Göös: 31–75.

Suhonen, Pertti. 1994: *Mediat, me ja ympäristö.* Tampere: Hanki ja jää.

Uskali, Turo. 2003. *Älä kirjoita itseäsi ulos. Suomalaisen Moskovan-kirjeenvaihtajuuden alkutaival 1957–1975.* Jyväskylä Studies in the Humanities, 6. Online at: https://jyx.jyu.fi/dspace/bitstream/handle/123456789/13417/9513915433.pdf?sequence=1 (consulted 02.04.2016).

Yurovsky, A. Ya. and R.A. Boretsky. 1966. *Osnovy televizionnoi zhurnalistiki.* Moskva: Izdatelstvo Moskovskogo Universiteta.

Zilliacus, Ville. 1981: 'Esipuhe' in Sinkko, Risto (ed.) *Televisio ja suomalainen.* Espoo: Weilin+Göös: 9–17.

Vesistönsuojelukomitean mietintö. Komiteamietintö no. 13 – 1958. Helsinki: Valtioneuvoston kirjapaino.

CHAPTER 11

Who's Framing Whom? Surrealism and Science in the Documentaries of Jean Painlevé

Kathryn St. Ours

Abstract

French scientist and filmmaker Jean Painlevé made his first documentaries in the nineteen-twenties, when surrealism was emerging as an avant-garde movement of intellectual, artistic and literary scope. Unlike other surrealists opposed to rational scientific methods, Painlevé demonstrates that empirical research can stimulate human imagination and creative expression by revealing the fantastic and mysterious aspects of nature. Painlevé's documentaries resort to "nonscientific" framings and are key to his popular success. Whereas the most famous surrealist films are overwhelmingly anthropocentric, Painlevé frames animals in order to foster knowledge and genuine appreciation of the creatures in and of themselves. His documentaries adopt a hybrid approach. On one hand, his films contain facts and figures; on the other, they make a clear appeal to emotion through music, voice-over, visual imagery, and humor. As a result, such shorts as *The Octopus* (1927), *Sea Urchins* (1928), *and Hyas and Stenorynchus* (1927) were well received in Parisian avant-garde movie theaters. By means of anthropomorphism and reference to myth and legend, *The Love Life of the Octopus* (1967), *The Seahorse* (1933), *and The Vampire* (1945) suggest that humans are in a sense framed by nature, that is, that our imagination may have an empirical basis.

1   Introduction

The unusual trajectory of zoologist and scientific documentarian Jean Painlevé (1902–1989) deserves a place in any discussion devoted to the framing of nature. First and foremost a scientist with an impressive academic background,[1] he created over 200 films during his long career and routinely made three versions of the same film corresponding to three ways of framing – one for researchers, another for educators and a third for popular audiences. Focusing primarily on marine fauna, these documentaries were shot within his laboratories in

---

[1]   Painlevé received degrees in physics, chemistry and biology from the Sorbonne in 1924 (MacDonald 2009a).

Roscoff, Brittany or in Paris and then on-site in the Atlantic Ocean once the adequate technology became available.

Early in his career, the nonconformist Painlevé's participation in the artistic avant-garde of nineteen-twenties Paris is particularly obvious in his documentaries targeting the general public. Collaborating with such figures as Antonin Artaud, Ivan Goll, Man Ray or Salvador Dalí and Luis Buñuel, the keenly intelligent and free-spirited Painlevé produced films in which surrealist aesthetics and scientific explanations are not mutually exclusive. When his first popular silent film *The Octopus* appeared in 1927, the young Painlevé had already played a role in the 1926 absurdist film *The Unknown Woman of Six Days* (based on a play of the same title by Ivan Goll) and in 1927, in *Mathuselah* (alongside Antonin Artaud). A year later, Man Ray incorporated Painlevé's footage of the starfish in *The Sea Star*. The unconventional scientist also allegedly served as chief entomologist (i.e., ant-handler) for Buñuel and Dalí's *An Andalusian Dog* in 1929. Contemporaneously, many of his silent films in black and white such as *The Octopus, Hyas and Stenorynchus* (sea crabs), *The Daphnia, or Sea Urchins* were, in fact, well received in Parisian avant-garde movie theaters because of their abstract, dreamlike imagery. Audiences were also fascinated by the strange and mysterious creatures, normally hidden from sight, viewed on screen for the first time.

This thumbnail sketch of the early period in Painlevé's career serves to affirm his nonconformist fancy for "non-scientific" film techniques, while explaining his take on genre:

> In the general-audience films, my goal was not outright didactic, I was applying the definition that I have always upheld, that is, one third reality and if possible new knowledge; one third to communicate something serious in a humorous way by means of contrast and artistry – mesmerizing or poetic – but all that has nothing to do with the scientific aspect. And then one third devoted to justifying the film: why the audience should watch.
> MICHEL n.p.

In other words, the mainstream scientific documentary is not merely a research tool that extends human knowledge by means of empirical observation. It also constitutes a *mise en scène* of science; cinematic and aesthetic techniques intentionally frame the viewer's responses. Thus, Painlevé's popular scientific shorts are not purely denotative and capable of scientific rigor, but also connotative, instigating associations and attitudes that shape the human/nature relationship.

Interestingly, surrealist cinema's use of scientific footage parallels Painlevé's adoption of para-surrealistic techniques in films of the 1920s. So we shall begin by comparing the distinct ways in which the two tendencies employ signs, aided by the semiotic theories of Charles Sanders Peirce. Application of Peirce's tripartite categorization of signs – iconic (real similarity to object), indexical (some direct relationship between sign and object) or symbolic (arbitrary relationship based on social convention) – reveals that the surrealist interest in the human alone stands in contrast to Painlevé's will to study the animal in and of itself and in relation to *Homo sapiens*, often in defiance of scientific strictures against anthropomorphism. Mainstream surrealism is not so much overtly anti-science as it is unconvinced of the scientific method as a means to attaining a higher plane of reality. Sleep and dreaming are essential and the poet is uniquely equipped to create images inaccessible to science. Painlevé, on the contrary, credits empirical science and the awakened state with the potential to create such images. In actual fact, the parasurrealist's methods and beliefs are perhaps more in line with the principle of communicating vessels, relying on a constant exchange between reality (science) and the imagination (poetry) in equal measure, than those of the mainstream surrealists.

In Painlevé's films of the middle period (1930–60), the tendency to anthropomorphize can once again be understood with reference to Peirce's theories concerning the pre-linguistic and extra-cultural dimensions of animal behavior, fundamental to his sense of semiotic naturalism or pansemiotism (all of nature perfused with signs). Peirce's semiotic triad of signifier (representamen) / signified (object) / interpretant (the understanding the interpreter has of the relation of the signifier-object relation) particularly emphasizes the ways in which a sign signifies its object in order to generate and shape the meaning derived by the viewer. The content/meaning dyad is rejected in order to highlight interpretation as an active process, as semiosis in the proper sense. Indeed, the meaning of a sign is not contained within it but arises in its interpretation.

As such, Peirce's semiotic theory has particular potential for the analysis of Painlevé's popular documentaries as scientifico-artistic hybrids that explicitly mediate the viewers' emotions and thoughts through the framing of signs. Consequently, the question "who is framing whom?" allows for multiple answers. From the technical standpoint, for example, the filmmaking (subject) frames the animal (object); on the other hand, oftentimes the documentarist's work (object) depends on unexpected or unpredictable animal (subject) behaviors, for which the cameraman must patiently wait. In addition, if some signs have a pre-linguistic origin, there may be a link between empirical phenomena and the human imagination. Peirce's extralinguistic sense of semiosis emerges from his early twentieth-century writings and correspondence.[2] Similarly, Painlevé suggests that human myths and legends may have an objective basis, that is to say, that our faculty of imagining is in a sense framed by nature.

2 André Breton's Surrealism

In 1924, two competing surrealist manifestos appear. By far the most famous, André Breton's discourse rails against the realistic attitude, informative and positivistic thinking, and the reign of logic. Surrealism is "psychic automatism in its pure state, by which one proposes to express – verbally, by means of the written word, or in any other manner – the actual functioning of thought" (Breton 1946: 24). Accordingly, the Bretonian surrealist method of creation must be automatic, unhindered by reason or any type of moral or aesthetic agenda. Artistic endeavors must proceed without any set plan, consumed by an irrational fever and indifferent to results. Perforce the new language of cinema is a medium considered to be capable of objectifying intense psychic forces. Through montage, dissolve, use of filters, of accelerated or slow motion, for example, cinematic signs combine to sublimate material reality and put the viewer in touch with forces that escape consciousness. In the cases studied here, early surrealist films make use of unedited scientific sequences in order to release the creative powers of the human imagination.

Man Ray's short *The Sea Star* (1928) actually includes a forty-second clip from Painlevé's documentary devoted to the starfish. The framework for this surrealist creation is in fact a poem by Robert Desnos, inspired in turn by a starfish in a jar purchased at an antique shop. According to the poet, the preserved creature perfectly crystalizes a lost love while objectifying a beautiful and moving memory.[3] Man Ray's use of scientific footage seeks to blur the distinction between present and past, lived experience and memory, reality and dream. Although Painlevé's live creature appears only once amidst other recurring shots of its mummified counterpart, the contrast is striking. Indeed, the clarity and definition of the scientific sequence stands in stark opposition to an otherwise aesthetically "fuzzy" film completely shot through a

---

2 As Peirce put it in an unpublished manuscript: "The action of a sign generally takes place between two parties, the utterer and the interpreter. They need not be persons [...] every sign certainly conveys something of the general nature of thought, if not from a mind, yet from a general repository of ideas, or significant forms [...]." (qtd. in Corrington: 163).

3 Man Ray's ability to provide an utterly flattering and moving image of Desnos himself and his dreams signified for the latter the triumph of artistry over technique (Cineclub de Caen).

jelly-covered lens. This series of frames within frames – from the lost love, to the poem, to the preserved starfish, to the real starfish, to the film – formalize and reactivate the affective charge of the original recollection. So whereas the documentary accents the starfish as an iconic sign, the surrealist text highlights its symbolic quality.

Similarly, Buñuel and Dalí's *An Andalusian Dog* (1929) contains several frames of a live sea urchin that materializes from a handful of ants and then metamorphoses into a woman's underarm hair by means of dissolves. Throughout the film, characters, objects, discreet scenes and body parts echo one another by means of analogy, metonymy or similarity; the iconic, indexical and symbolic sign functions are not mutually exclusive. The indistinct frontiers between fiction and reality seem reminiscent of an oneiric sequence where entrancing forms are coupled with unsettling and mysterious content. The viewer is literally invited to open her eyes (when the protagonist's ocular globe is sliced with a razor!) to the strange, symbolic, and yet transformative power of images, of which Painlevé's underwater creature is but one example. Here again, however, the scientific image is framed and dissolved within a surrealistic exploration of the unconscious.

One final example from the surrealist bestiary comes from *The Age of Gold* (1930) – actually a sort of sequel to *An Andalusian Dog* – the first three and a half minutes of which set the tone for the rest of the film. The opening sequence and accompanying intertitles depict the characteristics and habits of the scorpion: friend of the dark, inhabitant of torrid regions, this anti-social and solitary predator brandishes pincers and a venomous stinger located at the end of its tail. Close-ups of both anatomical parts are included and the segment ends once the scorpion has killed a rat many times its size. Such iconic images of the scorpion abruptly transition to the on-screen words "a few hours later" and to the surreal portrayal of strained sexual relationships in the face of bourgeois mores. Does the factual information about the scorpion serve any other purpose than to frame the subsequent narrative within an atmosphere of tension, conflict, and repressed impulses? Is the scorpion essentially a symbol, then, the elicitor of affective responses?

In the end, shots of the sea urchin, the starfish or the scorpion within surrealist film are meant to serve neither the interests of the animal *per se* nor those of science. In this sense, therefore, these authentic, tangible, living beings might be considered surrealist objects, that is, natural objects that undergo a role change and which, through framing, are intended to unlock human drives and to explore them uncensored (Breton 1965: 131). Placing an ordinary object in an unusual context de-familiarizes it and heightens our sense of the marvelous. The dominant discourse in surrealist cinema of the nineteen-twenties frames scientific images as mere muses for a preeminently irrational freedom. Iconic signs take a back seat to their indexical or symbolic counterparts.

Thus, despite Breton's familiarity with Freud's psychoanalytic theory as a rational way to study the irrational – his initial writings appear in French translation in 1921 and *The Interpretation of Dreams* in 1925 – the Austrian doctor fails to take the French poet seriously when the two meet in Vienna in 1921. According to Freud, Bretonian surrealism wrongly intends to bypass the constraints of the superego in order to liberate people from societal and political taboos; on the other hand, the psychoanalyst defies the poet to interpret dreams as effectively as would a scientist. Poetry and science – a way of life versus a therapy – are therefore at odds with one another. Well-known philosopher and psychoanalyst Jean-Bertrand Pontalis mounts a similar case in his essay "Les vases non communicants." He asserts that Breton's experience with psychiatric patients in Saint-Dizier in 1916 converted the surrealist's will to unleash the unconscious into a series of artistic techniques destined to evoke the irrational by means of a movement and techniques intended to enchant, stun, and shock (137).

3   Breton's Nemesis: Ivan Goll

Breton's surrealist manifesto can in many ways be considered a riposte to the one published by Ivan Goll a month earlier the same year in the first and only issue of the review *Surréalisme*.[4] The Goll coterie upholds conscious creation inasmuch as all that an artist creates originates in nature. Art should transcribe empirical events and basic matter, thereby recognizing the primacy of the physical organism. Hence surreality does not derive from the irrational, the occult, or the oneiric but from concrete reality; the surreal is the result of a more direct, more intense excavation of the material world, not liberation from reason. In Painlevé's films, the iconic sign serves to represent the creature accurately and pertinently, but may subsequently attain symbolic or indexical functions when mediated by film techniques such as music, sound effects, voice over, montage, etc. Despite this notable difference between Breton's and Goll's or Painlevé's conceptions of surrealism, all share many of the same general attitudes and favor similar aesthetic techniques. None is a champion of common sense; anti-bourgeois, anti-clerical, eager to shock, their

---

[4]   The Goll group looks to Guillaume Apollinaire, not Breton, as the founder of surrealism. It is, after all, Apollinaire who coins the term in 1917 in a letter to Paul Dermée: "Tout bien examiné, je crois en effet qu'il vaut mieux adopter surréalisme que surnaturalisme que j'avais d'abord employé." (Biro and Passeron: 28).

poetics hinges on weird associations, unexpected juxtapositions, and images of transgression and transformation. A case in point is one of the pieces published in Ivan Goll's review and penned by none other than the iconoclastic Painlevé. Entitled "Neo-zoological Drama," this satirical piece aims to illustrate that scientific observation and empiricism can unlock the uncanny and the mysterious that Breton claims to be the fruit of unconscious activity. Here is an excerpt:

> The plasmodium of the Myxomycetes is so sweet; the eyeless Prorhynchus has the dull color of the born-blind, and its proboscis stuffed with zoochlorel-lae solicits the oxygen of the Frontoniella antypyretica. He carries his pharynx in a rosette, a locomotive requirement, horned, stupid, and not at all calcareous [...]
> qtd. in BELLOWS and MCDOUGALL: 117

Painlevé attains the limits of reason – nonsense, in fact – by means of the scientific description of the mating ritual of the flatworm. The heavily jargonized language is no more than incomprehensible gibberish for the non-initiate, akin to the products of Breton's surrealist automatic writing and drawing experiments. Nonetheless, it is such extreme receptivity to the empirical and the quest for discovery through scientific inquiry and the minute description of natural processes – not chance, hypnosis or dreaming – that can increase our knowledge of the natural world and heighten our curiosity about what lies beyond the currently visible or known. So, whereas Breton invites us to cross into the dangerous waters of the "soluble fish," those territories where the human "soluble in his thought" is free to unfurl the flag of imagination (1946: 37), Painlevé, on the other hand, works and thinks underwater, adopting and inventing scientific and cinematic techniques that promote empirical research. His documentaries are visual avatars of the prose piece just quoted; they deepen our understanding of subaquatic fauna in and of itself but radically highlight esthetics. I now propose to examine three of Painlevé's films with a view to showing how and to what end he weaves avant-garde artistry into his scientific documentaries. Painlevé succeeds in extending the field of human perception by combining mystifying imagery and a de-mystifying positivism.

4   Three Early Silent Films by Painlevé

One of Painlevé's first popular silent films, *The Octopus* (1927), references surrealist symbols in direct as well as oblique ways. Is he debunking Bretonnian surrealism as in "A Neo-zoological Drama?" Whereas Breton explains the marvelous in his 1924 *Manifesto* as a collective revelation able to arouse a sense of the uncanny – such as dolls and mannequins for us moderns (17) – initial images of Painlevé's documentary feature an octopus climbing over a doll and swimming over a human skull. Whereas the surrealist poet describes the state of diving into some random auditory or visual apparition and the subsequent experience of re-emerging, having traced a tree or a wave and perceived the unseen, the para-surrealist documentarian films an octopus falling from a windowsill, a tree and then at last, plunging into the sea. At the very least, these unusual sequences seem to be more typical of the indexical and symbolic signs frequent in surrealist cinema than of the straightforward scientific documentary. And then there are the multiple shots of the ocean. But how many are required? Is the number of such shots – eight in all – not a bit excessive and unnecessary if the point is to remind us of the creature's native habitat? Needless to say, the sea's symbolic presence – the depths of the irrational and unconscious – abounds in the three surrealist films previously discussed.

Notwithstanding his unmistakable surrealist sensibility, Painlevé explores underwater creatures (normally hidden from sight) in an empirical manner. The gaze of the scientist concentrates on the material existence of the octopus by presenting magnified images of the animal's skin cells that purposefully change color depending on the creature's environment, making the octopus a sign-producing subject. Although the documentary is in black and white, the pulsating, rippling epidermis comes alive through shading and nuance. Lest such shots be interpreted as concretizations of a dream state or an invitation to surreal musings, however, intertitles clearly provide scientific data that frame these iconic and indexical images and make it clear that we are not within the realm of the imagination.

Likewise in 1928, Painlevé documents the life of the sea urchin in a manner undoubtedly loathsome to surrealists intrigued by the spiny animal's evocative power in *An Andalusian Dog*. In descriptive fashion, Painlevé first distinguishes between two kinds of sea urchin. Then, following sequences of the locomotion of the creature that would inspire marvel among the non-scientific, the viewer learns that suckers on the tips of the spines are the key to the movement of the rock variety. Furthermore, the documentary explains the self-interment of the sand urchin in terms of its alimentary canal. Indeed, a sense of unexplained mystery is dispelled once the animal is cut open and its digestive tract revealed. The demystified dance-like movements of the sea urchin may still entrance, but not in the non-didactic fashion of Bretonnian surrealism.

Also released in 1928, *The Daphnia* exposes the spectator to a world of abstraction that is actually the real creature magnified 150,000 times. We observe multitudes of Daphnia swarming in pools and streams much like fleas in the air and then zoom into the multidirectional eye, pulsing blood and muscle and serpentine intestine of the specimen. Here, visual poetry in motion provides proof of reality's ability to entrance us and to lead us into unchartered waters. The film's intertitles as indexical signs explain the captivating images without dispelling a sense of the mysterious: "All waters are brimming with Daphnia. [...] Its cyclopean eye bears brilliant crystallins. [...] All Daphnia are female and reproduce without fertilization." (Painlevé 2007, disc 2). In fact, as explained later in "Jean Painlevé au fil de ses films" (Painlevé 2007, disc 3, 28:48), the filmmaker was banking on the parthenogenesis of the Daphnia – asexual reproduction under normal conditions – to hold the interest the nonscientific viewer. Here, the iconicity or indexicality of the animal as sign vehicle or producer i.e., fresh water as signifier of the daphnia and vice versa, generates awe before nature thanks in part to the technique of enlargement.

Painlevé's tendency to re-enchant science remains unabated in the wake of the talkie, in which case he takes full advantage of the power of another indexical sign, namely sound, to frame nature for nonscientific audiences. He dares to deliberately combine cognitive and affective education by means of an explicit interest in the enigmatic and unexpected.

5 Painlevé's General Audience Films of the 1930s–1960s

Advances in technology necessarily transform science as well as the cinema. The so-called New Scientific Spirit formulated in large measure by Gaston Bachelard reframed the notion of reality and of surreality: modern science had undertaken the study of the irrational.[5] Thus surrealism's original rejection of positivism becomes moot; science no longer excludes what it cannot assimilate.[6] The following comment reflects Painlevé's appreciation of surrationalism as poeticized science and/or scientized poetry: "Does the complete understanding of natural phenomena strip away its miraculous qualities? It is

---

5 In *The New Scientific Spirit* (1934) and *The Formation of the Scientific Mind* (1938), Bachelard establishes a new paradigm that would allow the scientific mind to free itself from the epistemological barriers of the past, that is to say, intellectual habits and patterns that prevent science from accounting for inconsistencies and anomalies. In a later work, *The Poetics of Space* (1958), he applies this new paradigm to the study of the human imagination in terms of universal archetypes.

6 In all fairness to Breton, it is necessary to note that he, too, agrees that surrealism needs to be accompanied by a surrationalism. But the means to this end were dreams and poetry, not the scientific documentary (Breton 1965).

certainly a risk. But it should at least maintain all of its poetry, for poetry subverts reason and is never dulled by repetition" (Bellows et al. 2001: 119).

As for the films of Painlevé, the objective and the subjective had always been communicating vessels. Science for him must be a dynamic process whose inquiries develop new habits of mind, for the boundless realm of scientific investigation implies the constant evolution of the researcher's framing of hypotheses. The advent of the talkie heightens Painlevé's tendency to poetize science. It comes as no surprise then, that his popular documentaries of the 1930s–1960s explicitly mediate the viewers' emotions and thoughts through framing devices such as voice-over and music.

The Seahorse (1934) is replete with shots of this vertical fish complemented by the informative comments of a neutral narrative voice: the physical characteristics of the animal, its ability to change color, its anatomical dissimilarity to any other fish. This film is therefore not lacking in factual content. It is, however, the indexical signs that capture the audience's attention. Now, in principle, an index, caused by the object to which it refers, is not arbitrary.[7] But indexical signs can also consist of elements intentionally brought together within the same frame in order to engender an interpretant, in which case the sign determines an interpretant by using certain features of the way the sign signifies its object to generate and shape our understanding. Such implied and inferred modes of indexicality abound in *The Seahorse*.

First the animal is likened to a horse by means of the explicit voice-over: head held high with a pompous air, the triumphant military music in the opening and concluding sequences, and the photo finish to the documentary consisting of a superimposition of the seahorse on documentary footage of a horserace. Painlevé is counting on our human familiarity with and respect for the chevaline in order to teach us something about the seahorse by analogy, thereby creating new possibilities for our relationship to this unique fish.

Other indexical signs whose normally exclusively human object is diverted to refer to the nonhuman are prevalent. As the seahorses are filmed blithely swimming in calm, undisturbed waters accompanied by the lyrical music of Darius Milhaud, the narrator draws our attention to the prehensile tail and upright position: "We cannot help but describe this animal as possessing limbs when we observe the head held high, the vertical tail, reminiscent of a biped." Clearly, the film's invitation to anthropomorphize is deliberately heavy-handed in order to teach us something about the animal under investigation. Although an extensive discussion of anthropomorphism lies beyond the scope of this

---

7   See the discussion of Charles Sanders Peirce in *Semiotics: The Basics* (1974) by Daniel Chandler. London: Routledge.

study, it is worth noting that the heuristic possibilities of the practice are more and more widely accepted among ethologists. Franz de Waal, for example, point outs the dangers of what he calls "anthropodenial." Painlevé, for his part, feels that humans are allowed and indeed obliged to anthropomorphize. Otherwise, he claims, we would understand and appreciate nothing around us (Painlevé 2007, disc 3, 20:40).

Painlevé's penchant for anthropomorphism is readily affirmed when the documentarian's camera captures the gestation and coming into the world of the seahorse's offspring. The narrator emphasizes the anguished expression and rolling of the eyes – the convulsions of giving birth in many mammals – enhancing the anthropomorphic aspect. Of greater interest to the lay public, however, is the fact that the male carries the fertilized eggs and that it is he who delivers the progeny. In this instance, the consequent meaning becomes itself a sign within the semiotic process. This new signifying vehicle could promote a questioning of traditional gender roles, for example, in the mind of the viewer. In fact, Painlevé later confessed that *The Seahorse*

> was for me a splendid way of promoting the kindness and virtue of the father while at the same time underlining the necessity of the mother. In other words, I wanted to re-establish the balance between male and female.
> qtd. in MACDONALD 2009b: 166

One might also consider *The Seahorse* as an arrangement of signs framed in such a manner as to reiterate the myth of childbirth (with all its trials and travails).

The Love Life of the Octopus (1967) clearly frames the octopus by means of a series of symbolic indices intended to reinforce a mythological interpretation. Painlevé was undoubtedly well aware of the prevalence of octopus mythology throughout human history within a multitude of different cultures.[8] Symbolic indices signifying the octopus as a mysterious and horrific creature are imposed right from the start of the film: the unsettling percussion music of Pierre Henri, sound effects produced by unrecognizable instruments evoking an edgy mood, plus a hauntingly expressive voice-over (tremolo, elongated syllables and use of emphasis). All of which insist upon the creature's most disturbing

---

8 Roger Caillois examines the prevalence of octopus mythology from antiquity to the present in *La pieuvre. Essai sur la logique de l'imaginaire* (1973). As previously in *Le mythe et l'homme* (1938), he asserts that legend, myth and the human imagination in general are grounded empirically.

aspects – tentacles and suckers – ever-present in the mythology, as well. The myth not only makes the signified/signifier (object/sign) relation intelligible, however, it becomes a mediating sign within a new triad. The octopus as animal with its own evolutionary history possesses malleability, tentacles, suction pads, the ability to change color, etc., signifiers that the myth seizes upon in order to arise and to thrive through what French semiotician Roland Barthes calls a perpetual game of "hide and seek" (Barthes: 203–204). This to and fro framework determines the meaning and arouses the interpreter whose affective reaction is never intended, however, to empty the octopus of its empirical reality.

Painlevé generates another element of the octopus myth in similar fashion. The title of the documentary *The Love Life of the Octopus,* sets up the viewers' expectations and undoubtedly peaks the interest of a popular audience in the creature's legendary lubricity more than would, for instance, *The Mating Habits of the Octopus or The Reproductive Cycle of the Octopus*. Here again, the viewer witnesses empirical reality – images of the octopus in and of itself – framed by the manipulative use of symbolic indices or conventions that emphasize the mysterious, mythical status of the animal. The narrator highlights the very large suckers of the male right before filming him "violently grabbing a female who transports him on her back," eventually allowing him to "insert the end of his special arm into the female's respiratory cavity."

Now, we might readily agree that recourse to the legendary and mythical power of the seahorse or the octopus are conventional signs (symbols), that they are due only to human contrivance and independent of reality. However, a third important Painlevé film – *The Vampire* – suggests that myth may be linked to extra-human realities. For this to be true, conventional signs need to be motivated non-arbitrarily (in a physiological way) as extensions of natural signs, providing an empirical basis for myth.

The Vampire (1938–45) begins with a 2 minute and 40 second montage of several clips from earlier Painlevé films devoted to what the voice-over calls strange, terrifying or mysterious creatures like the seahorse and the octopus and that, according to the narrator, have provided "inspiration for countless legends among poets and artists." Next, the documentary moves to actual footage taken from a famous German horror film. The narrator's conclusion seems fair enough but the claim linking the human imagination to animal behavior is more than just a poetic analogy. Duke Ellington's *Black and Tan Fantasy* and *Echoes of the Jungle* serve as the soundtrack, for Painlevé found these jazz pieces perfectly suited to the terrifying and legendary aspect of the vampire (Painlevé 2007, disc 3, 1:13:00). For in the end, is the blood-sucking vampire not an avatar of the octopus myth that focuses on the life-threatening suckers of tentaculed creature?

According to mythologue Roger Caillois, this is most certainly the case. In his essay on the octopus, he notes that the aquatic animal drinks its nourishment (1973: 209) and that because of its suckers, is thought to have the power to drain the blood and life from its victims (222). In this way, claims Caillois, the octopus joins mythological ranks with the vampire and other blood-sucking creatures by means of "an unconscious selection of obscure yet necessary origins" (218). Moreover, Caillois concludes that fantasy has thus obeyed nature (226), thereby attesting to the continuity between matter and the imagination (227). Whereas Caillois' epistemology explicitly affirms the biological basis for myth, Painlevé's transgressive cinema inspires us in to explore the possible links between art and science in a more discreet manner.

It is suggested that the biosemiotic rhythms of the octopus or by extension, the vampire bat lay the grounds for human semiosis. Painlevé's implies that signs (in this case, the vampire myth) are what they are even though they move away from their initial potencies, making their continuity hard to detect. Consequently, the sign-producing power of nature could manifest itself in culture as well; myth remains natural although transfigured. Indeed, the octopus/vampire myth has been one of the most enduring throughout the world for centuries. This constitutes what might be called pan-psychism or mental continuity, the existence of a "quasi-mind" in non-humans, the human imagination being isomorphic to empirical reality. So who is framing whom if science is fiction and fiction can be science?

6 Conclusion

As we have seen, Painlevé's keen awareness of the semiotic impact of cinema explains his use of sign-vehicles to peak the non-scientist's interest in the animal through humor, anthropomorphism and myth. When empirical science is communicated this way, unlimited semiosis is more likely to occur. Such a stance has ecological implications. Are these animals not worthy of our respect? How different and alike are they and we? Painlevé's confession of his discomfort as a scientific documentarian certainly reveals what we might call an eco-sensitivity:

> I have often felt uncomfortable because of my ability as a man, the master, to capture animals, even microbes, and to do what I wanted with them. I find terrifying the fact that they must be subservient to me because I am the strongest. That really bothered me in all my films regardless of the subject.
>
> PAINLEVÉ 2007, disc 3, 20:10

Jean Painlevé challenges the human tendency to view the nonhuman as somehow inferior and shares with modern-day ethologists the propensity to empathize with the animals studied. He would agree with them that anthropomorphism can complement scientific investigation and is not simply the result of an anthropocentric failure to distinguish or differentiate. As a proponent of the new scientific spirit of the 20th and 21st centuries, Painlevé raises the question of icons and indices in a pre-linguistic order and suggests that cultural constructs are not necessarily independent of nature. In his general-audience films, rational science, modern technology and esthetics frame nature in uniquely in uniquely environmental terms, creating correspondences suggestive of the common origin of all terrestrial life forms. Once acknowledged, a bio-semiotic kinship between myth/legend and empirical nature could diminish our anthropomorphic claims of exceptionalism to the benefit of all living beings, leading us to ask ourselves "who's framing whom?"

Bibliography

Barthes, Roland. 1957. *Mythologies.* Paris: Seuil.

Behar, Henri. 2007. *Mélusine.* Lausanne, Switzerland: Éditions L'Âge d'homme.

Bellows, Andy, Marina McDougall and Brigitte Berg. 2001. *Science is Fiction. The Films of Jean Painlevé.* Cambridge, MA: MIT Press.

Biro, Adam and René Passeron. 1982. *Dictionnaire général du surréalisme et de ses environs.* Paris: Presses Universitaires de France.

Breton, André. 1946. *Les Manifestes du Surréalisme.* Paris: Éditions du Sagittaire.

Breton, André. 1965 [1936]. 'La crise de l'objet' in *Le surréalisme et la peinture.* Paris: Gallimard, 1965: 275–280.

Cineclub de Caen (n.d.). 'L'etoile de Mer.' On line at: http://www.cineclubdecaen.com/realisat/manray/etoiledemer.htm (consulted 15.03.2016).

Cahill, James Leo. 2012 'Forgetting Lessons: Jean Painlevé's Cinematic Gay Science' in *Journal of Visual Culture* 11: 258–287.

Caillois, Roger. 1973. *La pieuvre. Essai sur la logique de l'imaginaire.* Paris: Table Ronde.

Calcagno-Tristant, Frédérique. 2005. 'Jean Painlevé et le cinéma animalier. Un processus d'hybridation engagé' in *Communication* 24 (1): 117–149. n. 24 (1): 117–149.

Corrington, Robert S. 1993. *An Introduction to C.S. Peirce. Philosopher, Semiotician, and Ecstatic Naturalist.* Lanham: Rowman & Littlefield.

Fretz, Laure. 2010. 'Surréalisme sous l'eau : Science and surrealism in the early Films and Writings of Jean Painlevé.' *Film & History* 40 (2): 45–65.

Goll, Ivan. 1924. *Surréalisme.* Paris: n.p.

Hamery, Roxane. 2008. *Le Cinéma au Coeur de la vie.* Rennes, France: Presses Universitaires de Rennes.

Lombard, Gaëlle. 2008. 'Jean Painlevé: essai sur l'imaginaire de la matière vivante' in *Le court métrage français de 1945 à 1968*. Rennes: Presses Universitaires de Rennes.

MacDonald, Scott. 2009. 'Jean Painlevè: Going Beneath the Surface.' *The Criterion Collection: Current*. On line at: http://www.criterion.com/current/posts/1098-jean--going-beneath-the-surface (consulted 25.08.2017).

Magrini, James. 2007. 'Surrealism and the Omnipotence of Cinema' in *Senses of Cinema*. On line at: http://sensesofcinema.com/2007/feature-articles/surrealism-cinema/ (consulted 15.03.2016).

Michel, Jean-Luc. 2004. "La caméra d'un chercheur: entretien avec Jean Painlevé." *Éducation*, Feb. 3, 1978. On line at: http://www.cetec-info.org/jlmichel/Art.Painleve.html (consulted 15.03.2016).

Painlevé, Jean. 2007. Science is Fiction: 23 Films by Jean Painlevé. New York: The Criterion Collection.

Pontalis, Jean-Bertrand. 1988. *Perdre de vue*. Paris: Gallimard.

Riou, Florence. 2009. 'Jean Painlevé : de la science à la fiction scientifique.' *Conserveries Mémorielles* 6. On line at: http://cm.revues.org/350 (consulted 15.03.2016).

De Waal, Frans. 1999. 'Anthropomorphism and Anthropodenial: Consistency in Our Thinking about Humans and Other Animals' in *Philosophical Topics* 27 (1): 225–280.

CHAPTER 12

Cognitivist Film Theory and the Bioculturalist Turn in Eco-film Studies

David Ingram

Abstract

Following the approach popularised by David Bordwell and Noël Carroll, cognitivist film theorist Joseph D. Anderson proposes an 'ecology of the arts' that has no place for the 'Grand Theory' of Marxism and psychoanalysis. His argument is scientistic, in the sense that he both exaggerates the scientific status of his own approach, particularly its basis in evolutionary psychology, and dismisses humanistic approaches to film as unscientific and therefore worthless. However, despite reservations about the application of evolutionary psychology to film studies, the recent turn to a bioculturalist paradigm can be seen as a promising new direction for the discipline. Yet the question remains as to how compatible the bioculturalist paradigm is with so-called Grand Theory. Anderson and Torben Grodal criticise humanistic approaches such as Marxism and psychoanalysis that are concerned with the social and political dimensions of film. Though some of this criticism is well founded, a properly holistic approach to cinema will necessarily include thematic interpretation and attention to signification more generally. Textual hermeneutics, including the allegorical, thematic and ideological analyses derived from revised forms of psychoanalysis and Marxism, will thus remain an important part of a broadly inclusive, ecocritical approach to film.

1 Introduction

An important aim of eco-film studies is to understand how films and film spectators are shaped by particular societies and their wider ecosystems. Cognitivist film theory can play a useful role in this endeavour. The 'bioculturalist' paradigm on which cognitivist approaches to film are based draws on findings in the natural and social sciences, especially cognitive psychology, evolutionary psychology and neuroscience, to relate the mental and bodily components of film spectatorship to its social and cultural aspects (Grodal 2009: 4). Cognitivists argue that the older 'culturalist' paradigm that has dominated film studies since the 1970s frames the field inadequately and misleadingly by assuming that the perceptual processes involved in film viewing are entirely socially constructed. The new bioculturalist paradigm is thus providing an alternative frame for film studies that allows for a fuller understanding of both the film as text and the activities of the film spectator. This essay explores what the work of cognitive theorists David Bordwell, Torben Grodal and Joseph Anderson can contribute to eco-film studies, and proposes that a bioculturalist paradigm allows for a more thoroughly ecological approach to film, and is particularly useful for developing an ecological notion of the film spectator. However, the prospects of developing a political ecology of film depend on a broadening of the field into the social, historical and political aspects of cinema which tend to be of less interest to cognitivist theorists.

2   Beyond the Culturalist Paradigm in Eco-film Studies

Cognitivism differs from culturalism in the way it conceptualises the film spectator, which has important implications for eco-film studies. Bordwell focuses on the role that mental representations play in film spectatorship, arguing that viewers make sense of a film narrative by making inferences from the mental 'schema' they bring to the viewing experience (Bordwell 1989: 10). Other approaches to cognition augment these mentalist models of the mind with more biological explanations of perceptual framing. Grodal cites theories of 'embodied cognition,' drawing on the work of cognitive linguist George Lakoff, neurobiologist Antonio Damasio and evolutionary psychologists John Tooby and Leda Cosmides, amongst others. His model of 'PECMA flow' proposes that narrative comprehension in film is a linear movement from initial 'perception' to 'emotion' and 'cognition,' culminating in 'motor action' (Grodal 2009: 145–157). This conceptual framework is based on a fundamental assumption of evolutionary psychology: that we 'are able to watch films with brains and bodies that have evolved in a totally different environment,' and that many visual fictions thereby 'reflect core elements in the emotional heritage that enhanced human survival in the past' (Grodal 2009: 6). In effect, we watch films with Paleolithic brains and minds. In contrast to Grodal, Joseph Anderson more explicitly applies to film viewing the 'ecological psychology' developed in the 1970s by James J. Gibson, who assumed, in Anderson's words, that 'perception is direct and noninferential' (Anderson 2013: 80). He writes:

> The perceptual and cognitive activity involved in film viewing is the same activity we human beings engage in when interacting with the world at

large. As such, that activity must be viewed from the perspective of our ecological relationship with that world, our active search for meaningful patterns in an overdetermined environment, and our simultaneous perception of possibilities for action (i.e., affordances) in that world.
ANDERSON 1996: 136–137

What unites these two cognitivist approaches is the assumption that film viewing draws on everyday modes of perception which are not wholly or exclusively socially constructed. In this way, cognitivism departs from the culturalist assumptions about the self which in various guises came to dominate contemporary film theory since the 1970s. Althusserian-Lacanian film theory asserted that human subjectivity is wholly a product of ideology, and that the concept of a unified self is purely an ideological construct of patriarchal, capitalist societies. Against such notions, Grodal cites Lakoff and Johnson's argument 'that the concept of unified, conscious subjecthood is universal. The reason for this is functional: the conscious will needs to carry out unambiguous actions and therefore constructs a unified identity that can carry out those actions and, where necessary, suppress all experiences (identities) that conflict with the chosen course of action. Thus the motivation for constructing a centred subject is not ideological but practical' (Grodal 2009: 216). For cognitivists, then, extreme cultural constructionism neglects the role that biological and evolutionary factors play in the formation and development of the self. Cognitivists thus favour the explanatory power of evolutionary functionalism, according to which the concept of a unified self is a function of the dynamic relationship between human beings and their environment, rather than wholly a product of historically situated ideologies.

Bordwell developed his cognitivist critique of culturalism most influentially in his essay 'Contemporary Film Studies and the Vicissitudes of Grand Theory' (1996). Here he distinguished between two related areas of the 'Grand Theory' central to film studies since the 1970s: 'subject-position' theory, based on Althusserian Marxism and Lacanian psychoanalysis, and 'culturalism' itself; that is, the set of assumptions which variously underpinned Frankfurt School Marxism, postmodernism and Cultural Studies, the latter of which came to the fore in film studies in the 1980s. As Bordwell observes, there are in practice important continuities between these two approaches. The most significant shared assumption for our purposes is that, as he puts it, '*Human practices and institutions are in all significant respects socially constructed*' (italics in the original) (Bordwell 1996: 13). Bordwell argues that film scholars share with many social scientists 'the assumption that human behaviour is almost completely shaped by its environment. This premise leads to exaggerating the differences among individuals, groups, and cultures and to avoiding inquiry into the areas of convergence' (Bordwell 1996: 14). Bordwell argues that this extreme constructivism is 'empirically limiting' and supports his argument with reference to the critique of total 'human plasticity' in the work of evolutionary psychologists John Tooby and Leda Cosmides (Bordwell 1996: 31 n22).

The difference between culturalist and bioculturalist approaches to cinema may be illustrated by two interpretations of the same film. Grodal writes of Welles' *Touch of Evil* (1958) in terms of cognitivist theories of embodied cognition ('embedding') which seek to account for the emotional and cognitive relationship that the viewer has with the narrative events on screen, particularly as mediated by the central character, Vargas (Charlton Heston). Grodal's model of fiction is based on 'viewer identification with active and passive positions in narratives and on different types of cognition and affective identification with the narrative actants' (Grodal 1997: 157). His analysis of *Touch of Evil* therefore implies a prototypical viewer who responds to the way Vargas gains 'total control of the situation' in the course of the narrative (Grodal 1997: 244). As a detective-figure looking for his kidnapped wife, Vargas moves through a 'nighttime' world which Grodal describes as a 'run-down border town where the dark oil-derricks and steel constructions, the night clubs, and the hoodlum-ridden streets are frightening, but are, at the same time, fascinating symbols of heteronomy and the surrendering of free will' (Grodal 1997: 244). For Grodal, Vargas stands for a sense of psychological control against a background that suggests the opposite, and at the end of the film, he is 'in control, despite temporary transmitter fall-out and the brief moment in which he is held at gunpoint by Quinlan. The uncanny, dark oil-rigs and bridge pillars serve as backdrops' (Grodal 1997: 245).

Grodal's descriptive analysis of *Touch of Evil* thus interprets its *mise-en-scène* in terms of the psychological meanings available for the spectator. He is interested in concepts such as 'heteronomy,' 'free will' and being 'in control'; moreover, although he describes the ending as 'uncanny,' elsewhere in his book he is critical of Freudian accounts of the unconscious mind. He is also relatively uninterested in an ideological analysis of the film which would tie it to a particular social formation, preferring instead to speculate on human reactions to the environment that appear to transcend specific places and times. Hence he describes the objectification of Susan, Vargas' wife, which the film establishes with binary oppositions between white / dark, female / male and good / evil, in terms of her 'passivity,' without involving himself in any arguments about ideology, patriarchy or colonialism which the film may invite:

> The focus of attention has shifted from mind-control to body-object. In the film the object is (not surprisingly) an innocent, blonde, all-American girl, Susan, trapped in a desert motel and later in a sleazy hotel, whereas the evil forces are dark Mexican males who supposedly enjoy a tacit acceptance of their acts by the overweight and crooked 'cop,' Quinlan.
> GRODAL 1997: 244

In contrast to Grodal, Stephen Heath analysed the same film over fifteen years earlier at the height of the Althusserian-Lacanian era in film studies. Informed by Lacanian psychoanalysis through the writings of Christian Metz, he drew attention to binary oppositions that figure the power relations between men and women in the capitalist, patriarchal society in which the film was made. The main difference between the two interpretations is that, for Heath, ideology goes all the way down, and there is no possibility of a universal human nature beyond it. He writes that the narrative centres on 'the object to be restored'; that is, Susan. At the start of the film, the kiss between Susan and Vargas is interrupted by an explosion: 'henceforth, Vargas's action as hero of the narrative is the desire to get things back into place: re-establish Law in the light of Justice (defeat Quinlan); have his wife returned to him 'clean' (as a result of Quinlan's schemes, she has been arrested on murder charges)' (Heath 1981: 137). For Heath, as opposed to Grodal, these meanings are thoroughly social and ideological. Narrative is about 'transformation,' he writes, and 'the coherence of the transformation – with at the end of the film the narrative image – brings into play determinations that are fully cultural and ideological' (Heath 1981: 136–137).

Heath's understanding of ideology is shaped by the Althusserian notion of 'interpellation,' or subject positioning theory. In his 2013 essay 'Toward an Ecology of the Arts,' Anderson criticises the notion of ideological manipulation implied by this theoretical position; in doing so, he proposes his model of the film spectator over what he sees as the more abstract and simplistic conceptualisations of Grand Theory. He writes that the

> viewer of a motion picture presented a major problem for grand theorists. Their solution was to create a theoretical spectator who was not a real biological person but a construction and to define the film as a constructed instrument of exploitation. From this perspective film is more propaganda than art. It has nothing to do with aesthetics. Beauty is a trap, and narrative is dangerously absorptive. Such an ideology allowed for no

> adequate account of the actual interface between the viewer of the film and the fictional world of the film.
>
> ANDERSON 2013: 78

Anderson here objects to the simplistic determinism of subject positioning theory, which assumed that the spectator's response was in some way totally determined either by the form of a film or by the apparatus of cinema itself. Yet, as Bordwell notes, this 'extreme' and 'implausible' version of the theory may have been characteristic of film theory circa 1975, but was gradually superseded by a more nuanced conceptualisation of the spectator in later Cultural Studies approaches, according to which the viewer 'is less a subject of the dominant ideology and more in control of the process of identification and thus of his or her own meanings' (Bordwell 1996: 16). Anderson, writing in 2013, is thus perpetuating an older, straw man version of film theory. Despite this, however, his overall point about determinism in cinema spectatorship is important. According to cognitivism, he writes, 'a film spectator might be *cued* by a film rather than *positioned* by it,' so that the spectator's interpretation of a film is less deterministic and more open and contextual than Grand Theorists had assumed (Anderson 1996: 8). As Anderson puts it,

> We, as perceivers, are part of the ecological system, and in the world it is the meaning of events in relation to ourselves that we perceive. To put it another way, I perceive not what something *means* but what it means to me. We are programmed through evolution to perceive meaning in that way, as part of our environment.'
>
> ANDERSON 1996: 137

Unlike critics influenced by Marxism, such as Stephen Heath, Anderson thus tends to understand meaning as something that the viewer or critic constructs from a text rather than discovers in it. As Gregory Currie notes, Bordwell's version of constructivism also acknowledges the 'beholder's share' in film viewing and therefore stands 'in opposition to the orthodox view, which, with obvious Marxist antecedents, tends to see the viewer as a passive receiver of signification in need of the semiotician's skilful analysis of the film's (probably sinister) message' (Currie, 1995: 112).

The attempt by cognitivists to take into account the actual psychological experiences of real film viewers has been a genuine advance for film theory, as has their criticism of the crude determinism of Althusserian-Lacanian subject positioning theory. Yet the stand-off between cognitivism and Grand Theory described above is not fixed and inevitable: as we shall see in the following section, a combination of cognitive and cultural (as opposed to 'culturalist') approaches would be beneficial for eco-film studies.

3   Towards a Synthesis of Cognitive and Cultural Approaches in Eco-film Studies

Writing in 1998 of the recent 'biocultural synthesis' in anthropology, biologists Richard Levins and Richard Lewontin asserted the need for a dynamic mode of thought that sees 'interpenetration rather than rigid dichotomies, historicity rather than static universals' (Levins and Lewontin 1998: xv). Indeed, the theoretical incompatibility between cognitivism and culturalism begins to diminish when more moderate and nuanced versions of the respective approaches are proposed. An important objection to the evolutionary psychology on which Grodal and Anderson base their arguments focuses on what Barbara Herrnstein Smith calls its 'narrowly adaptationist' notion of human behaviour, derived from a version of evolutionary theory that has been contested by both biological system theorists and developmental psychologists (Smith 2001: 130, 132). It should be noted that recent developments in evolutionary psychology have taken on board such criticisms in order to seek less simplistic versions of the theory. Cognitive neurobiologist Johan J. Bolhuis concluded in 2011 that a

> modern EP (evolutionary psychology) would embrace a broader, more open, and multi-disciplinary theoretical framework, drawing on, rather than being isolated from, the full repertoire of knowledge and tools available in adjacent disciplines [...] The evidence from adjacent disciplines suggests that, if EP can reconsider its basic tenets, it will flourish as a scientific discipline.
>
> BOLHUIS ET AL. 2011: 4–5

Moreover, there are alternative theories of evolution that rely less on the concept of functionalism on which both Anderson and Grodal base many of their arguments. Evolutionary biologists Stephen J. Gould and Richard Lewontin observed in 1979 that the adaptationist program is itself a departure from Darwin's more pluralistic model of evolutionary development, according to which the 'current utility' of a particular trait could be 'an epiphenomenon of non-adaptive structures' (Gould and Lewontin 1979: 581). They argue that theorising about evolution benefits from 'a consideration of alternatives to the proposition that each part is 'for' some specific purpose' (Gould and Lewontin

1979: 586). Applied to film studies, this pluralistic notion of evolutionary development allows for a potential reconciliation between cognitivism and some aspects of the Grand Theory it criticises. Eco-film studies could therefore seek a synthesis of the two approaches which cognitivists tend to frame as incompatible polar opposites. In doing so, the discipline would expand beyond the self-imposed methodological limits that cognitivist theorists set for film studies. For even if we accept that the ecological psychology on which Anderson draws does grant reliable epistemological access to the experiences of what he calls the 'real biological person' in front of the screen, this still raises the question of how that person fits into the society of which he or she is a part, as well as the wider ecosystem or environment on which he or she depends. For an ecocritic, this question requires an act of conceptual framing that needs to be understood in social, historical and political terms. A fully ecological film theory will therefore explore not only the ways in which a film works on an individual spectator, but also what that spectator's place is within the wider ecosystem, knowledge of which is necessarily social, historical and political. Humanistic inquiry is needed to produce such a political ecology of film. As we shall see in the next section, however, some cognitivists have ambivalent attitudes towards some of the aims and methods of humanistic study and have questioned its role in film studies.

4   Humanistic Method in Eco-film Studies

Cognitivists have raised important questions about methodology in both film studies and the humanities in general which have important implications for eco-film studies. Bordwell's criticism of Grand Theory is ultimately aimed at what he sees as weak methods deployed within film studies as a whole. Accepting this critique of Grand Theory, Grodal nevertheless calls for a synthesis of approaches from the sciences and the humanities, arguing that the 'natural science research on the human brain and body and its evolutionary history and the humanities represent different approaches to the same object and they benefit from cooperation' (Grodal 2009: 5). In contrast, Anderson is more dismissive of humanistic approaches in general and asserts the superiority of the natural sciences over the humanities as means of understanding film. We will discuss each of these approaches in turn.

Bordwell's demolition of bad method in film studies is salutary yet contentious. He criticises four familiar 'routines of reasoning' which he sees as weakening argumentation in contemporary film studies: top-down inquiry, argument as bricolage, associational reasoning, and the hermeneutic impulse

(Bordwell 1996: 18). Although all of these are important criticisms, it is with the first that we are most concerned here, because it concerns the methods adopted by Grand Theorists regarding their ambition to include a social and political dimension within film studies. Bordwell criticises Rick Altman's suggestion that it is useful for film studies to think not in terms of an individual film but of a 'film event,' or, in Bordwell's words, an 'interchange' between 'all institutions, activities, texts, and agents that might pertain to cinema' (Bordwell 1996: 14). He comments that Altman's view 'can be criticised as simply restating the humanist's uninformative truism that everything is connected to everything else' (Bordwell 1996: 14). But an ecocritic may begin to object here. For even if such ecological notions may be 'uninformative' in some contexts, Bordwell's stance has the potentially negative effect of closing down potentially important avenues of inquiry and thereby limiting the scope of film studies in a way that ecocritics may find problematic. For an ecocritic, he may have thrown the baby of social and ecological concern out with the bathwater of Grand Theory.

Bordwell concludes his critique of the 'top-down application' of theories in film studies as follows:

> What could make people think that they *needed* a highly elaborated theory of ideology or culture in order to talk enlighteningly about a particular film or historical process? Partly, I suggest, an institutional routine which posited that every argument rested upon some larger assumptions about just such matters.
> BORDWELL 1996: 21

Yet an ecocritic might respond that there are indeed larger assumptions which need to be taken into account in order to produce a rich and complex account of a given film. The ecological and political implications of a film may necessitate bringing in ideas from disciplines outside of film studies. In contrast, Bordwell advocates middle-level research based on small scale, piecemeal theorizing. Such programs, he writes, 'have demonstrated that you do not need to understand a film by projecting onto it semantic fields 'privileged' by this or that theory. Most important, the middle-level research programs have shown that *you do not need a Big Theory of Everything to do enlightening work in a field of study*' (italics in original) (Bordwell 1996: 29). Nevertheless, ecocritics will surely want to draw on a wide range of semantic fields to understand how films and their audiences fit into the wider ecology: eco-film criticism will be necessarily both para- and intra-textual.

In 'The Bordwell Regime and the Stakes of Knowledge' (2001), film theorist Robert Ray responded to the rationalist methodology favoured by Bordwell by reasserting the claims of postmodernist Grand Theory. Ray criticised Bordwell and his co-authors for their faith in positivist science and rational argumentation, proffering instead an experimental yet non-empirical approach to knowledge production derived from irrationalist methods such as Dada, Surrealism, Situationism, post-structuralism and historian of science Paul Feyerabend's anarchist epistemology. For Ray, what is important in film studies is not a search for truth but the generation of new concepts to keep the subject 'revolutionary' in Thomas Kuhn's sense (Ray 2001: 46).

Although this may indeed be a creative direction for eco-film studies to take, the irrationalist and anti-scientific tendency in Ray's approach is surely questionable. In particular, he views Bordwell's interest in science as dogmatic and authoritarian, even though the opposite is surely the case. Indeed, unusually for a film critic, Bordwell acknowledges that his hypothesising may be wrong, and even ends his essay on cognitivism with the sentence, 'All this could turn out to be wrongheaded and useless' (Bordwell 1989: 15). Ray's postmodernist approach to knowledge may also seem inadequate for an ecocritic who wants to know which concepts may provide a better understanding of the world than others. As Lakoff argues about environmental communication, we need not simply new frames, but better ones (Lakoff 2010: 71). Although Ray is more interested in an idea's context of discovery than in its context of justification, an eco-film critic will want to know how a particular concept relates to the way actual ecosystems work in the real world. Whether an idea is revolutionary or novel in itself is not in this sense the most important criterion. It may be that cognitivism is currently one of the most plausible and productive ways of understanding how people watch films in real situations, and in this it has an advantage not only over more abstract and simplistic Lacanian-Althusserian models but also over methodologies that are less concerned with justification and empirical testing.

Anderson takes his methodological criticism further than Bordwell by arguing that, because Grand Theory is not grounded in science, it lacks a valid methodology of its own:

> The conglomerate of theories that constituted Grand Theory demonstrated that theories with no scientific validity could easily become disconnected from what is real and what is possible. Because there was no scholarly tradition for such theories to be tested in the real world, the only constraints were those of the ideology underpinning them.
> ANDERSON 2013: 78

In contrast to Grodal and Bordwell, then, Anderson's positivist view of science gives him an unfair and dismissive attitude towards the humanities. Barbara Herrnstein Smith notes that evolutionary psychologists tend to 'appear captive to an unregenerate Two Cultures mentality, with its familiar intellectual provincialisms and disciplinary antagonisms' (Smith 2001: 139). Yet method in the humanities is not always or necessarily as poor as Anderson makes out. Despite his sweeping dismissal, scholarly traditions have been established for testing knowledge claims in the humanities, even if they are not always adhered to by every humanist scholar. Stephen Toulmin's argumentation theory and Jürgen Habermas' theories of justification provide two pragmatist models for humanistic study which are rigorous and defensible, and place it on a par with scientific methodologies in terms of the provisionality and relative validity of its truth-claims (Toulmin 1958; Habermas 2003: 36–38). Discussing the epistemology of socio-historical research, sociologist John R. Hall writes that

> practices of inquiry that are dismissed in some quarters as 'unscientific' or 'anecdotal' have their own viable rationales which, if pursued rigorously, are capable of producing knowledge deserving of attention even by scientists. These conclusions imply neither that all cultural constructed knowledge is equally plausible, nor that any culturally constructed knowledge is necessarily untrue.
> HALL 1999: 4–5

Even if the humanities are not subject to the validity claims of the experimental sciences, as Anderson complains, they can still qualify as rational discourse if a pluralistic, inclusive model of knowledge production is adopted. As we have seen, this is what Grodal advocates in his call for the natural sciences and the humanities to be brought together in 'cooperation.'

In claiming that the scientific methods of cognitivism are superior to the methods of the humanities, Anderson is being 'scientistic' in the way defined by philosopher Tom Sorrel: 'the belief that science, especially natural science, is much the most valuable part of human learning' (Sorrel 1991: 1). This belief, he continues, often includes two further aspects: 'the belief that science is the *only* valuable part of human learning' and 'the view that it is always good for subjects that do not belong to science to be placed on a scientific footing' (Sorrel 1991: 1). According to this definition, the cognitivist theorists discussed in this essay are scientistic in various ways. Bordwell notes that scientism has become an easy and superficial accusation to make against cognitivist film theory, and goes on to defend the third idea mentioned by Sorrel, but not the first two: in other words, he supports attempts to put film studies on a scientific footing by drawing on insights from the experimental sciences, but, unlike Anderson, does not see humanistic study as necessarily inferior to the sciences. As he puts it,

We may eventually discard the belief that molecules, dna, and evolutionary selection are as real as anything can be, but as conceptual constructs they are indisputably superior to what preceded them and to all current rivals. Cognitive theory may produce something of comparable competitive strength.'

BORDWELL 1989: 4

From Bordwell's perspective, then, attempts to bring science into film studies are justified as long as they are informed by a fallibilist approach to scientific knowledge, rather than one based on dogmatic assertions of absolute fact or truth. In contrast to Bordwell, however, Anderson is also scientistic in Sorrel's first and second senses, which are less defensible.

5   Conclusion

Questions remain as to how much of the older Marxist-psychoanalytic paradigm may be both compatible with cognitivist approaches and useful for ecocriticism. The role of psychoanalysis is complex and beyond the scope of this essay. As for Marxism, Kate Soper has observed that, despite its adherence to industrialism, productivism and anthropocentrism, the greening of Marxism is underway, as histories of labour, power and exploitation are being placed within wider environmental histories, including a consideration of non-human agencies and attendant issues of biodiversity. Historical materialism can no longer assume that the Earth's resources are limitless or that human beings are infinitely malleable by social forces (Soper 1996: 83, 90).

Cognitivism is also reframing questions of aesthetics and politics in a way that is beneficial for eco-film studies. Again, it is doing this by providing counter-arguments to the assumptions of earlier film theory. 'Grand Theory and its constituents,' Anderson writes, 'were really no more than political agendas that were either promoted or thwarted by a film or a set of films. These theories were always on the outside of the art looking in' (Anderson 2013: 77). Anderson's main point here is an aesthetic objection to crude political readings of films. Applied to eco-film studies, we may acknowledge that it is tempting for eco-film critics to judge films according to whether they either 'promote' or 'thwart' their own political agenda. Yet the fact that ecocritics have political agendas, and tend to be committed to promoting a desired social good through their criticism, whether that is conceived of as, for example, environmental awareness, environmental justice, biophilia or ecological literacy, is not necessarily bad in itself. Ecocriticism can be defended as a form of moralist criticism, in parallel with the concerns of literary and cultural studies with other important and inter-related social issues such as class, gender and race. This ecocritical framing can be applied to film criticism in a way that is creative, exploratory and provisional, rather than dogmatic, stereotyped or fixed. Even if a critic has a political agenda, then, it does not mean that he or she has to judge a film crudely according to whether or not it conforms to it or not. A film could 'thwart' one's political views but still be considered interesting, challenging, well-made, or whatever indicator of aesthetic merit the critic chooses to apply. Such an open, pluralistic approach to eco-aesthetics may avoid the crudeness and reductiveness in criticism to which Anderson rightly objects, without a need to suppress the social, political and ecological interpretation of films completely.

As we have seen in this essay, cognitivism reframes important questions about what constitutes both the text and the spectator in eco-film studies. Julian Hochberg and Virginia Brooks write of narrative comprehension in film that 'in the case of motion pictures, it is the experience on first viewing – the *on-line* processing, or perception – that may be more important to the psychologist if not to the critic, the film student, or the cultist' (Hochberg and Brooks 1996: 270). They observe that film critics have tended to create a model of the film viewer that is an abstraction from the direct, 'on-line' experience of a person watching a film for the first time; in other words, from the typical way that people watch films in real life. In ways like this, cognitivist film theory is exploring a number of productive conceptual frameworks for analysing the aesthetic effects of films, and how these are cued for the viewer by particular formal techniques. In doing so, it downplays the socio-cultural context of a film, and shows more interest in *how* a film signifies rather than in *what* it signifies. Yet for an ecocritic, social and historical studies will remain important for hypothesising about the wider cultural and ecological meanings of these filmic effects. It is here that textual hermeneutics find a place after all.

In *Ecologies of the Moving Image* (2013), Adrian Ivakhiv understands that a theory of film based on perceptual ecology is not sufficient on its own. Instead, there is a need to add to what he calls the 'more restrictive understanding of perception and cognition' in the work of Joseph and Barbara Anderson. Their approach, he writes,

> is oriented toward identifying ways in which film viewing is undergirded by the reciprocal relationship between a perceiver and her immediate environment. The experience of film viewing, however, is both densely cultural and highly artificial, and a thoroughly ecological interpretation of film should recognize the many layers of relationship between viewers, the film medium (as it has historically developed), the culture

within which film objects exist as viewable objects, and the many 'realities' being referred to in the worlds portrayed by film.
IVAKHIV 2013: 351–352

Cognitive film theory should thus be 'broadened' to embrace a wider notion of ecology than that proposed by ecological psychologists. What begins in cognitivism as a justifiable critique of the limitations of textual hermeneutics, or what Bordwell calls 'Interpretation Inc.', should thus not become a total dismissal, as this works against broader ecological forms of criticism which relate films in complex ways to the wider environment or ecology (Bordwell 1989: 21). Eco-film studies might attempt to combine cognitivist theories with textual hermeneutics, including the allegorical, thematic and ideological analyses derived from revised versions of historical materialism, in order to create a more properly ecological film studies.

Bibliography

Anderson, Joseph D. 1996. *The Reality of Illusion: An Ecological Approach to Cognitive Film Theory*. Carbondale and Edwardsville: Southern Illinois University Press.

Anderson, Joseph D. 2013. 'Toward an Ecology of the Arts' in Shimamura, Arthur P. (ed) *Psychocinematics: Exploring Cognition and the Movies*. Oxford: Oxford University Press: 76–93.

Bolhuis, Johan J., Gillian R. Brown, Robert C. Richardson and Kevin N. Laland. 2011. 'Darwin in Mind: New Opportunities for Evolutionary Psychology' in *PLoS Biol* 9 (7). On line at: http://journals.plos.org/plosbiology/article?id=10.1371/journal.pbio.1001109.

Bordwell, David. 1989. 'A Case for Cognitivism' in *Iris*. 9. Spring: 11–40. On line at: http://www.davidbordwell.net/articles/Bordwell_Iris_no9_spring1989_11.pdf.

Bordwell, David. 1996. 'Contemporary Film Studies and the Vicissitudes of Grand Theory' in Bordwell, David and Noël Carroll (eds). *Post-Theory: Reconstructing Film Studies*. Madison: University of Wisconsin Press.

Currie, Gregory. 1995. *Image and Mind: Film, Philosophy and Cognitive Science*. Cambridge: Cambridge University Press.

Gould, Stephen Jay. 2001. 'More Things in Heaven and Earth' in Rose, Hilary and Steven Rose (eds). *Alas, Poor Darwin: Arguments Against Evolutionary Psychology*. London: Vintage.

Grodal, Torben. 1997. *Moving Pictures: A New Theory of Film Genres, Feelings, and Cognition*. Oxford: Clarendon Press.

Grodal, Torben. 2009. *Embodied Visions: Evolution, Emotion, Culture, and Film*. Oxford and New York: Oxford University Press.

Habermas, Jürgen. 2003. *Truth and Justification*. Oxford: Polity.
Hall, John R. 1999. *Cultures of Inquiry: From Epistemology to Discourse in Sociohistorical Research*. Cambridge: Cambridge University Press.
Heath, Stephen. 1981. *Questions of Cinema*. London: Macmillan.
Hochberg, Julian and Virginia Brooks. 1996. 'The Perception of Motion Pictures' in Friedman, Morton P. and Edward C. Carterette (eds.). *Cognitive Ecology*. San Diego: Academic Press: 205–292.
Ivakhiv, Adrian J. 2013. *Ecologies of the Moving Image: Cinema, Affect, Nature*. Waterloo, Ontario: Wilfred Laurier University Press.
Lakoff, George. 2010. 'Why It Matters How We Frame the Environment' in *Environmental Communication* 4 (1), March: 70–81.
Lewins, Richard and Richard Lewontin. 1998. 'Foreword' in Goodman, Alan H. and Thomas L. Leatherman (eds). *Building a New Biocultural Synthesis: Political-Economic Perspectives on Human Biology*. Ann Arbor: University of Michigan Press.
Ray, Robert. 2001. *How a Film Theory Got Lost and Other Mysteries in Cultural Studies*. Bloomington and Indianapolis: Indiana University Press.
Smith, Barbara Herrnstein. 2001. 'Sewing Up the Mind: The Claims of Evolutionary Psychology' in Rose, Hilary and Steven Rose (eds). *Alas, Poor Darwin: Arguments Against Evolutionary Psychology*. London: Vintage.
Sorell, Tom. 1991. *Scientism: Philosophy and the Infatuation with Science*. London and New York: Routledge.
Toulmin, Stephen. 1958. *The Uses of Argument*. Cambridge: Cambridge University Press.
Welles, Orson. 1958. *Touch of Evil*. Universal US. (Film).

PART 4

Teaching Frames

∴

CHAPTER 13

Framing the Alien, Teaching *District 9*

Roman Bartosch

Abstract

This essay argues for an ecocritical educational approach informed by and thriving on the tensions and ambiguities produced by textual engagements with nature and non-human beings and suggests the concept of 'framing' as a productive element of a more general environmental teaching methodology. Outlining the different levels on which framing as a conceptual and interpretive tool can be applied in an analysis of Neill Blomkamp's 2009 film District 9, the film and a selection of educational implications will be discussed in the context of intercultural competence and what is described in this essay as 'transcultural ecology.' The suggestions apply both to university-level classes on transculturality and ecology and to secondary level EFL classes at school for which the tasks described in this essay will have to be slightly adjusted in terms of demands of complexity.

1 Introduction

One of the crucial questions and hotly debated issues in environmental and ecocritical education – or 'ecodidactics' as it is called in Germany – is its very didactical nature: can we 'teach' consciousness and ethical awareness and if so, should we do so at all? Do we mistake teaching for preaching? And how effective is educational practice grounded in the superiority of our 'environmental capital' (see Parham 2006; for a recent debate over these questions, see Bartosch and Garrard 2013 as well Major and McMurry 2013)? As it were, ecocritical pedagogy is torn between the urgency of environmental crises, which we know requires immediate address and mitigation, and the ethos of a critical pedagogy 'that encourages free expression' and is grounded in a 'concern to engage students in an oppositional [...] critique of society' (Parham 2006: 7). Reconciling the pressing issue of environmental crises with the 'dialogic' imperative of modern pedagogy is more than an antediluvian liberal-humanist reflex; it is, as Greg Garrard and I have argued elsewhere, 'the only real preparation imaginable for a risky, exciting and unprecedented future' (Bartosch and Garrard 2014: 225).

My purpose here is to discuss the challenge of such a 'pedagogy of the unprecedented' (Garrard) by bringing together two likewise important aspects of ecocritical education: on the one hand, the focus is on a text that could be called 'environmental' in the sense of Lawrence Buell's definition – especially because 'human interest is not understood as the only legitimate interest' (cf. Buell 1995: 7). The South African science fiction film *District 9* is such a text. As I will argue, it is particularly suitable for an environmental classroom because of the complex narrative of the naturalcultural evolutionary process of its dehumanised and increasingly a-human protagonist and the moral aporia the contact between humans and extraterrestrials entails. On the other hand, however, I believe that it is necessary and reasonable to try to move beyond the context orientation of many ecocritical pedagogies and, instead of focussing on the *representation* of environments, animals, and ecological or biological entities, to address the forms of *presentation*, or *staging*, of the plot. This, I will argue, will emphasise the constructedness of the narrative and bring home the idea that the way in which we frame stories matters just as much as the 'content' of this story. Understanding framing as a crucial element of narratives thus allows for the critical distance required by a 'reflexive pedagogy' (Parham 2006) and teaches important insights into the workings of discursive formations generally, environmental or other.

A focus on the framing strategies that are pivotal for the film's narrative construction requires a film-narratological engagement with the narrative discourse of *District 9* (e.g., Faulstich 2008 and, of course, Chatman 1978). Such a primarily text-centred approach can and should be supplemented by context-related approaches as informed by new-historicist or postcolonial studies (cf. James 2012, Wolff 2008). In the case of *District 9*, however, the interpretive role of the context, which for instance allows for reading the aliens as metaphoric depictions of those South-African blacks dislodged from District 6/Distrik Ses in Kapstadt (see Schmidt 2013: 250–251), is less than clear, and it is this tension that can help to bring about fruitful discussions of the aesthetic discourse of the film. The notion of otherness and othering underlying the filmic engagement with the 'prawns,' as the extraterrestrial refugees are called by the majority of the human inhabitants of Johannesburg, is particularly helpful: while it clearly refers to historical events and developments in the South Africa under Apartheid, especially the forced removals in Kapstadt during the 1960s, it also develops a notion of alterity that through the motif of the alien creates a strong metaphor for the 'bare life' that Andrew Norris, drawing on Agamben, describes as a 'general exception' (Norris 2003). It is by virtue of this construction that alterity can be discussed as a near-universal condition and effect of othering rather than a characteristic of a particular ethnicity, species affiliation or group membership known to students through the empirical reality they are familiar with.

Surely, it is ambitious to attempt to engage with the film from a perspective that takes into account the very tension between sociocultural and historical reference to the postcolonial condition of South-Africa under and after Apartheid and the more general aesthetic staging of alterity. Having briefly commented on what I understand to be some general challenges of ecocritical pedagogy above, I now want to elaborate the concept of 'framing' as a means to this end of teaching film aesthetics ecocritically. After discussing both contextual and text-centred elements relevant for dealing with the film, I will then conclude this essay by suggesting tasks and projects with which students will not only learn to engage with the topic at hand but to do so in a cooperative and creative manner, which I believe is one of the central tasks of ecopedagogy as well as modern, reflexive forms of teaching more generally.

2   Framing and the Ecopedagogical Challenge of Complexity

Ecocritically engaged educators would probably agree that in the context of teaching literature and film, ecological issues are highly popular among pupils and students for various reasons: environmentalism, climate change and, maybe most importantly, animals are of great interest to them because of their intrinsic ethical appeal, their connection to the everyday experience of the pupils' environment as well as the coverage of most of these topics in the media (for a critical assessment, see Küchler 2014). At the same time, traditional educational approaches fall short of some of the most crucial ecocritical tenets: young adult dystopia and animal narratives may belong to the canon of obligatory texts in an English classroom (see Grimm and Wanning, forthcoming). Yet, units on animal fables – and, thus, the always already metaphorical nature of literary animals – are rarely concerned with actual nonhuman critters (see Bartosch 2014), and young adult cli-fi novels may not always offer much more than traditional thriller plots in green clothing (Kerridge 2010). The narrative solutions they offer cannot be reconciled with the ecocritical awareness of tension and ambiguity that should inform our understanding of 'nature' as both a reality and a construct. This critique notwithstanding, traditional ecocriticism has no easy solutions to offer: its emphasis on fundamental interconnectedness and its advocacy of ecocentric perspectives likewise rather pose a number of problems. Thinking everything at once and in its unending interconnectedness, as the so-called 'first law of ecology' (Barry Commoner) suggests, is impossible even for grown-ups. How, then, could such an ecocritical stance inform classroom activity?

In order for this question to be answered, I want to employ the notion of framing as an interpretive means and a pedagogical end. As Axel Goodbody has pointed out, framing 'directs our attention to particular parts and features of an issue, which has implications for its interpretation' (2012: 17). As I will argue, identifying frames and, possibly, developing a flexibility concerning one's own cognitive and even affective frames constitutes a central objective of (green) pedagogies because it allows students to grapple with the world's complexity in productive ways. Since framing, described and discussed as a specific cognitive strategy by George Lakoff and Erving Goffman, for instance, can be seen as 'a universal process' (Goodbody 2012: 17) that encompasses not only mediated and constructed 'strategic frames,' but also primal and often subconscious 'deep frames,' dealing with framing in the English classroom is likely to be difficult. Yet, since framing as a literary/filmic strategy foregrounds the very concept so evidently, discussing frames as part of film analysis eventually teaches not only the composition of a film but the ways in which 'frames work by linking an unfamiliar object or field of experience with a familiar one, mapping the values associated with the latter onto the former' (Goodbody 2012: 18).

The story of *District 9* blends alien film conventions and the aesthetics of both (mock-)documentary and action movie. Director Neill Blomkamp and producer Peter Jackson tell the story of a group of extraterrestrial refugees, 'clearly decoded and reminiscent of those unfortunate ill-treated Third World economic migrants' (Brereton 2013: 230),[1] and their arrival in Johannesburg, South Africa. This narrative takes the form of a retrospective that is part of a documentary about how, twenty-eight years later, the cunningly labelled MNU-corporation ('Multi-National United') sets out to dislocate the alien refugees and their ghettos from the centre of J-burg to the periphery. The ecological implications have been discussed by Pat Brereton in the context of Virilio's concept of 'grey ecology'; the complex enmeshment of xenophobic politics, migration and transnational corporations could form another point of entry to interpreting the film, which might be informed by recent debates about neo- or eco-colonialism and what Rob Nixon (2011) has discussed as 'slow violence.' In addition to these perspectives, I want to try to engage with the filmic strategies used by Blomkamp and discuss the criticism of the film, its collapsing into blatant action movie patterns, in light of an educational interest in framing and the question of how to deal with narrative techniques and paratexts in

---

1   For those unfamiliar with the film, I have added a short synopsis of the film at the end of this essay.

the context of teaching alterity in the context of a 'green cultural studies' (see Garrard 2012).

When teaching *District 9*, the concept of frames is helpful on three levels. Framing can, firstly, be understood as an epistemological premise that is foregrounded by the filmic self-referential play with strategies of framing and the aesthetic of found-footage, documentary and action movie elements. Secondly, framing plays a role on the level of characters and the representation of the alien creatures – it is, in fact, an act of framing to understand the inhabitants of District 9 as either extraterrestrial or subaltern, or both. Thirdly, the phenomenon of framing can inform a discussion of the role and function of the fictional discourse of the alien film as opposed to or in connection with the actual history of South-African apartheid and other forms of racist (and speciesist) discrimination. The ambivalence of such 'true fictions' and their dependence on narrative framing surely benefits an environmental classroom as a central teaching objective since almost no 'green topic,' from animals to climate change, can do without specific narrative patterns and tropes that help frame the stories we tell without necessarily making them less true (see, for instance, McHugh 2011 and Hulme 2009). Therefore, on all three of these levels, the concept of framing proves fruitful for a discussion of the workings of fictional texts, the relevance of art for forms of understanding the world, and the engagement with the 'alien' other. The interest in framing strategies employed in this film as well as by its viewers thus connects with the pedagogical aim of fostering critical thinking and self-reflection by enabling pupils to recognise frames and switch between them in order to explore the rich semantic textures of *District 9* and other real or imaginary environments.

3   *District 9* as Text in Context

The question of interpretive methodology most importantly revolves around the decision whether to foreground the structure and composition of a text as such or whether to emphasise the historical or social conditions of the discursive field of said text, its modes of production etc. *District 9* presents a rare case where the very tension between both approaches can – and should – be made the central objective of classroom activity. It may seem frustrating, or at least unorthodox, not to resolve the question of whether, for instance, the story is a political allegory and should be read in ways that render the aliens metaphoric, or if it is rather an ecologically minded science fiction fantasy. Yet, focussing on this constant tension and pointing out how reductive each either/or-approach to this text would turn out to be brings home the importance of forms of framing and creates awareness of the constructedness of discourse more generally. This should be the first ecocritical teaching objective: the filmic discourse frames the plot in ways that help us to distinguish but also to categorise and discriminate what we see in remarkable ways.

Students might very likely be surprised by some of the director's choices, such as the decision for Johannesburg (not New York or Los Angeles) as the location where the human-alien contact takes place, the representation of the aliens as weak and destitute, and, more importantly, the film's change from mock-documentary to action movie. In a first step, it is therefore important to formulate the expectations of students when watching an 'alien film' and to reflect on and discuss what these expectations imply: in particular a discussion of the wrong assumptions about the allegedly dangerous alien invaders who are in fact nothing but helpless and desperate refugees seems a good starting point for debates about perceptions of the other as well as expectations concerning stories about the other. The same can be said about the locale: what does it mean, what kind of expectations remain unfulfilled, and how does it possibly even hurt one's pride as an inhabitant of Europe or the US that the aliens 'chose' J-burg as their point of arrival? It is only after such questions have been addressed that it makes sense to move on to more specific discussions of the framing strategies of the film – that is, the decisions for a filmic discourse grounded in the genre of (mock-)documentaries and action films, respectively.

As for the second aspect, the significance of framing the alien characters, it is not only the stranded aliens but protagonist Wikus's transformation into an alien that will prove a fruitful starting point for analysis: what happens to Wikus's sense of identity and belonging, but also what is being done to him by media representation, the exploitation by political and military forces and xenophobic discourse in the most general sense, is highly interesting because it again points to the forms of framing with which we categorise and understand otherness. In the case of Wikus, it is the protagonist himself who experiences this fundamental transformation – which, in turn, has implications for the generic choice of narrative form: it is because of Wikus's becoming subaltern posthuman that at this point, the mock-documentary simply ceases to make sense and is replaced by the action narrative. This leads to my third ecocritical teaching aim, the link between filmic discourse and the representation of both South Africa and the nature of othering, which I will discuss in more detail in the next section where I introduce tasks and projects that try to deal with these teaching goals.

Before I do so, some remarks are due that leave the text-centred discourse analysis aside in order to situate the film in the actual historical and political context (for an overview of approaches to teaching postcolonial literature and culture, see Eisenmann et al. 2010). What does it mean that the film is 'South-African'? As Brereton remarks, it is important that Wikus's transformation is not only a transformation into a 'general' other, although '[t]he very pointed political allegory with other "dispossessed" and "unruly types" is so blatant, it would be virtually impossible not to be recognized by mass audiences everywhere' (Brereton 2013: 231). At the same time, 'it would not escape a South African ear for instance that the alien language incorporates "clicking sounds"' (Brereton 2013: 231; Brereton here draws on Roger Ebert's review of the film in *The Times*). 'The other' then stops being a generic term for subalterity and becomes a very concrete, very real entity. While its repugnant form thus becomes metaphorical explanation of the practice of othering implicated in the derogatory term 'prawns,' it likewise links with existing forms of ethnic slurs.

Understanding that this 'alien aesthetics' at the same time localises and dislocates the narrative of alterity can be engendered by a discussion of the acts of framing involved in the filmic discourse. As it were, click sounds and signs localise the film while at the same time, the radical alterity of the 'prawn' cannot be resolved by such localisations – we have both metaphor and 'a [...] visceral biological organism, which through human eyes at least remains ugly' (Brereton 2013: 231) and thus cannot be exhausted by a metaphorical reading of human subalterity since its meaning clearly touches upon the nonhuman, the nonsubjective and the nonrational elements of our world. Framing here reverses the heterotopic quality of science fiction dystopia and alien attack films and grounds it in the materiality of the world which is both real and constructed at the same time, as ecocritical work has repeatedly shown. As Brereton sums up this paradox for *District 9*:

> racist driven connotations remain more pointed [...] in this context, since the film is explicitly set in South Africa, rather than a more conventional alien futuristic time and place. Can the alien creatures be potentially 'humanized,' as in so many science fiction fantasies [...]? Or rather, as many critics appear to affirm, [...] are audiences essentially unable to make this necessary jump of imaginative empathy towards becoming ecologically connecting with an Othered species sharing their habitat [?]
>
> BRERETON 2013: 232

If the latter is the case, Brereton suggests that it is the film's 'not displaying a surfeit of anthropomorphic identification' (232) that prohibits identification and empathy – but since anthropomorphisation is not without dangers (yet, nevertheless, never absent from *District 9*) and framing provides much more helpful accesses to the filmic discourse, I doubt that it will be easy *not* to connect with the aliens. It is, moreover, Wikus's transformation into an extraterrestrial – his becoming-alien in multiple senses of this expression – which may point to the most important lesson when thinking about identification and feeling-with: identifying, literally becoming-one, and hybridisation. Both of these tropes might have been staples of traditional postcolonial studies but have more recently come to be discussed in more nuanced terms and as processes encompassing insecurity, pain, and doubt (a notion that has influenced recent research in transculturality and world literature significantly; see Doff 2009: 360–362; Schulze-Engler 2007). For Wikus, becoming-alien means becoming a hunted and detested creature, his contact with the other – or, rather, what his own species and its desire for profit makes of it – destroys his life and ostracises him for good.

4   Task Design

The teaching objectives that I mentioned above are meant to inform a whole unit, if not an ecocritical-pedagogical stance more generally, with regard to the role and importance of framing in literary and other narratives. In order for this stance to make a dent in the classroom, it is indispensable to think about specific tasks and task design that guarantees age-appropriate, inclusive and cooperative and/or open task formats (cf. Schäfer 2014). Besides the relatively large number of suggestions about the design of task formats and so forth in pedagogical literature, there exist numerous methodological deliberations all of which seek to maintain or foster the greatest possible impact by combining active, receptive, information-based and creative learning methods; examples include the UN's IEEP (UN 2003) or the tripartite educational model of 'awareness' / 'analysis and evaluation' / 'participation,' discussed and applied by Hayden Gabriel and Greg Garrard (2012) (for a discussion of these models, especially in the context of the European system of evaluation by PISA, see Grimm and Wanning, *forthcoming*). For my argument here, I will focus primarily on the well-established method of distinguishing, first of all, three phases of reception and analysis: a pre-, a while-, and a post-watching phase. It is important to understand the relevance of a structured engagement with the film medium which might overstrain those students whose listening competences and visual literacy may need to improve; at the same time, however, pedagogical engagement with films must not ignore the excitement and pleasure of film watching by presenting, for instance, too much information or too many small-scale tasks that, if anything, kill any *plaisir du texte*. As argued above, *District 9* in significant ways plays with and frustrates viewer expectations. Yet, it is not likely that each and every student is a competent viewer already; and if the film is used in a school setting, the same holds true to an even greater degree for pupils. The actual tasks and the level of complexity governing the pedagogical activity must of course vary accordingly. So, while 'the types of visual representations' used in the film, and even the montage of different media forms, 'constitute the vocabulary that the anticipated target group is exposed to on a daily basis' (Schmidt 2013: 244), if the film's play with receptive expectations is to be understood, it needs to be discussed in class. The pre-watching phase seems perfect for this: students/pupils could be asked to 'define' an alien or a sci-fi film and introduce specific elements to each other; or, if the film and not its presumed genre is the main focus of the lessons, the film's poster could be presented as a silent impulse upon which pupils might react spontaneously by telling what they see and, almost at the same time, reacting to this visual cue's framing strategies in that they categorise the film according to what the poster suggests *District 9* is about. Moreover, not only the film's generic affiliation can be discussed but it might be instructive to discuss some character or physical traits of the aliens; indeed, some of the character traits and visual cues of 'traditional' alien representation appear in the film, while others are challenged, and it may be worthwhile to speculate about the reasons for this. Moreover, at the end of the session or unit, a comparison between students' expectations and the film's critique of these expectations could provide a list of representational forms of othering and 'us' vs. 'them' dichotomies inherent to orientalist discourse, as Edward Said has described Western structures of perception of 'the West' and 'the orient' (see Said [1978] 2003).

While watching the film (or, depending on the specific learning group, sections of it), pupils might be asked to take notes when, in the documentary part, different inhabitants of Johannesburg explain their aversion towards the aliens. Who are these people? What exactly do they say? And is it possible to identify certain (visual and rhetoric) strategies such as specific discourse markers (academic intellectuals, people 'from the streets,' etc.) and visual framings (books in the background etc.)? Especially the parts of the film that follow the compositional and aesthetic protocols of a documentary invite lively classroom debate and activity because of the employment of various short snippets, interviews and other, that are brought together in a form of a montage: this means that it is possible to pause the film after one or two statements, discuss these statements and suggest counter-arguments or play with the information in any other way. After the role(s) of framing and the processes of othering and/versus the 'realistic' style of the documentary have been engaged with, pupils could be asked to think about ways in which the film goes on and ends. The second bit can then be shown in its entirety, while pupils take notes on their expectations and on the change in framing patterns.

In all these discussions, both in the pre- and while-watching phases, it is important not to lose sight of the embeddedness of the filmic fantasy in the real-life xenophobia of the Apartheid system. As argued above, it is this tension between fact and fiction that tells a lot about framing, and it helps to understand the role and significance of films and literature in the environmental classroom. Fortunately, there exist a number of informational sites on the web that pupils could access and work with: the real Distrik Ses, for instance, is discussed on the site of the District Six-Museum in Johannesburg (www.districtsix.co.za/frames.htm), the viral promotional campaign for the film can still be traced online, and the history of colonialism and racism and its connection with speciecism and a rhetoric of beastly degradation, as manifest in the use of the derogatory term 'prawns,' is nothing new to environmentally interested teachers.

The post-watching phase should bring together both these 'real-life' elements and the insights into the importance of framing. The overall guiding question could be a discussion of the transition from one framing pattern to the other, that is, from (mock-)documentary to action film. Students could engage with different options: it tells us about the 'always already' framed nature of linguistic and artistic communication. It could be discussed as a logical necessity because, once Wikus transforms, the idea of documentation does not hold any longer; the dehumanised creature must not star a documentary but has to be turned into prey that is hunted, which requires different narrative patterns. Or, from a different angle, the class could discuss this discursive move as a concession to the global audience and modern Western cinema; in this context, it might be useful to discuss what Graham Huggan has called the 'postcolonial exotic,' arguing that postcolonial (and the same holds true for environmental) scholars should be 'alert to its complicities with the capitalist world-system it affects to critique' (Huggan 2001: 229). Dealing with these issues does not necessarily mean classroom debate and nothing else, however. Following the idea of cooperative and inclusive learning, I suggest creative tasks and project work instead: if they are supposed to talk about empathy and otherness, or if they are to think about the human-alien transformation and what it means for the human subject and identity, pupils could be asked to write a letter of apology to Wikus (or to Christopher, the alien), telling him what happened or asking him if he is going to return and why (not), for instance.

5 Concluding Remarks: Towards Transcultural-Ecological Education

In my remarks above, I have concentrated on the significance of framing as both a general epistemological issue in ecocritical pedagogy and a particularly narrative and literary strategy of presenting textual information. As an educational element, framing moreover serves the ecocritical interest of bringing together text and reader, not in some abstract play of signification but because 'the reader is a fundamental part of this process [of understanding framing]' and the 'interaction between text and recipient is therefore assumed to be a dynamic process' (Schäbler 2014: 15–16) that helps understand the epistemological value of transcultural literary narratives. As frames in literature share 'one frame function, namely to guide and enable interpretation' (Wolf qtd. in Schäbler 2014: 18), they also point to the importance of interpretation for processes of understanding generally.

This, I believe, is nowhere more relevant than in the context of teaching English in a transcultural dialogue, as described by Antor (2000) or Freitag and Gymnich (2007). It must be noted that 'similar framing strategies can fulfil vastly differing functions depending on their cultural-historical context' (Schäbler 2014: 224); in any (pedagogical) case, however, framing helps us to understand that ecocritical learning isn't necessarily concerned with nature 'out there' but with the complex mesh and mess that is natureculture (cf. Grewe-Volpp 2008). And it does not have to discuss nonhuman animals or ecosystems: aliens and racist systems will do just as well (or better).

Appendix: A Brief Plot Summary of *District 9*

A huge alien ship had stopped over Johannesburg, South Africa, in 1982. That the aliens on board were almost starved, weak fugitives, that they had been brought into provisional camps that turned into ghettos during the following 20 years, and that the aliens now face a xenophobic, hostile social climate that obviously bears resemblance to the *Apartheid* regime is what the audience learns by means of a collage of filmic snippets, arranged in the way of modern 'docutainment' series.

The actual plot of events starts when Wikus van de Merve (Sharlto Copley), employed at the security company MNU, becomes head of an operation with the aim of re-settling the aliens from District 9, their current abode, to District 10, supposedly an improvement of their living conditions. The operation is not successful, however, and the audience can witness the organisation's amateurish and humiliating ways of communicating with the aliens. Moreover, it becomes clear that it is the aliens' advanced weapon technology, rather than their well-being, that the MNU is interested in.

When Wikus accidentally touches alien liquid he believes to be a part of a weapon, he starts transforming into an alien himself for the liquid contained genetic information that has the power of forming hybrid beings by forging human and alien DNA. Instead of helping Wikus, the MNU people soon realise that Wikus's altered alien DNA is the key to the weapons they were after: they plan to amputate Wikus's arm and, finally, vivisect him completely in order to obtain as much of his hybridised biological material as possible.

Wikus manages to escape, but he has become the hunted rather than the hunter now. He returns to District 9 where he meets an alien engineer, Christopher, and his son who are working on a means of returning to the alien planet. Wikus is informed that he may be cured, and offers his help.

In a final battle between MNU, criminal ghetto gangs and aliens, Wikus saves the aliens and enables them to escape, but he is stuck on earth and has to hide from the MNU's grasp. His transformation is not stopped; instead he completely turns into an alien. In order to be remembered, he occasionally sends flowers and other artefacts he has made from garbage to his wife but has to remain hidden, anyhow. The last scene shows him, now living in the garbage just as the aliens he tried to dislocate in the beginning, as he crafts a flower from some metal parts he finds.

Bibliography

Primary Source
District 9. 2009. Dir. Neill Blomkamp. Perf. Sharlto Copley, Jason Cope, David James. Wellington (NZ): Wingnut Productions; Culver City, California: TriStar Pictures.

Secondary Sources
Antor, Heinz. 2000. 'Postcolonial Pedagogy, or Why and How to Teach the New English Literatures' in Bernhard Reitz and Sigrid Rieuwerts (eds) *Anglistentag 1999 Mainz. Proceedings of the Conference of the German Association of University Teachers of English XXI*. Trier: Wissenschaftlicher Verlag: 245–262.

Bartosch, Roman. 2014. 'Teaching a Poetics of Failure? The Benefit of *Not*-Understand the Other, Posthumanism, and the Works of Shaun Tan and Wolf Erlbruch' in Roman Bartosch and Sieglinde Grimm (eds) *Teaching Environments – Ecocritical Encounters*. Frankfurt am Main et al.: Peter Lang: 59–73.

Bartosch, Roman and Greg Garrard. 2013. 'The Function of Criticism. A Response to William Myjor and Andrew McMurry's Editorial' in *Journal of Ecocriticism* 5(1): 6pp.

Brereton, Pat. 2013. 'Eco-Cinema, Sustainability and Africa: A Reading of *Out of Africa* (1985), *The Constant Gardener* (2005) and *District 9* (2010) in *Journal of African Cinemas* 5(2): 219–235.

Buell, Lawrence. 1995. *The Environmental Imagination. Thoerau, Nature Writing, and the Formation of American Culture.* Cambridge, MA: Belknap Press of Harvard University Press.

Chatman, Seymour. 1978. *Story and Discourse. Narrative Structure in Fiction and Film.* Ithaca: Cornell University Press.

Doff, Sabine. 2009. 'Inter- and/or Transcultural Learning in the Foreign English Language Classroom? Theoretical Foundations and Practical Implications' in Frank Schulze-Engler and Sissy Helff (eds) *Transcultural English Studies: Theories, Fictions, Realities.* Amsterdam: Rodopi.

Eisenmann, Maria; Nancy Grimm and Laurenz Volkmann (eds). 2010. *Teaching the New English Cultures and Literatures.* Heidelberg: Winter.

Faulstich, Werner. 2008. *Grundkurs Filmanalyse.* Munich: W. Fink.

Freitag, Britta and Marion Gymnich. 2007. 'New English and Postcolonial Literatures im Fremdsprachenunterricht' in Wolfgang Hallet and Ansgar Nünning (eds) *Neue Ansätze und Konzepte der Literatur- und Kulturdidaktik.* Trier: Wissenschaftlicher Verlag: 259–276.

Gabriel, Hayden and Greg Garrard. 2012. 'Reading and Writing Climate Change' in Greg Garrard (ed.) *Teaching Ecocriticism and Green Cultural Studies.* Basingstoke: Palgrave Macmillan: 117–129.

Garrard, Greg (ed.). 2012. *Teaching Ecocriticism and Green Cultural Studies.* Basingstoke: Palgrave Macmillan.

Goodbody, Axel. 2012. 'Frame Analysis and the Literature of Climate Change' in Timo Müller and Michael Sauter (eds) *Literature, Ecology, Ethics. Recent Trends in Ecocriticism.* Heidelberg: Universitätsverlag Winter: 15–33.

Grewe-Volpp, Christa. 2006. 'Nature "out there" and as "a social player": Some Basic Consequences for a Literary Ecocritical Analysis' in Catrin Gersdorf and Sylvia Mayer (eds) *Nature in Literary and Cultural Studies: Transatlantic Conversations on Ecocriticism.* Amsterdam: Rodopi: 71–86.

Grimm, Sieglinde and Berbeli Wanning. 2016. 'Cultural Ecology and the Teaching of Literature' in Hubert Zapf (ed.) *De Gruyter Handbook of Ecocriticism and Cultural Ecology.* Berlin: De Gruyter: 513–533.

Huggan, Graham. 2001. *The Postcolonial Exotic: Marketing the Margins.* London: Routledge.

Hulme, Mike. 2009. *Why We Disagree About Climate Change. Understanding Controversy, Inaction and Opportunity.* Cambridge: Cambridge UP.

James, Erin. 2012. 'Teaching the Postcolonial/Ecocritical Dialogue' in Greg Garrard (ed.) *Teaching Ecocriticism and Green Cultural Studies.* Basingstoke: Palgrave Macmillan: 60–71.

Kerridge, Richard. 2010. 'The Single Source' in *Ecozon@ – European Journal of Literature, Culture and Environment* 1(1): 155–161.

Küchler, Uwe. 2014. 'Where Foreign Language Education Meets, Clashes and Grapples with the Environment' in Roman Bartosch and Sieglinde Grimm (eds) *Teaching Environments: Ecocritical Encounters*. Frankfurt am Main: Peter Lang: 23–34.

McHugh, Susan. 2011. *Animal Stories: Narrating Across Species Lines*. Minneapolis: U of Minnesota P.

McMajor, William and Andrew McMurry. 2013. 'Reponse of William Major and Andrew McMurry' in *Journal of Ecocriticism* 5(1): 5pp.

Nixon, Rob. 2011. *Slow Violence and the Environmentalism of the Poor*. Cambridge, MA: Harvard University Press.

Norris, Andrew. 2003. 'The Exemplary Exception: Philosophical and Political Decisions in Giorgio Agamben's *Homo Sacer*' in *Radical Philosophy* 119: 6–16.

Parham, John. 2006. 'The Deficiency of "Environmental Capital": Why Environmentalism Needs a Reflexive Pedagogy' in Sylvia Mayer and Graham Wilson (eds) *Ecodidactic Perspectives on English Language, Literatures and Cultures*. Trier: Wissenschaftlicher Verlag: 7–22.

Said, Edward. [1978] 2003. *Orientalism*. New York: Vintage.

Schäbler, Daniel. 2014. *Framing Strategies in English Fiction from Romanticism to the Present*. Heidelberg: Universitätsverlag Winter.

Schäfer, Ulla. 2014. 'Englischunterricht für Schülerinnen und Schüler mit Lernschwierigkeiten' in Roman Bartosch and Andreas Rohde (eds) *Im Dialog der Disziplinen. Englischdidaktik – Förderpädagogik – Inklusion*. Trier: Wissenschaftlicher Verlag: 46–62.

Schmidt, Jochen. 2013. 'Neill Blomkamp, *District 9* (2009)' in Susanne Peters, Klaus Stierstorfer and Laurenz Volkmann (eds) *Teaching Contemporary Literature and Culture: Film (Part 1)*. Trier: Wissenschaftlicher Verlag.

Schulze-Engler, Frank. 2007. 'From Postcolonialism to Transcultural World Literature' in Lars Eckstein (ed) *English Literatures Across the Globe: A Companion*. Paderborn: Wilhelm Fink.

UN. 2003. *United Nations Environment Programme*. On line at: http://unep.org (consulted Mar 19, 2015).

Wolff, Martina. 2008. 'Intercultural Awareness and Film: Spielberg's *War of the Worlds* as post-9/11 Film' in Petra Bosenius, Andreas Rohde and Martina Wolff (eds) *Verstehen und Verständigung. Interkulturelles Lehren und Lernen*. Trier: Wissenschaftlicher Verlag: 187–207.

CHAPTER 14

The Nature Study Idea: Framing Nature for Children in Early Twentieth Century Schools

Dorothy Kass

Abstract

Nature study, a new subject for elementary schools throughout the English-speaking world in the late nineteenth and early twentieth centuries, introduced natural science to children through new methods of pedagogy, including direct observation and reasoning, and self-activity. The subject, however, was differentiated from elementary science by its embrace of aesthetic appreciation and an aim to foster an emotional response to nature, often referred to as "sympathy." Scientific observation and reasoning, aesthetic appreciation, and sympathy with nature clearly and consistently defined the subject, and may be seen as comprising a particular frame through which children could regard nature. Amongst its diverse aims, nature study included a conservation ethic: as children came to understand nature, they would want to care for and protect it. In the state of New South Wales, Australia, nature study was introduced to a new syllabus in 1904 as required teaching for all classes of the centrally administered public elementary schools. While various types of evidence allow the historian to analyse nature study in practice, in this paper rare examples of children's writing about nature are introduced as one way of approaching how nature study and its particular frame for regarding the natural world was received and responded to by children.

1   Introduction

Nature study was a new subject introduced to elementary school curricula throughout the English-speaking world in the 1890s and the early 1900s. An important component of the educational reform movement known as "New Education," nature study was supported by a considerable body of theoretical and practical literature. This literature informed what was widely referred to as "the nature study idea." Nature study introduced plant, animal, and geological studies to even the youngest children in elementary or primary schools.

* Some material in this chapter originally appeared in Dorothy Kass, 2018, *Educational Reform and Environmental Concern: A History of School Nature Study,* Abingdon, Oxon: Routledge.

Methodology was crucial to its definition, with direct observation from nature, questioning and reasoning, and active learning replacing older methods of passive rote learning.

Two recent histories, published in the United States, provided a much needed analysis of nature study in all its complexity. Both authors correctly state that they are addressing a previously neglected area of research. The works complement each other in that Sally Gregory Kohlstedt's *Teaching Children Science: Hands-On Nature Study in North America, 1890–1930* looks primarily at nature study as an educational movement while Kevin C. Armitage in *The Nature Study Movement: The Forgotten Popularizer of America's Conservation Ethic* is concerned with nature study as both a pedagogic and a popular idea that was important in the conservation movement (Kohlstedt 2010; Armitage 2009a). Nature study in other English speaking countries has received some consideration in articles (Jenkins 1981; Jenkins and Swinnerton 1996; Marsden 1998; McGeorge 1994). Environmental historian Libby Robin made important connections between the attention given to nature study in Australian schools and the fostering of national identification through indigenous fauna and flora (Robin 2001a, 2001b, 2002). The author's own research into nature study in Australian schools indicated how important the new subject was within educational reform in the early twentieth century. While its advocates outlined many aims for the subject, one prominent aspect was its conservation ethic. Educators and others expressed concern about the Australian environment which they hoped that the education of children, as citizens of the future, would address (Kass 2018).

This paper will discuss "the nature study idea" through a consideration of its development and definition. I argue that its ideology, advocacy, and practice represented a particular frame for the study of the natural world, a frame through which children were invited to view, study, and relate to nature. I then turn to nature study as it was practised in the Australian state of New South Wales, introducing samples of writing by school children as evidence of the particular way of perceiving the natural world which nature study endorsed. The paper will conclude with considerations as to the place of the nature study idea in a lineage of environmental thought.

2   The Nature Study Idea

The nature study idea developed its distinctive form in the United States in the 1890s and early 1900s. Prominent educators, many of whom had travelled to Europe and studied in Germany, were putting into practice new educational ideas, including the incorporation of natural science teaching at all levels of schooling (Kohlstedt 2010: 37ff; Armitage 2009a: 52ff). At Cook County Normal School in Chicago, a training school for teachers renowned for its progressive ideas, educator and science graduate Wilbur Jackman developed a distinctive course in natural science which was published as *Nature Study for the Common Schools* in 1891. "Nature study" was a term that had been in use for one or two years, but it was this influential book which gave it high visibility (Jackman 1891).

Nature Study for the Common Schools established many of the basic tenets of teaching nature study. These included: lessons arranged by the seasons; direct observation of, and contact with, nature by the child; the importance of relating nature study to other subjects; and the variety of modes through which the child could express his or her observations including oral language, written language and art (Jackman 1891: 26–28). *Field Work in Nature Study*, a later book by Jackman, stressed outdoor study and the need for plants and animals to be studied in relation to each other and their environment (Jackman 1894). Schemes for fieldwork within particular environments such as a river basin, a swamp, or a lake shore were included, along with the advice that "[t]he central point of interest in the study of either the animal or the plant is in its adaptation to the features of its environment" (Jackman 1894: 48). Jackman's writing witnessed the early association of the concepts of adaptation and ecology with the teaching of nature study.[1] Jackman and other advocates of nature study repeatedly used the word "environment," their texts indicating the significance of nature study for environmental history and the history of environmental education.

Nature study courses became increasingly widespread in the United States in the 1890s, and many authors produced practical handbooks for the guidance of teachers. These included those by Lucy Langdon Williams Wilson (1897) and Dietrich Lange (1898). Different approaches and schemes perhaps emphasised the need for a thorough, theoretical treatment of the new subject. Three important and influential texts were published at the turn of the century, providing deeply thoughtful analyses of nature study. These were: *Nature Study and the Child* (1900) by Charles B. Scott; *The Nature-Study Idea* (1903) by Liberty Hyde Bailey; and *Nature Study and Life* (1902) by Clifton F. Hodge.

Prominent educator Charles Scott chose his title to appeal to a wide interest in "child study." Progressive educators discussed findings of the new disciplines of child development and child psychology in their efforts to promote a new,

---

1 Environmental historian Donald Worster explained that the term *oecologie* was first used in 1866 by Ernst Haeckel. Gaining currency in the late nineteenth century as *ecology*, the term replaced the earlier usage *economy of nature* (Worster 1985: 191ff).

child centred education. In *Nature Study and the Child*, Scott argued that the subject provided a means of placing the child firmly within the natural environment. He stressed that the materials for study would be found in actual nature, and children would continue to study nature through the senses, as they had since infancy: "The laboratory for nature study is all outdoors; and the only instruments and appliances absolutely necessary are the seeing eye, the hearing ear, and the understanding heart" (Scott 1900: 97).

Scott stressed the gaining of knowledge through personal observation, investigation and reasoning, but continued by arguing:

> If we merely aim to interest the children in nature, develop their powers of observation, expression, and thought, and give them a better knowledge of their physical environment and stop there, the ultimate results may be of doubtful value [...] No; interest, power, knowledge, are not the highest aims in nature study. Preceding these, along with these, more important than these, must come the cultivation of the sympathies of the child [...] Most closely related to the cultivation of sympathy with nature is the development of the aesthetic sense in our pupils, the appreciation of the beauty of their environment.
> SCOTT 1900: 112–113

Scott perceived the subject as consisting of the acquisition of knowledge, the nurture of "sympathy," and the development of aesthetic appreciation. "Sympathy" for Scott and other advocates referred to the fostering of a close, caring understanding and an emotional attachment to the natural world. Intellectual historian Daniel Wickberg, in an etymological study of "sympathy," explained that the invention of the concept of "empathy" in the twentieth century actually redefined the meaning of "sympathy" which had formerly included those meanings later attached to "empathy" (2007: 135–136). Armitage, in discussing "sympathy" as used by the nature study advocates, referred to John Ruskin's definition of sympathy as "the imaginative understanding of the natures of others, and the power of putting ourselves in their place." The application of sympathy to non human nature remained something of a radical sentiment to which some critics of nature study objected (2009a: 6). The sympathetic aspect of the nature study idea deserves particular attention on the part of scholars studying the history of environmental thought.

Scott's "highest aim for nature study" was "to adapt the child to his environment" (Scott 1900: 119). In this section Scott outlined his concerns for the physical environment:

> We have adapted ourselves to our physical environment by stripping our land of its forests, our air of its birds, our waters of their fish, by using up in the most reckless manner our natural resources. Nature has been our slave, from whom we could take anything, to whom we owed nothing.
> SCOTT 1900: 123

Nature study, for Scott, would provide a new and better adaptation to environment, where children would wish to care for and protect natural resources.

Liberty Hyde Bailey, lecturer at the Agricultural College of Cornell University, had been involved in the teaching of nature study and its promotion for several years when he collected his writings for publication as *The Nature-Study Idea: Being an Interpretation of the New School-Movement to put the Child in Sympathy with Nature*. He chose the title and sub-title of his influential book with precision. For him nature study was a new ideology, a new movement, which aimed to place the child in a position of "sympathy" with nature. For Bailey, as for Scott, nature study was much more than science.

Bailey promoted the study of a "central theme in a scene of life" such as the brook, studied in its entirety. The brook would illustrate in miniature the forces which had shaped the earth's surface and allow the study of its plant and animal life (Bailey 1903: 26–27). Bailey, in effect, was promoting the study of an ecosystem and the adaptations and interrelationships of its components.[2]

Bailey's environmental vision appears surprisingly similar to those articulated by environmentalists much later in the twentieth century:

> It were better that we know the things, small and great, which make up this environment, and that we live with them in harmony, for all things are of kin.
> BAILEY 1903: 86

Bailey's philosophy embraced both a concern with the physical environment itself and man's place within it. As nature study led children to sympathy with nature, they would "learn to love all nature's forms and cease to abuse them" (Bailey 1903: 36). His was an optimistic view that saw evidence of a growing interest in the natural world in popular nature writing as much as in laws to protect the nation's flora and fauna. Societies for lessening cruelty to animals,

---

2 The term *ecosystem* was not available to Bailey, but *ecology* was listed in the glossary of his earlier book, *Lessons with Plants* (1897: 460). He defined ecology as "the science or study which treats of the relationships of organisms to each other and to their environments."

and a realisation that fashion was leading to the destruction of birds for their feathers and mammals for their fur also pointed to "an enlargement of our sympathies," and an "enlarging vision respecting our own place in the world" (Bailey 1903: 111–116).

Professor Clifton Hodge's *Nature Study and Life* presented a different underlying philosophy to that of Scott and Bailey. While they had absorbed a post-Darwinian view of humanity as embedded in nature, Hodge drew upon an older Judaeo-Christian tradition, where nature's chief function was to serve man's needs, where man had "dominion over every living thing that moveth upon the earth" (Hodge 1902: 1). Hodge traced human development and progress through the subjugation of nature represented by the domestication of animals and the cultivation of plants. For Hodge, nature study was important in order to achieve the Biblical injunction to exercise dominion over nature (Hodge 1902: 2–15).

However, Hodge was also a strong advocate of the need for conservation. If, as God's representative, man had been a little "severe," leading to extermination of species, then correction was necessary (Hodge 1902: 8). He promoted the preservation of land and forest conservation as necessary for future human utilisation of resources. Hodge stressed the economic advantages to be secured from the teaching of nature study and regretted that this aspect was often ignored by teachers. Nature study should allow identification of both "the beneficent" and the "evils in nature," such as insect pests, noxious weeds and injurious animals (Hodge 1902: 17–19).

The differences between the three exponents illustrate the complexity of the nature study idea and of the ideological contexts in which it operated. There were certainly many aims for nature study: educational, economic, social, moral, and environmental. Difference of opinion on the subject's purpose was perhaps inevitable. Some texts, while obviously promoting the study of nature and interest in the natural world, stopped short of expressing concern about the environment and advocating conservation of resources or preservation of natural landscape, flora and fauna. Charles McMurry (1904), for example, advocated the thorough enjoyment of nature, its woods, wildflowers, and song-birds, and the free and unstinted pleasure of children as they explored nature (McMurry 1904: 73). But he stopped short of expressing any concern about the state of that nature, such as its abuse, disappearance, or extinction. He focussed on the benefits of applied science in areas such as health, sanitation, and medicine and hoped for increased respect for science and scientists. (McMurry 1904: 60–62). Wilson's *Nature Study in Elementary Schools* (1897) and Lange's *Handbook of Nature Study* (1898), as pedagogical manuals, do not exhibit explicit concern about environmental degradation. Certainly concern about the environment developed and increased as time passed, influenced by the very popularity of the texts by Scott, Hodge and Bailey. In the United States, conservationists increasingly came to consider children and their education to be of importance in the conservation movement (Armitage 2009a: 4–5).

Analysis of a range of texts addressing nature study reveals that advocates, despite their differences, consistently endorsed three basic components. All stressed the importance of natural science as a topic to be introduced to elementary schools and to be taught through careful observation and problem solving. Additionally, all believed that aesthetic appreciation of nature and the development of a sympathetic understanding of the natural world were important. These two aspects clearly defined nature study and distinguished it from elementary science. For several decades in the United States, and for a longer period in other English speaking countries, the nature study idea provided a frame for teaching and learning about nature in schools. It was self-consciously distinguished from and, for a time, was dominant over an alternative frame of objective elementary science.

3 Nature Study in New South Wales, Australia

By the early years of the twentieth century, nature study was being talked about and introduced into schools throughout the English speaking world, with prominent British educator Patrick Geddes endorsing nature study as a movement that was "wide and general, one affecting the education of both sexes, of all ages, and all countries" (Geddes 1903: 113). In Australia, as elsewhere, advocates endorsed a range of purposes for the new subject. Adapted to the Australian context, these included nature study's potential for national, scientific, technological, industrial, and agricultural development. There were also its educational, moral, and health benefits. Victorian educator Charles Long, in his influential booklet *The Aim and Method in Nature-Study* (1905), analysed over a dozen outcomes for nature study. The subject as education in knowledge and appreciation of the distinctive Australian fauna and flora was important from the time of its introduction. The need for protection of that nature gained in prominence during the course of the first decade of its teaching, influenced by educators who were often also dedicated naturalists. As naturalists they were involved in debates surrounding the need for conservation of resources, protection of nature, and public education in those matters (Kass 2018).

Nature study was included in new curricula in each Australian state in the early years of the century. Australia became a federated nation in 1901, but the administration of education remained the responsibility of individual state governments. Within each state, the control of public elementary schools was highly centralised, and when new syllabuses were introduced, they applied to every school throughout the state. In New South Wales, nature study was an important component of the "New Syllabus of Instruction" of 1904 (New South Wales. Department of Public Instruction 1904). The subject was introduced to schools with enthusiasm and support from educators, administrators, politicians, scientists and naturalists (Kass 2014a, 2018: 98–110).

A range of sources may be used by the historian attempting to open the classroom door to see how the nature study idea was practically implemented in New South Wales in the years after 1904. Reports by teachers provide details of what was happening in particular classrooms, in school gardens, and on excursions made by classes to locales beyond the classroom. Inspectors' reports of schools are valuable, as are the rare surviving lesson registers kept by individual teachers (Kass 2014a, 2018: 128–129). Photographs give an enticing glimpse of children in their gardens, and involved in other activities beyond the classroom (Figures 14.1 and 14.2).

One particular type of evidence comes from occasionally surviving examples of children's writing. These may provide details of nature study in practice,

FIGURE 14.1   *Camdenville Public School, Sydney, NSW, 1909.*
SOURCE: SANSW: 15051_a047_002276

THE NATURE STUDY IDEA 229

FIGURE 14.2   *Chakola Public School, near Cooma, Southern NSW, 1920.*
SOURCE: SANSW: 15051_a047_002772

revealing the reception by children of the way in which nature study invited them to regard their natural environment. Such pieces have usually been published in journals or newspapers because they were considered exemplary rather than typical. For the historian this can be an advantage, as if the educators and teachers of the time had flagged these pieces of writing, saying: "This is what we wanted. This is what we tried to achieve." Three pieces of writing by Ethel, aged 12, written in 1906; Maggie, aged 12, written in 1914; and Edith, aged 15, written in 1921, are examples of children writing about nature (Ethel Packer 1907; Maggie May 1915; Edith 1922). These quite different compositions demonstrate the particular concerns of nature study.

"A School Excursion in the Bush", by Ethel Packer of East Kurrajong School, was entered into a competition held as part of a large nature study exhibition at Richmond, a country town west of Sydney, in November 1906. Her writing was described as having "remarkable literary merit" and won a prize for the best account of a school excursion.[3] Ethel described a bush ramble in which the pupils, accompanied by their teacher, observed the trees, plants, birds, insects, and streams. She described the gum, ironbark, and wattle trees, along with their economic uses. Then the children put their observational and reasoning skills into action:

> While we were walking along at our leisure we noticed a bush, for its leaves were eaten and riddled by something. We searched the bush to find the cause of this, and found a cluster of grubs; they were the grubs or larvae of the Gum Saw Fly. On other bushes were cocoons hanging from the branches [...] made of small sticks which the grub had bitten into suitable lengths, and then fastened together by silken threads which come from his body.
> PACKER 1907: 7

Nature study allowed Ethel to admire the "magnificent" ferns she observed near the stream: "some large and strong, some small and delicate [...] 'Oh, how lovely!' I exclaimed." In Ethel's description, we see several facets of nature study: observation and description; consideration of economic usefulness; aesthetic appreciation; and the freedom to rejoice in the experience and to conclude: "Oh! we had a glorious time wandering through 'Nature's Garden.'"

---

[3] Ethel was described as "a pupil of Miss Colvin's school." Elizabeth Colvin was an "accomplished and respected teacher at East Kurrajong School from 1898 to 1909" (Hawkesbury City Council 2011: 73). The Nature Study Exhibition was reported in *Windsor and Richmond Gazette* (1 December 1906: 6) and *New South Wales Educational Gazette* January 1907: 158–160.

Maggie May was a part Aboriginal child who attended Nanima Aborigines School, a one-teacher school in a cheaply constructed building at Nanima Reserve, four miles from the town of Wellington in central New South Wales. Maggie's essay, "The Autobiography of a Jacky Winter," won first prize in a literary competition for pupils under 13 years where children were asked to write an autobiography of any Australian native bird, and the instruction given that "preference will be given to work showing original observation on the part of the competitor."[4] The topic certainly demanded some degree of identification with the bird on the part of the child, but rather than encouraging an anthropomorphic story of children disguised as animals, the judges were looking for direct observation from nature of the bird's life cycle and behaviour. This is what Maggie wrote:

> I am going to tell you about myself. I was once in an egg shell, and my mother sat every day on the egg until I pecked a hole big enough to come out. When I was hatched I saw two other little birds in the nest [...] Then my mother brought us little grubs to eat, and we were all cosy together, my sister, my brother, and I [...] When my wings got stronger my mother taught me how to fly. When I was flying about I saw that there were a good many birds like us about. We are little birds, about the size of sparrows. We are brownish, grey above, and very light grey beneath, and the two outer feathers of our tails are white, and we have a hook on the end of our beaks, because we are fly-catchers. We make very small open nests [...] in Gum trees, Wattle, and Ti-trees, and we choose a dead limb, and place the nest in a fork of it.
> MAY 1915: 19

Maggie continued the life cycle as the young bird matured, chose a mate, laid eggs of her own, and then caught food for the young birds. Maggie gave more than what was asked by incorporating Aboriginal knowledge of the Jacky Winter:

> The old aborigines used to tell their children that if they threw stones at the little birds, the Great Spirit would turn them into stone. The Aborigines believed that we were people at first, and that the Great Spirit changed us into birds [...] The Aborigines call us the Murreibarng.

---

4   Information on Maggie's school from SANSW: NRS3829 School Files 5/17051.2 Nanima (2) Aboriginal. Competition rules from *Public Instruction Gazette* May 1914: 138.

> Murreibarng means – gathering at white ants' nests. We eat the white ants and their larvae too.
>
> MAY 1915: 19–20

Maggie seamlessly folded the Aboriginal sections into her essay. Was it these pieces which allowed her essay to stand out from others? At a time when indigenous nature knowledge was not highly regarded, the choice of Maggie's essay as exemplary writing is significant.

The final piece of writing, "Trees," was one of several compositions published in the *Education Gazette* in 1922, to illustrate the achievements of children living so remotely that they received their schooling by correspondence.

Edith wrote about a mountainous region known as "the Warrumbungles," today a national park located on the central western slopes of New South Wales. Edith demonstrated her close observation of trees and described their economic uses. But the strength of her writing was its aesthetic appreciation combined with her emotional involvement in the landscape:

> In the Warrumbungles you can climb up a tall hill and look away for miles and miles, over valleys and rivers and hills, and you can see the light green forests of fluffy apple-trees, and the dark green leaves and black trunks of iron-barks growing in the hollows. Then across a sort of dividing line you can see a still, blue green expanse of gum tops [...] You look beyond the near hills to [...] the horizon, blue in the distance, purple nearer to you, and merging into the sky to the far, far ranges a smoky-grey, and you know, though you cannot see them, the lights and shades that play on the beautiful, swaying, ever-moving forests of trees that clothe the hills.
>
> Then, because the beauty fills your heart with wonder, the glorious splendour of those endless hills, in their mantle of living green, brings a lump to your throat. You turn your head away for very aching, pain-filled happiness at this your world of hills and trees and stretching plains and winding rivers. And you may happen to look away to your left, where the country is "improved," where the hills are brown bare corpses [...] Immediately below you is a golden expanse of cultivated land, and it spreads for mile on mile in monotonous, grain-growing bareness, and wherever you look is yellow to brown, and the glaring sun strikes up from it, and a dusty road winds through, and in a corner of a paddock is a white weather-beaten house [...] You turn away once more, this time in [...] disgust and misery.
>
> EDITH 1922: 156–157

The three pieces of writing demonstrate the particular conception of nature study as elementary science, with close and questioning observation and reasoning, and its additional incorporation of aesthetic appreciation and the appeal to an emotional response to nature. Ethel, Maggie and Edith each demonstrate their perceptions of nature through such a frame. Ethel had no problem in talking of the utilitarian aspects of timber alongside her appreciation of beauty and her joy in the day's ramble through the bush in springtime. Nature study encouraged such associations. Maggie's "autobiography" followed the instruction to pay particular attention to actual observation from life of the habits of a native Australian bird. But the topic also required identification with that bird, in this manner clearly reflecting nature study's endorsement of "sympathy." Maggie's additional Aboriginal knowledge augmented the message, promoted by nature study advocates, that nature ought to be protected. Edith, too, demonstrated nature study's promotion of observation alongside emotional responses to the environment. Her introspective immersion and connection with the uncultivated landscape predates, but is not unlike, the writing of later environmentalists advocating official protection.

The writing of children such as Ethel, Maggie and Edith demonstrates that teachers could convey and children absorb a perspective on nature that was concerned at once with scientific observation and reasoning, aesthetic appreciation, and the encouragement of an emotional and caring affinity with the natural environment. Nature study represented an effective frame which had the potential to influence ideas and perceptions about nature, particularly because it was presented to children, future adults, in schools. In New South Wales, nature study remained part of the syllabus for decades and its legacy may be found within later syllabuses of Natural Science, Science, Human Society and its Environment, and Environmental Education (Kass 2018: 191–198). Environmental education for the present century might well take cognisance of the earlier subject matter, methodology and ideology of nature study.

There are already indications of this occurring, with nature study beginning to feature in broader histories of conservation, environmental thought, and environmental education. Michael Egan and Jeff Crane, in their collection, *Essays on the History of American Environmentalism* (2009), promote "a deeper and more nuanced reading of environmental activism" in contrast to the conventional history (Egan and Crane 2009: 2) and include a chapter devoted to nature study (Armitage 2009b). Thomas E. Smith and Clifford Knapp's *Sourcebook of Experiential Education: Key Thinkers and their Contribution* (2011) includes a section devoted to "Nature Study, Outdoor and Environmental Education."

Nature study undoubtedly influenced those children who would later become conservationists and environmentalists. Kohlstedt and Armitage both believe that education in nature influenced important figures, including Aldo Leopold and Rachel Carson, who shaped later environmentalist thinking (Kohlstedt 2010: 201–236; Armitage 2009a: 195–215). In Australia, bushman, nature writer, and supporter of Queensland's Lamington National Park, Bernard O'Reilly (1903–1975), in his memoir *Green Mountains* (1940/1990), recalled his small school in the Kanimbla Valley in New South Wales, where the creek rippled by and a variety of birds sang all day and built their nests in the trees. He loved nature study:

> The first lesson of the day was called Observation. We were required to write brief essays about any interesting natural phenomena or anything relating to natural history observed on the way to school; the subject was always of our own choosing. Two miles of varied bush track with many creek crossings, gave unlimited material for our young, greedy minds. I hope that Observation is still part of the curriculum of bush schools; it teaches children to discover Nature for themselves, and such intimacy with Nature's secrets nearly always leads to a strong desire to protect all beautiful and useful wild life.
>
> O'REILLY 1940/1990: 86–87

Conservationist and tireless worker for the declaration of national parks, Myles Dunphy (1891–1985), also appreciated nature study while attending school in Kiama, on the south coast of New South Wales, from 1903 to 1907. Myles augmented his interest in school nature study by rambling around the countryside and the beaches, these rambles developing into longer weekend trips, and later into extended walking excursions (Meredith 1999: 34–35; James 2013: 16).

Environmental historian Thomas Dunlap argued that environmental thought of the late twentieth century exhibited a dual legacy: the Enlightenment's rational approach to nature and Romanticism's concern with humanity's emotional ties to it. It looked to science for facts and backing for its understanding of the environmental crisis, and to romantic nature to guide a search for ultimate meaning (Dunlap 2004: 11–12). Dunlap perceived the historical continuity of these ideas, tracing an environmental tradition from the nineteenth to the twentieth and twenty first centuries: "Environmentalism emerged as a visible social movement and political cause in the 1960s, but its heritage stretched back into American history" (Dunlap 2004: 45).

Nature study should be considered as part of that heritage, not only in America but in a wider global context. The same dual legacy, described by

Dunlap, may be discerned within the nature study idea as defined and put into practice in the late nineteenth and early twentieth centuries in elementary schools throughout the English speaking world. With its inclusion of natural science, aesthetic appreciation, and sympathy with the natural world, nature study may well be considered as influential within the evolution of environmentalist thought.

Bibliography

Primary Sources

Bailey, L.H. 1897. *Lessons with Plants: Suggestions for Seeing and Interpreting some of the Common Forms of Vegetation.* New York: MacMillan.

Bailey, L.H. 1903. *The Nature-Study Idea: Being an Interpretation of the New School-Movement to put the Child in Sympathy with Nature.* New York: Doubleday, Page & Company.

Education Gazette (New South Wales Department of Education).

Geddes, Patrick. 1903. 'The Facilities for Nature-Study' in *Official Report of the Nature-Study Exhibition and Conferences* (1903): 111–123.

Hodge, Clifton F. 1902. *Nature Study and Life.* Boston: Ginn.

Jackman, Wilbur S. 1891. *Nature Study for the Common Schools.* New York: Henry Holt.

Jackman, Wilbur S. 1894. *Field Work in Nature Study: A Handbook for Teachers and Pupils.* s.l.: The Author.

Lange, D. 1898. *Handbook of Nature Study: For Teachers and Pupils in Elementary Schools.* New York: Macmillan.

Long, Charles R. 1905. *The Aim and Method in Nature-Study: A Lecture Delivered at a Congress of Teachers held at Daylesford, Victoria, April, 1905.* Melbourne: MacMillan.

McMurry, Charles A. 1904. *Special Method in Elementary Science for the Common School.* New York: Macmillan.

New South Wales. Department of Public Instruction. 1904. 'The New Syllabus of Instruction 1904' in *New South Wales Educational Gazette* March 1904: 234–242.

New South Wales Educational Gazette. 1891–1907.

Official Report of the Nature-Study Exhibition and Conferences held in the Royal Botanic Society's Gardens, Regent's Park, London July 23rd to August 5th, 1902. 1903. London: Blackie and Son.

O'Reilly, Bernard. 1990. *Green Mountains.* Sydney: Envirobook. (Originally published: 1940)

Public Instruction Gazette: Official Gazette of the Public Instruction Department of New South Wales. 1905–1915.

Scott, Charles B. 1900. *Nature Study and the Child.* Boston: D.C. Heath.

State Archives New South Wales. Department of Education; NRS 3829, School files, 1876–1979.

Wilson, Lucy Langdon Williams. 1897. *Nature Study in Elementary Schools. A Manual for Teachers*. New York: Macmillan.

Windsor and Richmond Gazette. December 1906–January 1907.

Primary Sources: Children's Writing

Edith. 1922. 'Trees' in *Education Gazette* July 1922: 156–157.

Ethel Packer. 1907. 'A School Excursion in the Bush' in *Windsor and Richmond Gazette* (5 January 1907: 7).

Maggie May. 1915. 'An Autobiography of a Jacky Winter' in *Bird-Life Supplement to the Education Gazette* October 1915: 19–20.

Secondary Sources

Armitage, Kevin C. 2009a. *The Nature Study Movement: The Forgotten Popularizer of America's Conservation Ethic*. Lawrence, Kansas: University Press of Kansas.

Armitage, Kevin C. 2009b. '"The Science-Spirit in a Democracy": Liberty Hyde Bailey, Nature Study, and the Democratic Impulse of Progressive Conservation' in Michael Egan and Jeff Crane (eds) *Essays on the History of American Environmentalism*. London: Routledge: 89–116.

Dunlap, Thomas R. 2004. *Faith in Nature: Environmentalism as Religious Quest*. Seattle: University of Washington Press.

Egan, Michael and Jeff Crane (eds). 2009. *Essays on the History of American Environmentalism*. London: Routledge.

Hawkesbury City Council. 2011. *Ordinary Meeting Business Paper* (13 September 2011).

James, Peggy. 2013. *Cosmopolitan Conservationists: Greening Modern Sydney*. North Melbourne: Australian Scholarly Publishing.

Jenkins, E.W. 1981. 'Science, Sentimentalism or Social Control?: The Nature Study Movement in England and Wales, 1899–1914' in *History of Education* 10 (1): 33–43.

Jenkins, E.W. and B.J. Swinnerton. 1996. 'The School Nature Study Union, 1903–94' in *History of Education* 25 (2): 181–198.

Kass, Dorothy. 2014a. 'Nature Study' in *Dictionary of Educational History in Australia and New Zealand (DEHANZ)*. On line at http://dehanz.net.au/entries/nature-study/ (consulted 02.04.2016).

Kass, Dorothy. 2018. *Educational Reform and Environmental Concern: A History of School Nature Study in Australia*. Abingdon, Oxon: Routledge.

Kohlstedt, Sally Gregory. 2010. *Teaching Children Science: Hands-On Nature Study in North America, 1890–1930*. Chicago: University of Chicago Press.

Marsden, William E. 1998. '"Conservation Education" and the Foundations of National Prosperity: Comparative Perspectives from Early Twentieth-Century North America and Britain' in *History of Education* 27 (3): 345–362.

McGeorge, Colin. 1994. 'The Presentation of the Natural World in New Zealand Primary Schools, 1880–1914' in *History of Education Review* 23 (2): 32–45.

Meredith, Peter. 1999. *Myles and Milo*. St Leonards: Allen & Unwin.

Robin, Libby. 2001a. *The Flight of the Emu: A Hundred Years of Australian Ornithology, 1901–2001*. Carlton South: Melbourne University Press.

Robin, Libby. 2001b. 'School Gardens and Beyond: Progressive Conservation, Moral Imperatives and the Local Landscape' in *Studies in the History of Gardens & Designed Landscapes* 21 (2): 87–92.

Robin, Libby. 2002. 'Nationalising Nature: Wattle Days in Australia' in *Journal of Australian Studies* 26 (73): 13–26.

Smith, Thomas E. and Clifford E. Knapp (eds). 2011. *Sourcebook of Experiential Education: Key Thinkers and their Contributions*. London: Routledge.

Wickberg, Daniel. 2007. 'The Sympathetic Self in American Culture: 1750–1920' in McClay, William. M. (ed.) *Figures in the Carpet: Finding the Human Person in the American Past*. Grand Rapids: Erdmans: 129–161.

Worster, Donald. 1985. *Nature's Economy: A History of Ecological Ideas*. Cambridge: Cambridge University Press.

CHAPTER 15

Matter, Meaning, and the Classroom: A Case-Study

Isabel Hoving

Abstract

This chapter discusses the pitfalls and best practices of teaching a key-issue in the environmental humanities. It is based on an experimental, co-taught course entitled "Matter and Muck" which was part of the 2013–2014 Research Master program Arts and Culture/ Literary Studies of the University of Leiden, Netherlands. One of the course's points of departure has been dark ecology's suggestion to acknowledge the unpleasant shapelessness and meaninglessness of our material surroundings. The course opted for a radically interdisciplinary approach: (Deleuzian) new materialism was brought into dialogue with Lacanian psychoanalysis and the life sciences. As their final assignment, the students were asked to create a virtual exhibition of art works and performances relating to the topic, and write a contribution to the catalogue. On the one hand, the course showed that the institutional context may not be favorable to the teaching of the relation between matter and meaning in its full complexity–during their previous studies, the master students had not been enabled to study the necessary critical theories (e.g. psychoanalysis, Marxism). On the other hand, the course itself brought to the fore the need to consistently ask critical questions about knowledge production, including the (seemingly) most critical forms of knowledge production. It also showed that an international, intercultural, and interdisciplinary group of advanced students is well equipped to remedy the lack of a systematic intellectual preparation for such a critique. They only need the space for independent research and intensive debate, in addition to relevant reading materials and all necessary teacher's support. The students' collaboration showed that intercultural theoretical insights can be as productive as interdisciplinary dialogue.

---

* I would like to thank Nuno Galego Marques Atalaia Rodrigu, Sonia de Jager, Thao Nguyen, Nadieh Rijnbergen, Anna Volkmar, and Rob Zwijnenberg, whose brilliant intellectual work made this course, and this essay, possible. I extend my thanks to all the other courageous and bright students who shared this adventure.

1 Introduction

The environmental humanities are not just concerned with the study of a *topic*; they define themselves as a field that addresses, with a sense of urgency, a complex global crisis that will have catastrophic impact if it is not adequately responded to. Scholars working in this field often understand their interdisciplinary research as relevant to the wider world: their research would be an indispensable aspect of a much broader range of political, social, technological, scientific, and cultural actions. New theoretical approaches to, and new imaginations of, the relations between humans and the more-than-human world, or between matter and meaning, are often presented as critical practices that may help to enable social and political action.

These ambitions may seem high-strung, and the challenges in our field overwhelming. One of the most immediate problems we face lies in our need to develop alternative approaches within the context of an institute for knowledge production that is organized around the very approaches we aim at criticizing. Of course, the departmentalization of the academy allows us to develop our research within the relative safety of, say, English departments. But this departmentalization also threatens the intended social relevance of our work. While many of us solve this problem by participating in interdisciplinary research projects, here I would like to discuss another path. One way in which we can explore the broader significance of our field is through teaching.

Academic teaching will inevitably be concerned with the reflection on knowledge production, and with the relation between knowledge production and questions of (political, social) power.[1] Within the classroom, the institutional constraints I identified above – the possible dominance of theoretical approaches we aim at criticizing – stop being constraints; they can become a productive object of study. Especially when a class consists of students from different disciplines, a discussion about the history, context, theoretical productivity, and social relevance of different theoretical approaches becomes not only an option, but a necessity. In this essay, I want to discuss one particular case study: an experimental, co-taught master course which was part of the two-year Research Master program Arts and Culture / Literary Studies at the University of Leiden, Netherlands, in 2013–2014. This case study will allow me to reflect on the question if, and in what way, teaching can help to explore the critical force of the different theoretical approaches relevant to

---

1 Gayatri Chakravorty Spivak's *Outside in the Teaching Machine* is one of the most thorough reflections on this topic.

the environmental humanities. I will argue that the classroom is an ideal environment to produce insights about the ways in which theory can engage with social and political practices.

2   The Design of the Course

The course, which was entitled *Matter and Muck: Bio-art, Ecocriticism, and the Material Turn,* was taught by a colleague from the department of Art History, a specialist and pioneer in bio-art studies, professor Rob Zwijnenberg, and myself, a cultural analyst dedicated to ecocriticism, with a background in postcolonial literary studies. We started our course description with the observation that "[a]rtists and writers seem increasingly fascinated by the shapeless, abject, matter, muck – and zombies. Theorists follow in their wake." Our general research question was:

"What are the historical and political reasons for this 21st century urge to engage with disintegration and abjection? Can we already discern a counter-linguistic or material turn in the humanities? According to those who hold that this is so, we should seek the reasons [in] the multiple crises of the early 21st century [that] necessitate [...] a radical rethinking of a range of foundational concepts, such as, for example, language, the real, the human, and the environment. Art and literature play an important role in that re-imagination."

The course aimed at discussing "the theories of (bio-) art and literature (ecocriticism) that ponder the aesthetic fascination with matter," and the art that evokes "nature as the zero point of life, the ungraspable site of the 'real.'" The course was meant to "test the productivity of exhilarating new (or not so new) approaches such as phenomenology, psychoanalysis, Deleuzian new materialism, etc."

The interdisciplinarity seemed unavoidable. Because of the sheer philosophical or scientific complexity of most approaches, many teachers will have a difficult time deciding whether they will present a variety of (perhaps conflicting) interdisciplinary approaches, or whether they will offer their students one consistent theoretical frame instead. One of our points of departure had been dark ecology's proposal to acknowledge the unpleasant shapelessness and meaninglessness of our material surroundings, so we might have decided to test the merits of that particular approach–which would already be a major task. We opted, however, for a radically interdisciplinary approach. Three different theoretical fields seemed essential for the research of matter and materiality. Lacanian psychoanalysis – a long-standing interest for critical literary theorists – theorizes materiality in relation to the difficult concept of the Real.

As (Deleuzian) new materialism represents a highly influential response and alternative to psychoanalysis, and is more and more prominent in ecocriticism, it must be addressed in a course that aims at reflecting on all relevant approaches. It rethinks matter within the frame of a non-transcendental ontology; while matter does not have a fixed identity (and therefore exceeds discourse and fixed meanings), it is the site of potentiality, that is, the unfolding of possibilities. Finally, the life sciences inquire into the nature of the materiality of living organisms; their research of its semiotic interactions with its environment invites yet another way of thinking the relation between meaning and matter. Bio-artists respond to their inquiries in ways that exceed the theories we offered. These were the fields we felt we had to address. To avoid offering a starkly reduced version of these theoretical approaches, the course was taught by two teachers with different specializations (philosophy/life sciences; cultural analysis/psychoanalysis). To bring out the social relevance of the course, we also decided to invite artists and visit exhibitions.

The master students that participated in the course were an international group of slightly over thirty advanced art historians and literary theorists, with highly varied backgrounds in theory. Many of them would have already been acquainted with some of the issues surrounding bio-art (an art practice that uses live organisms and tissues), but we did not expect any shared previous knowledge of ecocriticism, new materialism, object-oriented ontology, or even phenomenology. Nevertheless, we were convinced of the intellectual talents and scholarly independence of these young scholars, and that is what we told them during the first class. We also explained that the aim of the course was to work through these issues by inviting all students to participate in the creation of a virtual exhibition (with the title of the course), and produce a catalogue that would meet academic standards. After a series of seven weekly lectures that would build a solid theoretical foundation and introduce a range of relevant art works (bio-art, literature, graphic novels, paintings, environmental art, etc.), students would work in six small, independent groups, which would meet over a period of six weeks during weekly tutorials under the supervision of one of the teachers, towards their contribution to the catalogue. Students were asked to form groups around themes they could select themselves – though in the end, the six groups adopted four of the six themes the teachers had suggested (the Anthropocene, Human Enhancement, Thing Theory, Edible Matter). The course would be concluded with a student conference, in which the students were expected to present their work to each other, and to an interested audience.

During the first two classes we gave an overview of the genealogies of what we had decided to call the material turn. Against the background of different academic overviews of this development,[2] and the talk Timothy Morton gave in January 2012 at the MLA conference on melancholic objects, we sketched the development of structuralism and poststructuralism, partly as a critical response to phenomenology; we then moved on to the critique of social constructivism that emerged from gender studies and performativity studies. We discussed the radical shift in perspective proposed by Deleuze's return to a pre-Kantian philosophical tradition, and his revival of Spinozian thought; we discussed the huge impact of his return to the ontological questions that had been considered out-of-bounds in most mainstream philosophy. We presented this as a key insight in the course: poststructuralism had been the most radical movement that had declared matter as inaccessible without semiotic mediation; through such interventions, matter had been opposed to meaning. We discussed the drawbacks of an approach that sees matter as fundamentally outside meaning, while insisting on the continuing merits of poststructuralist thought. We showed how the opposition between matter and meaning was now being revised, and opened the debate about the agency and vibrancy of matter. To remind our students of other contemporary developments that highlight the need to address matter, we referred to the ecological crisis, neuroscience and the technologizing of the body.

After these two introductory classes, we proceeded with five weekly three-hour classes that discussed the concepts of the real and of matter from, respectively, a psychoanalytical and posthumanist, new materialist view; we discussed the concepts of matter and muck within the context of an African American cultural critique; and continued the discussions within the context of bio-art and human enhancement. To stimulate active engagement with these theories, students were asked to give a presentation in which they explained and defended one of the (often conflicting) views elaborated in the reading materials for that class, and to write a portfolio in which they were to offer a critical and analytical self-reflection of what they were learning throughout the first seven lectures of the course. We explained that "the portfolio is meant to facilitate your reflection on the radical shift that is currently taking place in the humanities, to keep track of your varying response, and allow you to develop and document an intense engagement with the relevant bodies of theory and the art work. In addition, this reflection on your own learning process will help you to formulate clear and productive research questions that may form the

---

2 One written by two Dutch new materialists, Dolphijn and van der Tuin (2012), and the other by Serenella Iovino (2012); these texts were complemented with a chapter from Jane Bennett's *Vibrant Matter* (2010).

point of departure of your contribution to the catalogue" (which was their final assignment).

3 The First Problem

We expected a wealth of obstacles. What we did not foresee was that our very introduction would already land us in deep trouble. What kindled immediate enthusiasm and awe was less the grand overview we offered our students, but rather Morton's opaque, concise, grandiose 2012 lecture. This abrupt introduction to object-oriented ontology had an ambivalent effect on our students. Many of them were immediately spell-bound, and eager to know more about this – for many of them – almost incomprehensible, but seemingly visionary alternative approach to the world. In terms of pedagogy, however, our decision to present Morton's idiosyncratic lecture by way of an introduction turned out to be a double-edged sword. The positive effect was that our students, henceforth, would be willing to engage with the most sophisticated and complex theories we would offer (and this was indeed what we had hoped for). On the flipside, however, the course was not at all meant as an introduction to object-oriented ontology or speculative realism, approaches we had not adequately studied, and often found highly problematic. What we had aimed at, was furnishing our students with adequate insight into the *variety* of the theoretical approaches they would need to analyze the highly complex contemporary artistic response to the social and ethical desire to relate to matter. We did not want to lead them into a highly abstract movement of which they – and we – would not be fully able to judge the merits. As our students began to clamor for more, however, we felt obliged to expand our own knowledge of the field, and share our insights with them. I dedicated one tutorial of two groups working on "thing theory" to a more sustained exploration of object-oriented ontology and speculative realism, in the second part of the course. I did so reluctantly, in an open exchange, and shared my reservations about these approaches.

4 The Second Problem

Before the tutorials, we had already offered other possible theoretical frames for the study of the fascination with chaos and meaningless matter. We did succeed in convincing the students of the need to consider more approaches than the one encountered through Morton's talk. The third class delved deeply into psychoanalysis. As stated above, Lacanian psychoanalysis understands matter through the concept of the Real; language, discourse, and meaning are predicated on the subject's transition from the Real into the Imaginary and the Symbolic order. As Slavoj Žižek has it, the Real will return to disturb the precarious structure of meaning, while it is on the other hand also the very support of the Symbolic order. It seems to me, as a literary scholar, that a lot of popular art can very well be analyzed with the help of this approach (perhaps with some revisions).

What I had not realized, was the fact that a majority of the students in this interdisciplinary, international class had never encountered any form of psychoanalytic reflection on art before. Many though not all students were completely overwhelmed by Lacan's and Žižek's texts. I realized – not for the first time – that the academy fails to profit from different crucial intellectual traditions that allow for an insight into the complex ways in which human beings endow life with meaning: psychoanalysis in the first place, and modernized, revised forms of Marxist thought, in the second. Without any knowledge of these traditions, it is very hard to contextualize and historicize semiotic practices, and articulate a cultural critique; they offer a wealth of tools to explore the relation between knowledge production, power, and desire. Even if they must be thoroughly problematized, they can be a very useful safeguard against reductive assumptions about matter (as readily available, neutral, objective). But they are both highly complex forms of reflection, and they are not easily appropriated.

My own pedagogical approach is informed by the wish to stimulate my students to historicize and contextualize – intellectual moves which, in these times dominated by hyper-individualist discourses, they find increasingly difficult to master. While our own bachelor program, taught at the Film and Literary Studies Department, offers space and time to work on this, we were not fully prepared for the different academic positions of the master students that were trained in another context. All too easily, we had assumed that the other courses in the Master program would offer a thorough introduction to literary theory and cultural analysis. Not all students had already taken that course, however. What happened then should not have been a surprise. Lacking a grounding in political analysis or psychoanalysis, the students took recourse to an ethical approach, instead of a political analysis or psychoanalysis. Looking back, we can see that this response was stimulated by our early session in the course on different case-studies; a reading of Hurricane Katrina (2005) within an African-American, postcolonial, and materialist context; provocative instances of bio-art where animals were used; the debate on human enhancement. It is only after these classes that we, as teachers, realized that, while we had scheduled a lot of dense readings on psychoanalysis, posthumanism etc., we had not offered any theoretical texts on *ethics*. This is a main theoretical point we intend to address the next time we will offer this course. In addition to the material turn (and to the many other "turns" happening in these turbulent academic times), we can witness a broader *ethical turn*, and, as this ethical turn can also be witnessed in society, where it is fed by a growing dissatisfaction with the workings of the *political* system, we should have expected that our students would already have digested some of it. We cannot afford to neglect this intellectual and social context. A way to give the ethical turn a useful place in our classes, would be through a critical consideration of the relation between ethics and politics.

A starting point could be the observation that "the ethical has come to substitute, and subsequently annihilate the possibility of, the political," as Graff Zivin has it in an online essay published in 2013, which opens with some comments on a more general skepticism towards ethics in literary studies and philosophy: "What did it mean to posit the ethical as a new position from which to approach the literary, or the question of the subject? Would so-called 'politics' be obliterated as a productive locus of criticism, not to mention action? Was the 'face-to-face' of the ethical encounter to replace the possibility of collective agency, resistance, or revolution?" Following one of Graff Zivin's suggestions, I think that Alain Badiou's work on ethics, and Peter Hallward's introduction to his work, could well serve as a way to open a discussion on the relation between ethics and politics, not in the least because both scholars are also inspired by Marxism. Badiou would also be extremely useful because of his critical comments on Deleuze, and his more positive engagement with Lacan, and Lacan's theorizing of the Real. On moments like these, we find that teaching calls as much for interdisciplinary collaboration as any ambitious, innovative research project – we would certainly have to ask a sympathetic philosopher to teach this particular class with us. But we cannot afford *not* to offer such a class, if we want our students to critically reflect on the advantages and the disadvantages of an ethical approach to the issues at hand.

5   The Strength of a Cultural Analysis Approach

We need not have worried, though. By the time we offered our tutorials, the students were already passionately engaged in exploring concrete works of art and literature, and were less interested in hyped-up, abstract philosophies that seemed less immediately relevant to their concerns, than in social and cultural critique.

We will rethink the design of our course, especially with regard to the theoretical context we will offer the students. One of the strong points in our design was, however, that it complied with the lessons taught by cultural analysis. Good research is triangular; it consists of an intimate interaction between the object of inquiry, a body of theories, and the researcher(s) with their own intellectual and personal agenda. None of these agents is stable, all are in need of being problematized. The nature of our case studies, and those selected by the students, strongly called for a critical, ethical, or political response.

The students were encouraged to consider different possible theoretical approaches. While they embraced aspects of Deleuzian materialism, for example, they also insisted on the need to take into account epistemological questions such as the nature of human knowledge – they also asked critical questions about the project to radically do away with anthropocentrism. As such, they avoided a reductive understanding of the material turn as the decisive, definitive *next step* in the environmental humanities.[3]

We were very much encouraged by the insistence with which some students asked questions about knowledge production. A good example is Sonia de Jager's contribution. She was part of the Anthropocene-theme group. As teachers, we were quite surprised by the emergence of noise as the theme through which the group of students wanted to elaborate the relation between materiality and meaning, within the framework of the Anthropocene. But they made their point very clear, as can be seen in this quotation from Nuno Atalaia's paper:

> Noise provides a productive and likewise disturbing starting point to think the Anthropocene as an epoch dominated by meaningful human agency [...] Noise itself, following its etymological root in Latin and early french nausea, is always thought as 'disturbance' or 'uproar,' hence attacking, blurring or destroying a meaningful structure. Likewise, in mathematics noise designates "a random error or variation in observations which is not explained by the model" (Oxford Reference for Mathematics, 2009)

For Sonia de Jager, the focus on sound represents a shift that had already been theorized by Michel Foucault in 1963. An auditory instead of the privileged

---

3 But then again, this is one of the very points of new materialism, as Dolphijn and van der Tuin point out: new materialism is not polemically opposed to earlier approaches, as it is not based on linearity, and therefore not on a linear notion of the development of theoretical debates either (89–92).

visual attention to an object leads to *a different kind of knowledge*. Sonia de Jager offers a felicitous case: "in 1964, due to a shift in mode of attention [that is: from visual to auditory, IH], astronomers Arno Penzias and Robert Wilson made a discovery which drastically changed humanity's understanding of our place in the cosmos: it rendered the edge of our universe a glowing curtain of plasma – as opposed to that which we had always known to be a dark, endless void." While de Jager here emphasizes the insight that knowledge production occurs through material interactivity (produced through material technological practices, here: the radio telescope), she also brings to the fore the "intrinsically relativistic, unavoidably subjective" nature of the human relation to the universe. She quotes Bruno Latour's remark that there is no "direct access to truth without any mediation" (2011), and insists on the need for self-reflexivity. A certain form of anthropocentrism, for her, is still indispensable.[4] Paying attention to noise changes the relation between humans and the non-human universe. She criticized mainstream notions of knowledge production by pointing out that sound (as "shapeless, dynamic, undelineable") problematizes the quest for a controllable, accurate means for human knowledge production. One might conclude that these observations lead away from anthropocentrism, but they also lead to a very useful epistemological self-reflection on the ways in which we produce knowledge.

The theme of noise tied in quite well with our course's focus on matter and muck – if matter, like noise, is understood as the meaningless aspect of the material world. According to the students who worked together on the theme, sound and noise are material in more than one sense. The point of departure of Nuno Atalaia's paper was the insight that "the Anthropocene as a concept is defined by a certain taking of conscience (rather than quantity, quality or intensity) of the material impact of human production and techniques." He then found this material impact in the empty stone quarries of the French region of Soissons, from where the specific sort of limestone came which was used to build the rhizomatic network of French cathedrals. These cathedrals followed the system of proportions invented by Pythagoras, which also informed the harmonic structure of Medieval and Renaissance musical composition. "This allows us to read both cathedrals and the quarry as both composition and noise," says Atalaia. "[t]he quarry can be seen as the primordial chaos [...] where the empty noise of construction would be left, all that which the harmonic system did not take into account." The group of students working on the

---

4   This insight springs from her examination of the interactive (if not intra-active, to use Karen Barad's term) nature of the agency involved in the act of listening to the universe.

Anthropocene, through the concept of noise, decided to use this quarry as the virtual site for a string of events. One of these would be a sound performance evoking the acoustic gothic textures of the cathedral network in the very emptiness from where their materiality had emerged.

One particularly promising aspect of their work was how it related noise to the notion of feedback: "one could envision the loosely defined Anthropocene as a feedback system; the Anthropos being both the soundemitting and noise-receiving entity" (Atalaia). The strong point here is that it locates agency not in human beings alone, but in the broader material world. At the same time, human agency is taken into account very explicitly. The proposal for such a performance is poetically convincing and intellectually well-founded. We were also struck by the potential of this approach as a materialist counterpart to social constructivism: in this case, the "real" (that what exceeds signification) is a highly *material* emptiness, fully tactile and audible.

Anna Volkmar, who participated in the same group, also subscribes to the need for epistemological self-reflexivity, and a critical form of anthropocentrism. She follows J.P. Rafferty's suggestion that the Anthropocene began with the emergence of radioactivity from the first atomic bomb tests "in the geological record" (Rafferty), and points, with Timothy Morton, at the fact that radioactivity "profoundly affected our understanding of objects as such and their agency in 'human social and psychic space'" (2014: 11). She then proceeds to discuss an artistic documentary on the 2011 Fukushima disaster (*The Radiant*, 2012 by the Otolith group) that uses distorted electronic noises to intensify the experience of a crashing wave to such an extent that "the screen of Kantian aesthetics between object and observer" is broken down; "the protective technical equipment that separates human from nonhuman, camera man from viewer," is attacked. For Volkmar, too, the main insight here relates to the impossibility of knowing that is the condition of the Anthropocene. The documentary does not just result in the "physical immediacy" of the noise and the objects that caused it, but, more importantly, it also leads to our realization of "*our existence in it* [the nuclear object, IH]," while we are at the same time pushed out, and unable to grasp the nuclear object – which is exactly the condition of the Anthropocene.

What these students brought up was threefold: first, the need for a different kind of knowledge production which would address the agency of matter while also criticizing mainstream forms of knowledge; second, the need for a critique of anthropocentrism *and* a need for a certain wariness of such a critique; and, third, the need for both ontological *and* epistemological questions. Their selection of case studies ensured an open, creative engagement with the tensions and problems in the field. This, in our eyes, was far more productive than had we asked them to work within a single, fixed theoretical framework.

6 Why Epistemological Questions are Crucially Important

Looking back, we can see how these meta-reflections could have been more central to the course.

We could have elaborated the main insight that there are different ways to contribute to the critique of the long philosophical tradition that puts reality between brackets. The first is embodied in the ontological orientation that can be found in new materialism, Deleuzian philosophy, object-oriented ontology, etc. The other sticks to epistemological questions: how do we understand matter today, and, more importantly: what are the social and political interests and desires that inform theoretical projects that, as in this case, want to re-establish contact with reality?

This is the excellent question asked by Alexander Galloway, who expresses his nervousness about the political project at the heart of speculative realism in a 2010 discussion: "we need to acknowledge that this current round of realism is in fact a direct response to – and a desire to do away with – projects that were themselves extremely political, projects like identity politics" (2011: 23). "I'm just nervous when explicitly political projects are kicked out, and what's left is a series of scientific claims to the real [...]. I think realism is dangerous. And until we can hear a more sophisticated explanation for why it is ethically, politically, or morally advantageous to talk about the pure real, I'm nervous about it" (2011: 23–24).

We were happy to find that many of our students saw the need for a critical perspective, even without having been introduced to Galloway's valuable observation. They confirmed the need for a delicate balance between these two positions: the ontological effort to endow the real with meaning, on the one hand, and the epistemological insight that these efforts will not escape their own historical, subjective nature on the other.

The fact that the learning process was largely shaped by the participants themselves, and their objects of inquiry, also led to a sophisticated reflection we had not foreseen. In this sense, history itself leads to thorough self-reflection. Our class was relatively international; apart from a majority of Dutch students, eight non-Dutch European and American students participated, and five Asian students. I was thrilled to see how many of the latter opened the debate on the interaction between the critique of Western dualist philosophies, and non-dualist Asian philosophies. Thao Nguyen, who participated in a Thing Theory-group, discussed the case of Buddhist relics within the frame of Bill Brown's Thing Theory. Bill Brown's work is very helpful when it comes to exploring the relation between object and thing; as Thao Nguyen had it, "thingness," according to Brown, [is, IH] "the amorphousness out of which objects are materialized by the (ap)perceiving subject." Buddhist relics–the jewel-shaped remains of the Buddha and other spiritual masters, recovered from the ashes after their cremation – present a case that problematizes this definition, as they seem to "actually remain forever foreign things" to the onlookers, whether they revere the relics, or whether they do not believe in their sacred nature at all. In a comparable vein, one of our Thing Theory-students, a Dutch yoga teacher who had spent long periods in India (Nadieh Rijnbergen), wondered whether the concept of the "hyper-object" might be helpful in analyzing the objects in the Indian-American animation series *Little Krishna* – such as when the universe is shown to be inside Krishna's mouth. Such tentative interventions address the often implicitly spiritual reading of new materialist insights, and they may well help to problematize them.

Our course was designed to find answers to the question what theories we need to analyze and understand the contemporary globalizing world, which is threatened by environmental and other crises. We are convinced that we need a community of creative, critical academics and professionals with an interdisciplinary training to analyze the crisis in its full complexity, and address it in a sustainable manner. If we want our students to make sense of the interaction between the human efforts to endow the more-than-human world with meaning, and the agency of matter that disturbs, shapes, or allows these efforts, we have to teach them the crucial insights of past critical approaches as well as the radical new theories on matter and meaning, including old and new and Asian and other non-dualist insights. Our experience has shown us that this is a very difficult task. The present-day organization of the academy often fails to offer an adequate context for the necessary critical reflection. We can however only help to build the necessary expertise to address the crisis if we start training our students to critically engage with a wealth of relevant theories from their very first year onwards.

The fact that the environmental humanities are concerned with a global issue can be a guiding principle not just in the contents of the course, as in this case; it can also be a guiding principle in the learning process, especially in an international classroom. Perhaps even more than the encounter with demanding interdisciplinary theories, it may be the encounter with different cultural perspectives that stimulates students – and more advanced scholars – to question the systems of knowledge production that can hamper, or support, our shared efforts to make theory relevant for the world.

Bibliography

Bennett, Jane. 2010. *Vibrant Matter: A Political Ecology of Things.* Durham and London: Duke University Press.

Brown, Bill. 2001. "Thing Theory." *Critical Inquiry* 28(1): 1–21.

Dolphijn, Rick and Iris van der Tuin. 2012. *New Materialism: Interviews & Cartographies.* Ann Arbor: Open Humanities Press. On line at: http://openhumanitiespress.org/new-materialism.html (consulted 02.04.2016).

Galloway, Alexander R. 2011. "Quentin Meillassoux, or The Great Outdoors." *French Theory Today: An Introduction of Possible Futures.* Pamphlet 4. New York: TPSNY/ Erudio Editions. Online at: http://cultureandcommunication.org/galloway/FTT/French-Theory-Today.pdf (consulted 02.04.2016).

Gayatri Chakravorty Spivak. 1993. *Outside in the Teaching Machine.* London: Routledge.

Graff Zivin, Erin. 2013. "Politics Against Ethics." *Politica Comun* 4. Online at: http://quod.lib.umich.edu/p/pc/12322227.0004.009/--politics-against-ethics?rgn=main;view=fulltext (consulted 02.04.2016).

Iovino, Serenella. 2012. "Theorizing Material Ecocriticism: A Diptych." Part 1. *Interdisciplinary Studies in Literature and the Environment* 19(3): 448–460.

Lacan, Jacques. 1992. *The seminar of Jacques Lacan. Book VII: The ethics of psychoanalysis, 1959–1960.* New York: Norton.

Latour, Bruno. 2011. "Summary of the AiME project: An Inquiry into Modes of Existence." Online at: http://www.bruno-latour.fr/node/328 (consulted: 02.04.2016).

Rafferty, J.P. 2014. "Anthropocene Epoch (geochronology)." *Encyclopædia Britannica. Encyclopædia Britannica Online.* Encyclopædia Britannica Inc. Online at: http://www.britannica.com/EBchecked/topic/1492578/Anthropocene-Epoch (consulted 02.094.2016).

Žižek, Slavoj. 1991. "The Real and Its Vicissitudes." *Looking Awry: An Introduction to Jacques Lacan Through Popular Culture.* Cambridge, MA: MIT Press: 21–47.

CHAPTER 16

Postscript: Framing the Environmental Humanities

Hannes Bergthaller and Peter Mortensen

In our introduction, we argued that the essays in this book are linked by a shared interest in how nature is framed – that is to say, in the ways in which different cultural and linguistic traditions, narratives, technologies, media, or institutions, shape how people perceive and interact with nature. As any reader who takes a closer look at the chapters will quickly recognize, this is itself a rather broad way of framing them – and one that may seem intent on disavowing their striking heterogeneity. In closing this volume, we should therefore emphasize that we do not consider this heterogeneity to be something that ought to be dissembled, in the first place, as it is no more than an accurate (albeit partial) reflection of the different approaches and conceptual vocabularies employed across the environmental humanities – differences that obtain no less between academic disciplines than between national or institutional traditions. What counts as good scholarly practice is not the same in ecocriticism and environmental history; and environmental history in Estonia is not the same as environmental history in Australia.

The eagerness with which many scholars have embraced the label "environmental humanities" in recent years makes it sometimes too easy to overlook or ignore these fissures. In our home disciplines, ecocriticism and Anglophone literary studies, it has become quite common for scholars to claim that they now do "ecocriticism *and* environmental humanities" – yet if one reads their work, it quickly becomes clear that very little has changed since the adoption of the new moniker. It is probably fair to assume that similar things are happening in other fields. To be sure, we do not wish to suggest that this is necessarily problematic or constitutes false labelling. After all, there are no agreed upon criteria for membership in the environmental humanities other than the very loose ones set by the designation itself, and there are perfectly legitimate reasons why scholars (especially early in their career) wish to conform to the conventions that define their respective home discipline. Interdisciplinary work is often difficult and frustrating. It entails a time-consuming effort to familiarize oneself with different research practices and bodies of knowledge. Even so, it may not find much recognition in any of the disciplines which it attempts to bridge. And the idea that the environmental humanities could somehow "sublate" or transcend the areas of research which contribute to them makes very little sense – not only because it would put at risk whatever respectability such relatively young fields as environmental ethics, environmental history, or ecocriticism have been able to win within the more established disciplines of which they are and will remain a part.

But as Harvey Graff has argued, disciplinarity and interdisciplinarity should not be construed as standing in opposition. Rather, they are mutually dependent – they "stimulate, shape, and inform each other" (2016). The value of interdisciplinary work does not lie in the fact that it would overcome the limitations of specialized fields of inquiry, but in how it allows particular insights to migrate between fields, such that they can be put to use in different contexts, to help address questions and problems as they are defined by specific disciplines. Ecocritics will do well to pay attention to what is happening in environmental history or geography – not primarily because it will enable them to contribute to the general advance of the environmental humanities, but because it will make them better ecocritics. Where and when an interdisciplinary transfer of ideas will be fruitful is not something that could be determined in advance. It will necessarily involve an element of serendipity, the sudden spark of insight that sometimes occurs when we recognize the familiar in something that had seemed strange, or the strangeness in something that we thought familiar.

That is not to say, of course, that the purpose of the environmental humanities should be to facilitate chance encounters between umbrellas and sewing-machines (Lautréamont 1965: 263). We do believe, however, that there is not only a certain kind of beauty, but also a distinctive practical value in juxtaposing, as this volume does, such seemingly disparate issues as medieval bestiaries and contemporary political party programs, Finnish Cold War television and early twentieth century Australian nature pedagogy, or cognitivist film theory and toxic fear in the United States of the 1980s. It reminds us of the vast number of different ways in which nature has figured across discourses, cultures, and historical periods, and of the almost equally great diversity of ways in which humanists try to make sense of this multiplicity. Ultimately, what holds the environmental humanities together is the understanding that in order to find a way out of the current ecological mess, we also need to come to terms with the tangled mess that is human culture. This has become obvious even to many natural scientists, although they continue to enjoy something close to a monopoly on what counts as relevant knowledge in public debates over environmental issues (cf. Sörlin 2012). If humanists whose work concerns the environment wish to find a hearing beyond the confines of their respective disciplines, their best chance is to make common cause. The environmental humanities, then, are indeed a matter of "framing" our work, not only insofar as it concerns the question how we negotiate disciplinary boundaries, but also in in the particular sense of a strategic decision about how to effectively communicate with a wider public. Whatever audience this book will reach, we hope that it contributes to this important enterprise.

Bibliography

Graff, Harvey. 2016. "Interdisciplinarity as Ideology and Practice." *Insights from the Social Sciences*. Online at: http://items.ssrc.org/interdisciplinarity-as-ideology-and-practice (consulted April 4 2017).

Lautréamont, Comte de. 1965. *Maldoror (Les Chants de Maldoror)*. Translated by Guy Wernham. New York: New Directions.

Sörlin, Sverker. 2012. "Environmental Humanities: Why Should Biologists Interested in the Environment Take the Humanities Seriously?" *BioScience* 62 (9): 788–789.

Index

Abram, David 109
African American Literature 35, 46
African American cultural critique 242
Agency 17, 32, 41, 242
Alterity 208–209, 213–214
Althusser, Louis 192, 194
Altman, Rick 198
America and Americans (Steinbeck) 146
Anderson, Joseph 191–196
Animals 22, 78–79, 103–121
    Managerial discourse about 104, 106, 115, 116, 118
Animal ethics 104, 106, 109, 121
Anthropocene 246, 248
Anthropocentrism 36, 43, 106, 109, 119
Anthropology 37–39
Anthropomorphism 36, 177, 184–188, 213, 231
Apartheid 208–210, 216
Apocalypse 58
Aran Islands 52–63. *See* Robinson, *Stones of Aran*.
Armitage, Kevin C. 222
Artaud, Antonin 176
Australia 227
    Aborigines of 231–233
    Education system of 227–228

Bachelard, Gaston 183
Badiou, Alain 245
Bailey, Liberty Hyde 223, 225–227
Barthes, Roland 186
Bentham, Jeremy 25
Bean, Robert 39
Bednář, Kamil 141, 148–149, 151–152
Bennett, Jane 242fn
Bio-art 241, 244
Biophilia 201
Biosemiotics 188
Blomkamp, Neill 210
Boas, Franz 36, 39, 40, 43, 46
Bolhuis, Johan J. 196
Bondy, Egon 142
Bordwell, David 191–201
Breton, André 178
Brinton, David 37, 38

Brooks, Virginia 202
Brown, Bill 250
Buddhist relics 250
Buell, Lawrence 128–129, 208
Buñuel, Luis 176, 179
Bush, George W. 6

Caillois, Roger 187
Carson, Rachel 5–6, 126, 134, 163, 234
Chemophobia 127, 129, 130
Cílek, Václav 144
Civil religion 86, 88, 89–91, 98–99, 100
Clark, Timothy 55, 57, 62
Climate change 6, 26–30, 52, 58, 209, 211
Cold War 126, 128
Crace, Jim 23–24, 29, 31. *See Harvest*.
Critical discourse analysis 104, 108, 114
Cognitivist film theory 190–201
Cold War 126, 132, 139, 167. *See* Iron Curtain.
    Czechoslovakia during the 139–152
Cosmides, Leda 191, 193
Crosby, Alfred W. 3
Cultural constructionism 192

Dalí, Salvador 176, 179
Damasio, Antonio 191
Deconstruction 1–2, 44
Deep ecology 109
Deleuze, Gilles 71, 242, 245
Derrida, Jacques 1–3
Desnos, Robert 178
De Waal, Frans 185
Dickens, Charles 24–26, 31. *See Hard Times*.
District 9 (Blomkamp) 207–218
Dolphijn, Rick 242fn., 246fn.
Douglass, Frederick 41
Dualism 68, 83
Dubská, Irena 149–150
Dunlap, Thomas 234
Dunphy, Myles 234

Ecocriticism 2, 35, 46, 50, 198, 201, 207, 252–253
Ecological psychology 191
Ellington, Duke 186

Energy narratives 16–22
　　Relations to literature of 19–22, 29–32
　　Typology of 18–20
Environmental crisis 68, 127, 132
Environmental ethics 104
Environmental humanities 1, 124–125, 136, 239, 252
Environmental justice 201
Environmental literacy 16, 201. *See* scientific literacy.
Environmentalism 2–3, 5–6, 57, 109, 127
Estonia 88–100, 157–168
　　Attempted Coup d'Etat (1991) 157
　　Civil religion of 89–91
　　Romantic nationalism of 90, 91, 95, 96–97
　　Sacred natural sites of 88, 91–100
　　Sillamäe atomic complex 166
　　Television in 157–162
Eutrophication 158
Evolutionary psychology 191, 199–200

Feyerabend, Paul 199
Finnland 157–168
　　Television 157–162
Fish 106, 115–116, 163–164
Fleischmann, Josef 149
Folk culture 36, 43, 46
Foucault, Michel 246
Frames and framing 1–6, 18–22, 36, 52–53, 79–81, 87, 89, 96–100, 107, 191
　　Communication and 4–5
　　Environmentalism and 2–3, 5–6
　　Fluidity and 40–46
　　Literature and 16–32, 40–46, 217
　　Media studies and 18–22, 210
　　Philosophy and 1–3
　　Power and 68, 81, 210
　　Truth and 5, 211
Frankfurt School 192
Freud, Sigmund 180, 193
Fukushima nuclear disaster 248

Gamson and Modigliani 5, 18–22, 26, 29–30
Galloway, Alexander 249
Garrard, Greg 59, 207
Geddes, Patrick 227
Gibson, James J. 191
Goll, Ivan 176, 180–181

Goffman, Erving 4, 36, 210
Goodbody, Axel 52
Gottwald, Klement 140
Gould, Stephen J. 196
Graff, Harvey 253
Grapes of Wrath (Steinbeck) 140, 145, 147
Grodal, Torben 191–194
Guðmundsson, Jón 69, 71–83
　　Life and writings of 71–75
　　Organicist worldview of 75–83

Habermas, Jürgen 200
Hall, John R. 200
Hallward, Peter 245
Hard Times (Dickens) 24–26, 31
　　Critique of Utilitarianism in 25
　　References to coal burning in 25–26
Harvest (Crace) 23–24, 29, 31
　　Treatment of enclosure in 23–24
Heath, Stephen 194
Heidegger, Martin 3–4, 61
Heise, Ursula 52, 56, 57, 60, 62
Helsinki Convention (1974) 159
Herrnstein Smith, Barbara 196, 199–200
Heston, Charlton 193
Hochberg, Julian 202
Hodge, Clifton F. 223, 226, 227
Hodrová, Daniela 141
Holub, Miroslav 151
Howard University 40
Huggan, Graham 216
Hulme, Mike 5
Hurricane Katrina 244
Hurston, Zora Neale 34–36, 40–46. *See* "John Redding Goes to Sea," "Under the Bridge," "Magnolia Flower."

Iceland 69–71
Indigenous knowledge 231
Industrial pollution 127–128, 158, 163–164
Ingold, Tim 71, 81
Iovino, Serenella 242fn.
Iron Curtain 158, 160, 164
Ivakhiv, Adrian 202

Jackman, Wilbur 223
Jackson, Peter 210
Jeffers, Robin 141–152
　　Images of rocks in 141–145

Images of the ocean in   148–151
Images of trees in   145–148
Jirous, Ivan Martin   145
"John Redding Goes to Sea" (Hurston)   40–42, 46
   De-anthropocentrized agency in   41
Johnson, Roswell   38
Johannesburg   208, 210, 216

Kapstadt   208
Kohlstedt, Sally Gregory   222
Kuhn, Thomas   199

Lacan, Jacques   192, 194, 240, 243–244, 245
Lakoff, George   6, 191, 192, 199, 210
Landscape   86–88, 91–93, 96–100
Lange, Dietrich   223, 226
Latour, Bruno   247
Lautréamont, Comte de   253
Leopold, Aldo   234
Levins, Richard   196
Lewontin, Richard   196
Long, Charles   227

Macfarlane, Robert   56, 58
"Magnolia Flower" (Hurston)   44–45
   River as narrator in   44
Manuscript culture   71, 73
Marxism   192, 201–202, 244–245
McEwan, Ian   26–32
McMurry, Charles   226
Metz, Christian   194
Milhaud, Darius   184
Merchant, Carolyn   3
Minamata mercury disaster   163
Monument   86–88, 91–96, 99
Morton, Timothy   3, 52, 53, 58, 59, 60, 62, 242, 243, 248
Müller, Timo   52

Næss, Arne   104
Nationalism   88, 90–92, 95–100
Nature   67–69, 77–83, 86, 87–88, 90, 107
   Qualitative conception of   67–68, 79, 81
   Romantic images of   90
   Scientific objectification of   68, 81, 83
Nature study   221–235
New Deal   141
New Materialism   241

Neoliberalism   127–128
Nixon, Rob   210
Noise   129, 246
Norway   103–121
   Attitude to animals in   104, 106, 109, 120–121
   Political system of   105–106, 108
   Progressive image of   104
Nuclear weapons tests   158, 162
Nussbaum, Martha   20
Næss, Arne   104, 109

Object-oriented ontology   241
Oil pollution   158, 162–167
Oral tradition   86, 90, 92, 97, 99
O'Reilly, Bernard   234

Painlevé, Jean   175–188
   Para-surrealistic techniques of   177
Pan-psychism   186
Paradise Lost (Milton)   60
Peirce, Charles Sanders   176
Pontalis, Jean-Bertrand   180
Postcolonial studies   214, 244
Powell, John Wesley   37
Procházka, Vladimír   145
Psychoanalysis   241–243
Pythagoras   247

Race   37–39, 135
Radioactive fallout   126, 158
Rationalism   83
Ray, Man   176, 178
Ray, Robert   198–199
Reindeer   115–116
Renewable energy transition   15, 29–32
Rhizome   71
Robin, Libby   222
Robinson, Tim   51–63. See *Stones of Aran*.
Romanticism   90, 91, 95, 96–97

Sacred natural site   86–88, 91–100
Saga literature (of Iceland)   70–71
Said, Edward   215
Scientific Atheism   145
Scientific literacy   127–129
Scientific Revolution   68
Scott, Charles B.   223–225, 227
Sea of Cortez (Steinbeck)   144, 150

Semiosis   177–178, 186, 241
Social construction of reality   20–22
Solar (McEwan)   26–29, 30, 32
    Skepticism of   28
    Use of humor in   26
Soper, Kate   201
Sorrel, Tom   200
Soviet Union   157–168
Spivak, Gayatri Chakravorty   239fn.
Steinbeck, John   143–152
    Images of rocks in   141–145
    Images of the ocean in   148–151
    Images of trees in   145–148
    Jungian elements in   150
Stones of Aran (Robinson)   51–63
    Deep time thinking in   57, 62
    Aesthetics of dwelling in   53, 61, 62
    Derangements of scale in   52, 62, 65
    Ecocosmopolitanism in   52, 54–55
    Localism in   54
Subjectivity   192
Superfund sites   128. *See* industrial pollution.
Surrealism   177–185, 199

Television   157–168
The Beginning and the End (Jeffers)   146

Thing theory (Brown)   250
To a God Unknown (Steinbeck)   143–144, 146
Tooby, John   191, 193
Toulmin, Stephen   200
Toxic fear   125–136
    1980s culmination of   127–128, 132
    Distinctiveness of   125–126
    Historical origin of   126–127
    Measurement of   130–132
    Questions about   135–136
Toxic substances   126–129, 158

"Under the Bridge" (Hurston)   42–43
    De-privileging of humanity in   43
Utilitarianism   25

van der Tuin, Iris   242fn., 246fn.
Vernacular religion   86–87, 94, 96–97

Water pollution   158, 162–167
Welles, Orson   193
Wilson, Lucy Langdon Williams   223, 226
Whaling   104, 109
Worm, Ole   68, 74, 79–80, 81

Zivin, Graff   245
Žižek, Slavoj   244